THE BYRONIC HERO

THE BYRONIC HERO

TYPES AND PROTOTYPES

Peter L. Thorslev, Jr.

University of Minnesota Press, Minneapolis

Printed in the United States of America at the Lund Press, Inc.

Library of Congress Catalog Card Number: 62-16632

PUBLISHED IN GREAT BRITAIN, INDIA, AND PAKISTAN BY THE OXFORD UNIVERSITY PRESS, LONDON, BOMBAY, AND KARACHI, AND IN CANADA BY THOMAS ALLEN, LTD., TORONTO

Permission to quote from W. H. Auden's "Letter to Lord Byron," in *Letters from Iceland* (1951), has been kindly granted by Faber and Faber (London) and Random House (New York), owners of the world and American copyrights

Til Moder og Fader

ACKNOWLEDGMENTS

I OWE a personal and intellectual debt to Professor G. Robert Stange, who first suggested to me that the genesis of the Byronic Hero has not been so definitively studied as most scholars suppose, and who guided this essay through its first draft; and to those of my teachers or colleagues who have read the manuscript in whole or in part and have offered valuable scholarly or editorial suggestions: Professors Jacob C. Levenson and D. Burnham Terrell of the University of Minnesota, and Professors Jean H. Hagstrum and Arthur Nethercott of Northwestern University. I owe an intellectual debt greater than footnotes could express to the work of Professor Walter Kaufmann of Princeton, our best interpreter of Nietzsche, and of course to Nietzsche himself; the remainder of my intellectual debts are, I hope, adequately acknowledged in the Introduction, the Notes, and in the Appendix.

The University of Minnesota, Northwestern University, and the University of California have been generous in providing funds for research assistance and for the typing of the manuscript at its various stages.

P. L. T.

Los Angeles, California
March 1962

CONTENTS

≼§ THE BYRONIC HERO

MOOR: Pfui! Pfui über das schlappe Kastraten-Jahrhundert, zu nichts nütze, als die Taten der Vorzeit wiederzukäuen und die Helden des Altertums mit Kommentationen zu schinden und zu verhunzen mit Trauerspielen. Die Kraft seiner Lenden ist versiegen gegangen, und nun muss Bierhefe den Menschen fortpflanzen helfen.
SPIEGELBERG: Tee, Bruder, Tee!

Schiller, *Die Räuber*

Aber dass ich euch ganz mein Herz offenbare, ihr Freunde: wenn es Götter gäbe, wie hielte ich's aus, kein Gott zu sein! *Also* gibt es keine Götter.

Nietzsche, *Also Sprach Zarathustra*

INTRODUCTION

TO SAY that the most popular phenomenon of the English Romantic Movement and the figure with the most far-reaching consequences for nineteenth-century Western literature was the Byronic Hero is no overstatement of the case. In Victorian England or in the nascent American literary culture Byron's influence was perhaps less important, but still the young Tennyson wept on hearing of Byron's death; Arnold testifies that the collective English soul "Had *felt* him like the thunder's roll"; certainly the Brontë sisters' Heathcliff and Rochester attest the continued appeal of this awesome hero; and the most terrible figure in our classical American literature, Captain Ahab, has much of the Byronic Hero's aspect, of his dark soul. Lamartine and De Musset carried Byronism into the belated French Romantic Movement, and the Byronic Hero is the direct ancestor of many of the pessimistic or nihilistic heroes and philosophical rebels in French Romantic and decadent literature. Goethe received Childe Harold, Manfred, and Cain with overwhelming enthusiasm, and these heroes left their mark on many lesser German poets, from the youthful Heine to the brooding Lenau. Even Russia's first national poet, Pushkin, moulded his Eugene Onegin in Childe Harold's image. In Italy Byronism inspired poets and patriots from Manzoni to Mazzini; in beleaguered Greece and in Eastern Europe his influence is not yet dead. A few years ago, curious to find out what English or American authors were still taught in eastern European schools, I questioned a Hungarian refugee (an engineer) through a friend and interpreter. "Howard Fast and Jack London, of course," the refugee volunteered. After some elucidation Shakespeare drew a response, but when I dropped Byron's name, the "Freedom Fighter" didn't wait for the interpreter. "There was one," he replied eagerly, "who would have been with us."

The vast post-Byron literary and cultural influence would alone justify a study of the origins and development of the Byronic Hero, and there is further justification in the light that such a study should throw on Romanticism itself. Certainly no poetry in English affords a better opportunity for the study of the Romantic hero than that of Lord Byron; he is the one poet in the Romantic Movement whose hero was his poetry, or whose poetry existed for his hero. Furthermore, the Romantic heroes epitomize many of the most important aspects of Romanticism, and the Byronic Hero shows the elements of every major type of Romantic hero. One can find the "child of nature" in *Harold* and in the early romances; the Hero of Sensibility shows up not only in the *Childe*, but in such later works as *The Bride of Abydos* and *Sardanapalus*; Conrad and Lara are Gothic Villains turned sympathetic; Manfred is in some ways the English Faust; and finally, the concern with social and metaphysical-theological problems of a Cain or Prometheus type of hero is evident in many of the later dramas.

There have been studies of the Byronic Hero in Victorian literature, in French Romanticism, in Mary Shelley's novels, in the poetry of Heine or Pushkin, in the novels of Lermontov – but no definitive study of the Byronic Hero's antecedents in the literature before Byron, or of the hero in Byron's poetry itself. It would be difficult to find a sound explanation for this lacuna in literary scholarship, although one can assign some reasons. In the first place, the life of Byron has always been more fascinating than his poetry, at least to judge by the effort spent in chronicling it. For every book on Byron's poetry there have been at least five on his life; in the decade following the Byron centenary in 1924 not one book-length study of his poetry was published, but there were no less than twelve book-length biographical studies, six of which covered the whole span of his life. A second reason might be that Byron's influence on later literature stems not only from his works and perhaps not even principally from his works, but rather from his life and legend. For this reason, those who look upon him as of primary importance because of his influence rather than because of his intrinsic merit as a poet are far more likely to concentrate on the Byronic Hero in legend, and in European literature after Byron's death.

There has nevertheless been some discussion of the Byronic Hero as he exists in the master's work, although only one of these studies, and that the oldest, is a treatment solely of the hero and of his literary ancestors. The other studies concern the Byronic Hero only incidentally in search for bigger game: for a definition of the Gothic elements in English fiction, of the erotic element in world-wide Romanticism, or of the essence of German pessimism.

Heinrich Kraeger published his dissertation, *Der Byronsche Heldentypus*, in 1898.[1] He gives first credit for the source of the Byronic Hero to the "Titanentypus" as exemplified in the Satan of *Paradise Lost*, whom he associates with Prometheus. But, as could perhaps be expected of a German scholar, Satan turns out to have been a very distant ancestor, and we must look for the Byronic Hero's immediate paternity in the dramas of Klopstock and Schiller, particularly in the latter's *Die Räuber*. Now Karl Moor of *Die Räuber* is indeed an outlaw-hero of the type of Conrad or of Lara, but Byron did not read Schiller's drama until 1814 (see *LJ*, II, 388), and by that time *Childe Harold* I and II, *The Giaour*, *The Bride of Abydos*, and *The Corsair* had already been written. Moreover Byron could read no German, and there is not much evidence that he was influenced until after 1816 by what he read in translation. The works of early German Romanticism which Kraeger cites were influential in England, of course, but for the most part indirectly on Byron, through his predecessors and contemporaries.

The two best studies in English relate the Byronic Hero to the villains of the Gothic tradition: first in the novel, and second, in the drama.

Eino Railo, in *The Haunted Castle*, is interested in our hero only as an outgrowth of the villains and heroes of the Gothic novel, the paraphernalia of which are his major concern; however, in a short chapter entitled "The Byronic Hero" he does elaborate the close connection between Mrs. Radcliffe's villains and Byronic heroes, especially in the romances.[2] Conrad, Railo believes, is a direct descendant of the Manfred (Walpole's *Otranto*)–Montoni-Schedoni line, but he also points to the heroes of Scott's metrical romances (especially Marmion) as possible intermediaries between Mrs. Radcliffe and Byron. As is perhaps inevitable in a volume devoted largely to the tricks, devices, and physical settings of the Gothic novel, Railo places more emphasis on the Byronic Hero's physical characteristics than on his psychology, and he is interested only in the heroes of the romances, not of the dramas.

The second of the Gothic-Villain studies points to *Manfred* rather than to the romances, for it is specifically concerned with the Gothic drama rather than with the novel. In the first thorough investigation of this little-known field, *Gothic Drama from Walpole to Shelley*, Bertrand Evans points out that the villain on stage had a development markedly different from that of the villain of the novel.[3] The dramatic villain's remorseful repentance was increasingly emphasized at the expense of his villainy, and by the turn of the century he became sufficiently sympathetic to appear as a peculiar hybrid "hero-villain" or villainous hero. The influence of this sentimentalized Gothic Villain on the Byronic Hero, particularly on Manfred, must have been profound, especially considering the fact that as a member of the governing committee of Drury Lane (in 1814–15) Byron read these Gothic dramas by the score.

The study which has been by far the most influential, however, partly because of the notoriety of the book as a whole, and partly because of the scholarly reputation of its author, is Mario Praz's chapter on Byron in *The Romantic Agony*.[4] I think its total effect has been very misleading, however, by adding to the sins of the Byronic Hero vices of which he could never justly be considered guilty, and by extending and besmirching the Byronic legend so that the true nature of Byron's works becomes completely obscured.

The thesis of Praz's work is that there appeared in the Romantic

Movement a new erotic sensibility, a perverse sensibility, in which pleasure and pain, love and hate, tenderness and sadism, are inextricably blended—what is technically called "agolagnia." According to Praz the Romantics were the first group in the history of art to take delight in the horrid, to see beauty in the grotesque, even the bestial. In tracing this new sensibility Praz follows two figures through European literature (especially English, French, and Italian): the "fatal lovers," male and female. That such a sensibility existed (or exists) Praz amply proves; still, the book has two serious faults, it seems to me: the very weight and mass of evidence makes it seem as if Praz is reducing Romanticism to a perverted sensibility; and he seriously distorts some authors or their works to make them fit into his rather limited scheme.

The first charge Praz himself takes pains to refute in the prefaces to later editions of his book. He is not attempting to circumscribe Romanticism, he maintains, but only to emphasize one aspect of it which needs to be taken into account. These concessions, however, are not borne out by the book as a whole. On the second page of the first chapter he quotes at length from Faust's gruesome description of his *Walpurgisnacht* vision of a pale young witch with her throat slit, who resembles Margrethe, and Praz comments: "Here, one might say, through the lips of Faust, *speaks the whole of Romanticism.*" [5] And this candid contention—that this vision epitomizes Romanticism—is unfortunately true of the book as a whole. If this is only one thread of Romanticism, Praz should leave room for the rest of the fabric; if this is but one figure in the carpet, he should demonstrate occasionally that he is aware of other patterns.

In short, Praz has made a Procrustean bed of "erotic sensibility," and if the Romantic Movement will not fit, it will be chopped until it does, even if this means decapitation. And what he does to the Romantic Movement in general, it seems to me, he does particularly to Byron. In his chapter on Byron, Praz is concerned to prove three points: that the Byronic Hero is descended from Milton through Mrs. Radcliffe; that he is a fatal and cruel lover, linked with the Marquis de Sade; and that he was the progenitor of a long series of nineteenth-century vampires.

The first part of this thesis – the descent of the Byronic Hero from Milton through Mrs. Radcliffe – is not particularly novel, since it was a common contention even before Railo developed it in his work just mentioned. Praz, however, goes farther, and largely on the basis of an important parallel between the descriptions of Lara and of Schedoni, he writes that "Byron might be said to have derived all these characteristics [of Conrad, the Giaour, and Lara], by an almost slavish imitation, from Mrs. Radcliffe."[6] Here there is at least one obvious point which Praz seems to gloss over: Mrs. Radcliffe's villains are, after all, villains; Byron's heroes are heroes. Montoni and Schedoni cannot stand music or women, they have no understanding of virtue or of human sympathy, and consequently they never have any real sense of guilt or of repentance. In other words, they are personifications of evil, entirely unsympathetic and quite unbelievable; no attempt was made to give them depth of heart or soul. The Byronic Hero, on the other hand, is invariably courteous toward women, often loves music or poetry, has a strong sense of honor, and carries about with him like the brand of Cain a deep sense of guilt. He is almost invariably sympathetic in spite of his "crimes," none of which involve unnecessary cruelty, as do the crimes of the Gothic villain. Although the Byronic Hero bears a strong physical resemblance to Mrs. Radcliffe's Gothic Villains, he has been ensouled and humanized, and this is a crucial difference.

Praz's most important purpose, however, is to prove his second point: that the Byronic Hero is a fatal and cruel lover, linked with the infamous Marquis. Now this is admittedly a difficult point to prove by references to Byron's works, since the typical Byronic Hero, with the possible exception of Manfred, is a man of courtesy and sensibility toward women: he is as tender and loving as any hero in Romantic fiction. In some cases, as is the case with Conrad in *The Corsair*, it is this very chivalry which causes his defeat (Conrad tries to save the women of the harem in his raid on the Turkish port, and the delay causes his capture). Fatal the Byronic Hero may be; cruel he most decidedly is not. And he is not even in any very significant sense "fatal to his women," except in that he is often a "star-crossed lover"; but then so were Romeo and a hundred other heroes of Romantic story. Praz then shifts adroitly to a discussion of Byron's life (a woefully common practice with Byron critics), particularly of his relationship with his wife. There is certainly good reason to doubt Lady Byron's testimony on Byron's cruelty in his relations with her, although Praz accepts her word without question, but in any case this is a different matter entirely, since Byron is not his heroes, in spite of a hundred years of confusion of the two. This biographical evidence could scarcely even have contributed to the legendary Byronic Hero (admittedly an amalgamation of Byron and his poetry), since the testimony on Byron's supposed cruelty did not become public gossip at least until Mrs. Stowe's "revelations" of 1869.

Finally, Praz maintains that for the fashion of Vampirism, too, "Byron was largely responsible," and, sure enough, a few pages later the Byronic Hero has an added attribute, and we read of "the vampire loves of the Byronic Fatal Man." [7] This attribute Praz bases on a passing reference in one poem and on the fragment of a ghost story written as a joke. The passing reference to vampirism in the *Giaour* (755f.) is part of a Mohammedan curse on the hero, complete with references to his wife and daughter (when so far as the poem shows, he has neither); Byron obviously intended the curse as a bit of "local color," and there is no evidence whatsoever that the passage became at all notorious in Byron's time. The fragment of a ghost story Byron wrote as his part of the now-famous evening's entertainment with the Shelleys – the evening which produced *Frankenstein*. Byron's fragment, elaborated by Dr. Polidori and published as *The Vampire*, is a small fraction indeed of the complete tale – in his portion of the story Byron had not even introduced the vampire – and, in any case, the whole matter has nothing to do with the Byronic Hero. For the most part the Byronic Hero was a typical romantic lover, and nowhere in all of the poems is he referred to either literally or figuratively as a vampire-lover.

Praz's study seems to me to illustrate very well the typical difficulty which a critic encounters who does not distinguish between Byron, his heroes, and Byronism in legend and literary history, but his study has nevertheless been very influential. Even Samuel C.

Chew, perhaps the foremost contemporary Byron scholar, referred recently to "the Byronic concepts of the daemonic male and the *femme fatale*." [8] (And the *femmes* in Byron, so far as I can see, are sometimes spaniel-like, but never fatal.) And Cedric Hentschel, in his book-length analysis of *The Byronic Teuton: Aspects of German Pessimism 1800–1933*, has to a large extent attempted to fill in the gap on German literature left by Praz's concentration on the literature of England, France, and Italy.

Hentschel's analysis is obviously quite Prazian: "the Byronic Hero is a tripartite individual: he is the type of the satanic, sadistic dandy. Insofar as he is satanic, he is a descendant of Prometheus-Lucifer; insofar as he is a sadist, he stands in the shadow of 'the divine Marquis'; as a dandy, he manifests a fastidious exhibitionism." [9] For evidence of the dandiacal element in our hero, Hentschel points to Sardanapalus, perhaps the least typical of all of Byron's heroes. For the thesis of sadism Hentschel is obviously indebted to Praz, but he strains for further evidence in Byron's works. We find that "the sadistic element in Byron's works is large . . . Byron . . . reveals his will to sadism under the thin guise of vampirism, in his fondness for ruins as a poetic backcloth (*Childe Harold's Pilgrimage* is a necrophilistic orgy), and in certain tricks of style, such as his studied applications of the metaphor of the gladiator to his heroes." [10] Of Byron's alleged vampirism enough has been said; I can find only one instance of the gladiator metaphor in the romances (*Lara*, I, 13); and the judgment on *Childe Harold* is undoubtedly one of the most singular in critical scholarship. If a "fondness for ruins as a poetic backcloth" is to be used as evidence of sadism and necrophilia, Parnell and the gentle Dyer must have been at least sadists *manqué*, and the latter half of the eighteenth century must indeed have been one long necrophilistic orgy.

Several conclusions emerge from even so brief a review of these studies of the Byronic Hero. If we are to do him justice, we must study him more objectively, and not call him to account for all the sins of the last one hundred fifty years, from those of the Marquis de Sade to those of Nazi Germany. Also, and perhaps most important, he must be studied first in the context of the literature of the

Romantic Movement – the poems, plays, and novels of his own time – not in the context of the work of Heine or of Swinburne or of Count von Platen. And finally, he must be studied as he exists in Byron's works; we have no clear right to foist on him the characteristics of his creator without clear evidence.

This last point deserves some emphasis, I think, since with no other English poet has the identification of poet and poetic characters been so often made. Many of his contemporaries made this identification, and it is amusing to see Lady Caroline or the Countess of Blessington or even Annabella Milbanke looking forward to seeing Childe Harold, and being disappointed and a bit piqued when all they met was Byron. And in spite of Byron's protestations to the contrary, the literary critics of his own day – Scott, Jeffrey, Hazlitt, or, later, Macaulay – all insisted that Byron portrayed himself under the thin guise of the Giaour or of Lara. Georg Brandes and Hippolyte Taine, Byron's staunchest admirers at the close of the last century, carried on this theme, and even Oliver Elton, in our own century, writes that anything but a biographical approach to Byron is "impossible."[11] With the advent of the New Criticism, with its doctrines of the impersonality of poetry, one could perhaps have expected a new turn in Byron criticism, but even T. S. Eliot tells us that the romances ultimately fail because Byron did not know himself well enough and therefore made his heroes inconsistent, and *Don Juan* succeeds because in this poem "we get something much nearer to genuine self-revelation." For Don Juan is not heroic, and his "innocence" and his "passivity" in his relationships with women illustrate the truth of Peter Quennell's "contention" (presumably that Byron was dominantly homosexual).[12]

Now of course there are autobiographical elements in the Byronic Hero; every poetic character is to an extent a projection of his author's personality, if for no other reason than that the author must have felt moods and attitudes analogous to those of his heroes in order to understand and express them. It is even true that after the initial success of *Childe Harold* Byron sometimes assumed this role in public, but no more than Sterne, for instance, assumed the character of Parson Yorick, even to the point of manners and of dress, and to signing his letters with his hero's name. But Sterne of course had an existence quite independent of that of his whimsical parson, and so Byron is much more than, and self-consciously distanced from, any of his heroes. One can see this in the multiple roles he played in his letters: to Lady Melbourne he was the Regency rake; to Lady Caroline (at first), a moonstruck lover; to Hobhouse, a lively extrovert and party wit; to Augusta, an affectionate and loving older brother. At the end of his life, when he was setting off on the serious and chivalric expedition which was to mean his death, he could tell Trelawney that "if things are farcical, they will do for *Don Juan*; if heroical, you shall have another canto of *Childe Harold*."[13]

The main point, however, is that all the elements of the Byronic Hero existed before him in the literature of the age. This hero is unique, in one sense, in the powerful fusion of these disparate elements into a single commanding image; but he did not spring by a miracle of parthenogenesis from Byron's mind; he is to a large extent a product of a Romantic heroic tradition which was a half-century old before he appeared. Byron may in some sense have become his hero after the fact, but his hero was no mere outgrowth of the poet's personality. Byron did not project life into literature nearly so much as he projected literature into life.

In making this study, then, I have had three major purposes in mind. First, and most important, I have attempted to seek out the origins of the Byronic Hero, not in Byron's personality, but in the cultural and especially the literary milieu of the age in which he lived. Second, I have attempted to define and briefly to trace the Byronic Hero's development in Byron's works, limiting myself in this part of the discussion to *Childe Harold*, the four first and most important romances, and the two "metaphysical" dramas – *Manfred* and *Cain*. Finally, in a concluding chapter, I have attempted to place the Byronic Hero in the Romantic tradition, especially in the light of recent studies of the cult of the hero in the nineteenth century.

I have nowhere included more than incidental discussion of Byron's last great satire. When I first began this study I thought some apology for this omission might be necessary, but I no longer think so. The term "Byronic Hero" has been common coin in literary criticism for more than one hundred and thirty years, but in all this time it has never been used, so far as I can discover, to refer to Don Juan. This satire was not widely read or highly esteemed in Byron's own day or through most of the nineteenth century; even Matthew Arnold rests Byron's fame largely on *Childe Harold.* But a more important reason for excluding Don Juan from the family of Byronic Heroes is that he does not seem at all to share a common paternity: he is, if anything, far more closely related to Tom Jones or to Candide than to any of the Romantic heroes. He is, of course, overshadowed by the more powerful personality of the narrator, and it can be argued that the narrator takes on some of the characteristics of the earlier heroes. But even he has no Gothic coloring and little of their metaphysical rebellion, and surely his dominant trait is a pervasive irony and a sense of humor – characteristics not notable in any of the earlier heroes, from Childe Harold to Cain. And, in any case, a discussion of the problems in *Don Juan* would deserve another and a very different essay.

1 OUR LAST GREAT AGE OF HEROES

OUR ordinary twentieth-century working concept of the Romantic Movement is by no means strictly historical, but is based on a value judgment. When we think of the great names among the English Romantic poets we think first of Wordsworth, Coleridge, Keats, Shelley, Blake, and Byron – and probably in that order. The names of Scott, Southey, Campbell, and Moore rise only as second thoughts, if at all. We need occasionally to be reminded that this value concept of the Romantic Movement was built up only very gradually over a period of almost a century, and that it was most emphatically not the picture which rose to the minds of the people of the age.

Of the estimate of the general public of the period there can be very little doubt. While Keats was wondering where his next meal was coming from, while Shelley was living on his "inheritance" and paying for the publication of his poems, while Coleridge was making a precarious living as a public lecturer and public prophet, and while Wordsworth was living on an annuity as a stamp-distributor, Campbell and Moore were making comfortable livings as London Society Poets; Scott was offered £1,500 for *Marmion* and £4,000 for *The Lady of the Lake*, and later built Abbotsford with the sale of his anonymous Waverley novels (by 1818 his annual profits had risen to £10,000); and Byron, even after his exile and social disgrace, was earning an average of £2,500 a year from his works all the while he was in Italy. It is obvious that the heroes of the general reading public were Marmion, Roderick Dhu, Childe Harold, Conrad (ten thousand copies were sold the first day), Lara, and Manfred; not the Ancient Mariner, Alastor, and Michael, much less Peter Bell, or Simon Lee with his swollen ankles.

There is perhaps no accounting for the taste of the general public – but these judgments were also shared quite broadly by the literary critics of the day. In a review of Moore's *Life of Byron*, Macaulay, one of the first to recognize a distinct period of English literature after 1780 (although he did not call it a "Romantic Movement"), called Byron and Scott the "great names" of the age.[1] In a debate at Cambridge in 1829 over the relative merits of Wordsworth and Byron, the latter won handily, but the wonder is that Wordsworth was considered at all. A month later, when the "Cambridge apostles" defended Shelley *versus* Byron at Oxford, the Oxford dons professed never to have heard of Shelley, and thought that their opponents were defending Shenstone. And when as late as 1846 Thackeray made a bitter attack on Byron's reputation, largely because of the "immorality" in *Don Juan*, he felt it necessary to add, "Woe be to the man who denies the public gods."[2] Matthew Arnold, it is true, finally placed Wordsworth above Byron, but only with evident hesitation and after voicing the highest praise for the "second-ranking" poet's merits.

Anyone attempting a historical rather than a value concept of the Romantic Movement must come to terms with popular and literary taste of the day and with the problem of the Romantic age's conception of itself. Some of the reasons for this taste are adventitious: Byron was considered a fascinating personality even before he became the center of public scandal; but the same can certainly not be said of Scott or of Moore. Then, too, the public was of course intrigued with the exotic tone and setting of heroic verse tales and novels (Scott's Middle Ages, Moore's Orient, Byron's Mediterranean); but these tales are no more exotic than *The Ancient Mariner* or Keats's *The Eve of St. Agnes*. I think a far more important reason for the popularity of these heroic tales was that since the age was one of rebellion – social, moral, and philosophical – it was also an age of heroes. These poems and novels therefore satisfied the taste of the age: they gave it a surfeit of heroes, all passion and fiery energy, all moral, intellectual, and political rebellion.

Now whatever the virtues of the early eighteenth century, it was not an age of heroes. Perhaps this is so because it was still dominated by the idea of the "Great Chain of Being," and through most of the century, at least, this order was conceived of as essentially static; and heroes, especially Romantic heroes, have the quality of always aspiring, or at least of never remaining quietly in place. Or to put it another way: the early eighteenth century was the age of analytic reason, of common sense, and increasingly of sentiment – of what Lovejoy calls, paradoxically, "rationalistic anti-intellectualism," culminating in an ethics of "prudent mediocrity." [3] It takes no more than a cursory reading of the great satirists of the Augustan age, for instance, to see that overweening pride, or *hubris*, was still a cardinal sin. It is not difficult to see what Swift and Pope were against. They were against "eccentric" individualism in whatever manner it appeared: antiquarianism and "modernism"; linguistic scholarship and the "new science"; metaphysical speculation and "enthusiasm" in all its forms. What they were for is perhaps not so clearly defined, but perhaps it would be fair to say that they were generally for excellence in established forms and within established bounds, and above all they were for order and common sense.

Such an age could and did produce great literature, of course, but generally speaking it did not produce heroes, for there is always something of rebellious individualism, of pride, of *hubris*, about heroes. In the full bloom of the Romantic age, however, these were no longer cardinal sins: they had become instead the cardinal virtues.

For the Romantic Age was our last great age of heroes. It was the era of political and military heroes: heroes of revolution from Washington to Kosciusko, celebrated by most of the Romantic poets; or popular military heroes like Wellington, von Blücher, or Lord Nelson; and, of course, above all, Napoleon, who left his shadow across Europe not only in his lifetime, but through the entire nineteenth century, and whom every hero-worshiper from

Beethoven to Nietzsche has at one time or another taken for a god. It is not merely that these men were actual heroes, since every age has its great men (and the Age of Queen Anne had Marlborough); what is important is that these men were all admired, even loved, and that they became legends and myths while they were still living. The same preoccupation with heroes shows up in the arts of the period: with those two awesome robber barons, Götz von Berlichingen and Karl Moor, Goethe and Schiller initiated Germany's literary revival, and Werther and Faust, those cosmic egoists, continued it; in England terrifying Gothic Villains shared the stage with Shakespeare's great tragic heroes, and prepared the way for the Byronic Hero himself; and all over western Europe multitudes of rejuvenated Lucifers and triumphant Prometheuses filled the air with majestic defiance and majestic suffering. Even in music: Beethoven wrote the Egmont and Prometheus overtures and celebrated a heroine of freedom in his only opera, and the first great Romantic symphony, initially dedicated to Napoleon, has come to be called "Eroica."

To speak of the Romantic Movement as the "Age of Heroes," of course, is to say also that a key characteristic of Romanticism is individualism, that this lies at the heart of the movement and is the reason for this preoccupation with the heroic. Individualism may at first seem a negative concept, and to an extent, of course, it is. But the term should connote more than mere eccentricity, whether social or intellectual. Both Romantic poets and their heroes were isolated from the society of their day; they were all in some degree rebels and outsiders.

The concept becomes clearer, I think, with a contrast between the Romantic poets and some of their Augustan predecessors. Dryden, Swift, Pope, or Samuel Johnson were severe critics of the society in which they lived, to be sure, but they were always critics from within that society; they never at any time considered that they had some inner vision of truth not visible to the common readers of their age. They were quite convinced that all men could see as they did, if they but looked at Nature in the light of their common reason and common sense. This was most certainly not so with the Romantic poets: one article of faith in every Romantic's creed was that the artist was solitary and superior, a hero and leader above the common herd. In the Preface to the *Lyrical Ballads* even Wordsworth, who was closest of all the Romantics to eighteenth-century theory, viewed the poet as a man "possessed of more than usual organic sensibility" with a "greater knowledge of human nature, and a more comprehensive soul" than that of the common man, so that even if Wordsworth is very much concerned to show the poet as a "man among men," in actuality he sets him as far outside the common run as his dalesmen were from the normal society of nineteenth-century England. And with the other Romantic poets this feeling of isolation and alienation becomes so obvious (and sometimes so painful) that there is no need to illustrate it. Keats in his letters says he will undertake to live like a hermit, and even thanks the English world for being cruel to poets, so that they can be free to compose. For Shelley, the poet is the "unacknowledged legislator" of the world; for Byron, of course, he is the outcast who learns through years of suffering that he loves not the world nor the world him.

As the poets considered themselves alienated, isolated from society because of their greater sensibilities, because of their greater closeness to nature or to God, or merely because of their radical ideas in the areas of social, theological, or moral reform, so also they alienated and isolated their heroes. Their heroes were solitaries, like Northumberland dalesmen or disillusioned hermits; they were intellectual rebels like Faust; they were moral outcasts or wanderers like Cain or Ahasuerus; or finally they were rebels against society and even against God himself, like Prometheus or Lucifer.

Of course individualism is not the sole defining characteristic of Romanticism. Organicism is certainly another: it appears in expressionism as opposed to imitative or "empirical" esthetic theory; in organic as opposed to atomist or associationist psychologies (von Hartmann, and later, Freud freely acknowledged their debts to the Romantic poets); in organic philosophies of hylozoism, panpsychism, animism, and pantheism; and especially in organic theories of world or national history (originating with Herder in Germany, or in England with Burke), and in visions of organic societies – of the past, especially in the reinterpreted Middle Ages, or in future Utopias. Moreover, organicism may seem at odds with the Romantic emphasis on the individual, since the former is often taken to imply determinism, or even fatalism, as anti-Romantic critics are so quick to point out (see Yvor Winters on Romantic esthetic theory, or Kierkegaard on Hegel, or contemporary critics of Freud). Perhaps more reasonably, organicism is often taken to imply a view of man as too integral, indeed too organic a part of society or of the universe for him to remain an alienated outsider.

There may be an ultimate contradiction here, although I am inclined to think it is more apparent than real. Every alienated poet, I suppose, attempts to build some dream-world in which he or his hero can feel more at home. In any case, the fact remains that Romanticism was the age of individualists and also the age of organicism: many of the poets and philosophers who saw visions of organic societies or of organic universes were also the men who saw history in terms of heroes and hero-worship. Even Rousseau, closest to the eighteenth-century analytic-democratic tradition, had his theory of the "general will" and of culture leaders who were to apprehend it and execute it. Hegel had his *weltgeschichtliche Mann* and his admiration for Alexander and Caesar (and of course for Frederick). Carlyle had his vision of Ygdrasil, of Abbot Samson, and of Cromwell. And even the mild-mannered Emerson, with his borrowed pantheistic view of the universe, saw history as the shadow of great men.

A study of heroes and of hero types must then be an important, even an indispensable, factor in an understanding of the Romantic Movement, but I believe that such an approach through the hero is useful in understanding the culture of almost any era. The hero as he appears in literature bears with him the ethos of the age, the unspoken assumptions, the philosophical presuppositions in the context of which his existence becomes meaningful. His life mirrors not so much the events of the age as its tastes, its values, its aspirations and hopes for the future. One has understood a great deal of cultural history if one understands the rise of Satan from his uneasy and equivocal position in Milton's epic, through the increasingly hesitant condemnation of eighteenth-century critics, to his absolution and near-apotheosis among the Romantics. And one can learn even more, I feel, by tracing the "Hero of Sensibility" from the self-assured "esthetics of feeling" of Yorick, through the profound *Weltschmerz* and *Sehnsucht nach Unendliche* of Childe Harold or of Faust, and the tragic disillusionment of Arnold's "Empedocles on Aetna," to the knowing skepticism and recurrent passivity and resignation of Clough's "Dipsychus" (the "little Victorian Faust") or of that representative esthete, Marius the Epicurean. Whether the hero in literature precedes the specific philosophic formulation of his creed or not, does not matter very much; each reflects and complements the other. But I believe that one must also concede that the hero gives one the broader and often the deeper perspective of the spirit of the age which he represents. To understand the doctrine of sensibility in its fullest sense one must turn to Yorick or to Harley, not to Shaftesbury's *Moralist*, and Faust and Childe Harold give us a far clearer picture of what it means to be a Romantic than do innumerable treatises of Hegel or of the brothers Schlegel.

For the purpose of this study, then, I will outline and discuss in the succeeding chapters a range of heroes of the "pre-Romantic" eighteenth century and of the Romantic Movement proper. The heroes will appear in an order neither strictly chronological nor strictly logical, but which combines both approaches. There are definite logical and chronological relationships between the individual heroes, and some of the types can even be said to "fade into" one another, as do colors in the spectrum – the Gothic Villain into the Noble Outlaw, for instance – and the possible combinations, as is the case with the primary hues of the spectrum, provide an almost infinite variety of types and shades. Most of the heroes in this list have been typed and classified before, and some of them, like Faust and the Gothic Villain, have been the subjects of detailed scholarly studies. Still, to summarize the characteristics of these types, to distinguish them clearly, and to show something of their complex interrelationships, should serve an important purpose in characterizing both pre-Romanticism and the Romantic Movement proper.

Such a range of heroes will also provide antecedents and a context, a scheme and a terminology, for the discussion of the Byronic Hero himself, who is always a combination of these elements, sometimes unified and sometimes not; and this will be a terminology not derived from an analysis of Byron's personality or of his biography, but firmly rooted in the literature of the times. In brief, an analysis of these types will, I hope, enable us to see the Byronic Hero in an age of heroes, so that we may also see the age in the Byronic Hero.

This, in summary, is the list: The pre-Romantic eighteenth-century types are the Child of Nature, the Hero of Sensibility, and the Gothic Villain. All will be defined in some detail in the following chapters, so it should be sufficient to say here that in the Child of Nature I mean to include all of the naïve, unsophisticated, usually impulsive and somewhat aggressive types, with primitivistic or at least "close-to-nature" origins; the Heroes of Sensibility will include the relatively well-bred and sophisticated cultivators of feelings – feelings ranging from graveyard gloom through the merely tearful to the whimsical; the name of the Gothic Villain is of course self-explanatory. The Romantic types are the Noble Outlaw (matured in Scott's Marmion or Byron's Lara), the Faust-figure, Cain and the Wandering Jew, and Satan-Prometheus.

Certain relationships both within the two major groups and between the members of both groups become, I believe, immediately apparent.

Two of the major eighteenth-century types – the Child of Nature and the Man of Feeling – presuppose the doctrines of the essential goodness of human nature, and of the practicability or even the necessity of all moral suasion being effected through an appeal to the emotions. But neither of these types is really a thoroughgoing rebel in his society. The Man of Feeling is set apart from common men because of his peculiar and exacerbated sensitivity, although he shares the professed moral and social codes of his neighbors; the Child of Nature, sometimes used as a critic of society, is also shown in the process of adjusting to its demands (one thinks of Belcour in *The West Indian* or, in another situation, of Tom Jones). Even the Gothic Villain, certainly an outlaw and a moral renegade, takes his colors and his personality from the society around him; he acknowledges his wickedness as motivated by cupidity or lust, and he never makes appeals to the reader's sympathy on the grounds that he has been persecuted by an unjust society or by repressive social or moral codes.

The Romantic Heroes, on the other hand, from the Noble Outlaw through Satan-Prometheus, stand firmly as individuals outside of society. Thoroughgoing rebels, they invariably appeal to the reader's sympathies against the unjust restrictions of the social, moral, or even religious codes of the worlds in which they find themselves. This transformation can be seen most clearly in the passage from the Gothic Villain to the Noble Outlaw. The two have, first of all, much in common: in their physical appearance and bearing – dark, handsome, but with a cool reserve or even austerity of manner; in the sense of mystery and frequently of destiny which surrounds their every appearance; in the frequent flashes of a guilty conscience. But there is a large and important difference: the pre-Byronic Gothic Villain (of the novel, at least) is never sympathetic; if anything, he and his crimes are made to appear even more monstrous and grotesque by the addition of gratuitous acts of cruelty or sadism; the Noble Outlaw, on the other hand, is always first a victim of, and only then a rebel against, society; his sins, if not completely exonerated, are at least palliated by reference to his innate gentleness of nature, shown especially in his courteous treatment of women. There is a significantly parallel development, on the supernatural level, in the metamorphosis of Satan, from the publication of *Paradise Lost* to the Romantic Movement. He comes into gradual favor first as the exemplar of the sublime, and then as the prototype and almost the patron saint of Romantic rebels, first against an unjust society, and finally against an unjust God. The other two Romantic heroes – Faust and Cain-Ahasuerus – are Romantic revivals rather than gradual developments from eighteenth-century types. Faust has no important forebears in eighteenth-century England, and one must go back to the Renaissance for his last significant appearance. One can readily see why: the thirst after infinite knowledge which he represents was *hubris* to a neoclassical age: "presume not God to scan; / The proper study of Mankind is Man." And Cain and Ahasuerus, villains or buffoons to former ages, come to figure forth that recurrent Romantic concern with the eternal and solitary wanderer, who had always an air about him of the mysterious and the supernatural and above all of destiny or tragic fate.

It can of course be readily seen that the typing or classification of these heroes entails a great deal of oversimplification. Heroes are almost never found to be "pure" and unalloyed in their conformity to a type except perhaps in works of the most minor literary figures; one might say that the relative "impurity" of the character as a type is in direct proportion to the relative genius of the author. Great poets do not deal in types; they deal only in representative individuals. Even so, such a classification is still useful, first of all as an end in itself in the organization of literary history, and more important, in that it provides us with concepts which will enable us to understand the products of genius.

Still a note of warning seems in order here: this study is concerned with the major hero types of the Romantic Movement and with their interrelationships, especially the heroes which were to be important in the works of Byron, and I make no attempt to indulge in that kind of scholarship which has become known from the country of its origin as *Quellenstudien.* Much work of this sort has been done in the Romantic movement, particularly with Byron, since he has been so popular on the Continent among German scholars, who are or were the most intrepid of searchers for *Quellen* in the arid wastes of unknown and unread works of literature. Such studies undoubtedly have a place and an importance in literary history, although sometimes running to absurd extremes. They have also, however, a more fundamental limitation: in piling up parallels of plot detail or of verbal reminiscence, scholars are very likely to overlook other more important factors in the works they consider. Just as in discussing *Manfred* some scholars search diligently in Byron's biography for evidence of incest or of an unforgotten romance with Mary Chaworth, so other scholars spend their time looking for verbal echoes of *Faust* or *René* or *St. Irvyne*, and overlook far more important problems of literary history or tradition.

In the next two chapters, then, I will deal with these heroes individually, first with the eighteenth-century pre-Romantic types, and then with the four Romantic figures. I will attempt to sketch in broad outline the major characteristics of each species, to fill in the general cultural or intellectual milieu which gave individual heroes their significance or even their existence, and to exemplify their appearance in certain popular works of the day. Many of these works, like many of the heroes whose lives they tell, have long since faded into oblivion except for occasional brief resuscitation in graduate seminars. For the most part widely influential in their time, some of them – Mrs. Radcliffe's novels or Scott's romances, for instance – were certainly far more popular than the poems or novels of the same period which we still read. Whether or not Byron read the works in question is, as I say, not of great importance in this study, since I am not attempting to prove any direct literary influences; the works I will discuss are chosen only because they represent types of heroes of whose importance in the age and of whose general influence on Byron there can be little doubt. Byron was quite well-read, perhaps especially in the contemporary popular literature which seems no longer of much importance to us. Like the youthful Shelley, he devoured Gothic novels by the score; he never missed a Scott romance, or, later, a Waverley novel; and in his semi-official connections with the theater (one remembers that he personally encouraged Coleridge to finish *Remorse* for the stage) he must have read or seen produced a hundred long-forgotten melodramas and "Gothic" tragedies. One can take it for granted that he was perfectly familiar with all the heroes of this list, although, if proof is needed, there is ample evidence in his works.

PART ONE. EIGHTEENTH-CENTURY HERO TYPES

II THE CHILD OF NATURE

IN A monograph entitled *Nature's Simple Plan*, Chauncey Brewster Tinker gives an amusing and informative account of primitivism in the eighteenth century. He covers such peculiarly "age of reason" phenomena as Lord Monboddo, the "Scottish Rousseau" with his primitive notions of evolution and his fanciful searches for caudal appendages, and the enthusiastic reception and eventual disillusionment with imported "noble savages" on the one hand, such as Omai or Prince Lee Bo, and on the other with native peasant bards such as Stephen Duck, the Thresher Poet, or Mary Collier, the Poetical Washerwoman. Professor Tinker then concludes: "the 'noble savage' was the offspring of the rationalism of the Deist philosophers, who, in their attack upon the Christian doctrine of the fall of man, had idealized the Child of Nature. Man in a state of nature . . . untutored, was . . . the noblest work of God."[1]

At the outset, however, I think it is useful to distinguish, as Professor Tinker and others do not, between the older, neoclassical and stoic Noble Savage and his son and literary heir in an increasingly sentimental age, the "romanticized" and far more ebullient Child of Nature.

The Noble Savage has the oldest and most classical family tree of any of the heroes of the age. The roots of his genealogy can of course be found in the legend, as old as history and celebrated even in classical literature, of a prehistorical "golden age," a time of primeval innocence and joy, of golden leisure and abundant fruitfulness. This conception survived through the Middle Ages as a stock classical reference, and paradoxically enough, considering its pagan origins, it was frequently fused with visions of prelapsarian Eden.

The idea, thus blessed, was found especially useful by philosophers and critics, even in the Renaissance, who were for one reason or another attempting to castigate what they viewed as the corruptions of contemporary civilization. Erasmus was perhaps only half serious in his criticism of "school knowledge" and in his praise of the state of nature in the *Encomium Moriae*, but Montaigne for once seems quite in earnest in his full-dress portrait of noble savages in his essay "Of Cannibals" (see also "On Coaches"). From the Renaissance through the eighteenth century the legend found a final reinforcement in "romanticized" accounts of explorations, especially to America and to the South Seas. These accounts were popular reading throughout the period, and if the savages found by the explorers were not always noble, they were usually made to seem so by chroniclers responsive to a popular taste which demanded these idyllic visions of primeval innocence.

Still, as long as the intellectual climate remained essentially orthodox and Christian, the "natural man" could not become a hero. Nostalgic references to a golden age could be used for decoration, as a stock classical device, or to describe the blissful state before the fall of Adam, but there could be no full-blown noble savages. It is worth remembering that in his description of the state of nature as a state of war Hobbes was not considered and did not consider himself un-Christian. The Noble Savage needed a new philosophy of optimism, a philosophy not inimical to ideas of "natural" goodness and "natural" religion.

Such a philosophy was found in the increasingly deistic *Weltanschauung* of the eighteenth century. The doctrines of the Cambridge Platonists and the increasing Arminianism among late seventeenth-century latitudinarian divines helped to do away with the idea of the innate depravity of man. John Locke, often called the father of eighteenth-century optimism (although he was certainly no primitivist), made natural reason the common property of all men – including untutored savages – and his list of "causes of error," with its emphasis (following Bacon) on prejudices and preconceptions and on the acceptance of authority and received opinion, could easily be given a primitivist interpretation. In any case, with the rise of eighteenth-century deism there arose also the new "Natural Man," abstract, certainly idealized, and a bit too naked, stripped as he was of all of the "prejudices" of civilization, and thus stripped also of most of his individuality and human diversity.

The first "natural man" to appear in literature is this older, more reserved, Noble Savage. He tends in general to be either stoically laconic, or sententious, even somewhat priggish, given to lengthy comments on contemporary civilization, always contrasting it unfavorably with the simpler culture of his native land. Given his abstract background of rationality, and given his somewhat shadowy and colorless character, in which there can of course be no development, this type of hero generally is used only for brief appearances in long descriptive poems such as Thomson's *Seasons*, or as a convenient persona for the satirist. Such are the American Indian "kings" who appear briefly in the *Tatler* and *Spectator*, for instance, and it is easy to see the relationship between this type and the host of "ideal observers" who appear in satirical essays and poems all through the century. For the most part this older "natural man" does not survive into pre-Romanticism, but he must be kept in mind, since some of his characteristics do appear even in Romantic Children of Nature. The heroes of the radical "Jacobin" novelists, Godwin and Bage among them, are sometimes prone to the same sort of pregnant and sententious commentaries, and Outalissi, the Oneida chief in Campbell's *Gertrude of Wyoming*, although greatly sentimentalized, maintains the same stoic front of forbearance as the earlier more classical figure.

The second "natural man" to appear in literature was the younger, more sentimental, and distinctly naïve Child of Nature. Although as a hero he has the same cultural origins as his older classical counterpart, he is nevertheless genuinely distinctive, in youth, appearance, and temperament. Thrust into a strange adult society with nothing but his native innocence and ignorance, the Child of Nature could easily be sentimentalized and romanticized, and, unlike his older counterpart, he was capable of considerable development of character and therefore of being used in plots of the "initiation-into-evil" tale or of the *Bildungsroman.*

Since this hero was of great importance for the Romantic Movement, it may be worthwhile to review in the abstract his significant characteristics before discussing a few of his literary incarnations. His origins are usually humble, but there is almost always some obscurity or mystery connected with his birth; often he is an orphan brought up by strangers who have concealed his true parentage. If he is not actually a savage by birth (and frequently he is not), he has been raised in some relatively wild and uncultivated place, perhaps among American Indians (Bage's Hermsprong) or in the West Indies (Cumberland's Belcour), or nearer home, in Wales (Godwin's Fleetwood), or the Highlands of Scotland (Beattie's Edwin or Norval in Home's *Douglas*). In any case, he is always depicted as a being close to nature and to natural life, and this association has given him moral principles and love and natural generosity, and has developed his innately acute sensibilities. These natural sensibilities become more tender and sentimental as the century progresses, until some Children of Nature (Godwin's Fleetwood, for instance) refuse to hunt or fish because they cannot stand to harm their animal friends. Their love of natural scenery runs usually to the sublime – nature in her wilder or more formidable aspects. In appearance the Child of Nature is handsome, of course, but with none of the effeminacy of the Man of Feeling. He is physically strong and healthy, and has a temperament to correspond. As contrasted with the older Noble Savage, the Child of Nature is naturally ebullient, even aggressive, and it is this aggressiveness, combined with his naïveté, which gets him into so many scrapes and often provides the substance of the *Bildungsroman.* "Natural" reason is more typical of the older classical type; the young Child of Nature is either incapable of or hostile to analytic reason, and depends upon instinct, emotion, or native intuition, and, of course, on his natural goodness of heart. Finally, unlike his earlier counterpart, he is almost always in love, and in love he is always unreasoning and romantic. Love and marriage as mere social conventions or social conveniences are inimical to his very nature.

Once this hero has been characterized it is easy to see that Tom Jones, the most famous hero of the century, is also a Child of Nature, even if he is of course much more. He passes through most of the novel as a humble orphan, although, as frequently happens with heroes, he turns out to be the eldest son of a gentleman. But most characteristic is his naïveté and natural goodness of heart, as contrasted with the greed, hypocrisy, and snobbery of the social world in which he moves. Then, too, although his love affair with Sophia is tender and frequently as sentimental as in Romantic fiction, his sensibility never overcomes his natural good spirits or aggressive temperament. Even in the most tenderly trying of circumstances, he is capable of eating a good meal, and in his own day he became notorious for the fact that even his sexual appetite remains unimpaired.

But as usual, it is with the minor literary figures that the Child of Nature as a "type" hero becomes most obvious.

In 1771 Garrick produced a sentimental comedy at Drury Lane which immediately made the fame and the fortune of its author, Richard Cumberland. The play was greeted with "extraordinary enthusiasm," it was performed twenty-eight nights in its first season, and it "survived longer than any other sentimental comedy of this period." [2] This comedy, so popular in its day but long since forgotten, was *The West Indian*, and its hero, Belcour, born and raised on a West Indian plantation, was a Child of Nature. His origin is a mystery and he is ostensibly an orphan, although as it turns out he is actually the son of a wealthy London merchant. But his naïveté, his goodness of heart, and his ebullient and passionate nature are all ascribed to the fact that he has been raised a Child of Nature. We are forewarned of his appearance by the arrival of his baggage and of his menagerie: "two green monkeys, a pair of grey parrots, a Jamaica sow . . . and a Mangrove dog"; and in his first scene he tells us that "my passions are my masters; they take me where they will." Because of his warmth of nature he insults the girl with whom he has fallen in love at first sight and is thereupon challenged to a duel by her brother, and because of his ignorance he is duped by a rather transparently wicked old harridan who makes off with his money and jewels; but all of this is excused by Charlotte, who blesses "the torrid zone forever, whose rapid vegetation quickens nature into such benignity!" The latitudes of London, we find, "are made for politics and philosophy; friendship has no root in this soil." His patron warns his friends that Belcour's "manners, passions, and opinions are not yet assimilated to this climate; he comes amongst you a new character, an inhabitant of a new world. . . ." After he has been initiated into the evils of London society and into the mysteries of Romantic love, Belcour (the pun on his name is of course obvious), with "his heart beaming with benevolence, an animated nature, fallible, indeed, but not incorrigible," passes into the hands of his new-found father and his new-found bride, who will, we are assured, temper his passion and benevolence with common sense.[3]

Three minor novelists at the end of the century, all of them "Jacobins"—Thomas Holcroft, Robert Bage, and William Godwin—created Child of Nature heroes who are especially interesting in that they are less sentimental and more sententious than Belcour; they seem in part to be "throwbacks" to the older neoclassical natural man. The first of these virtuous radicals, Frank Henley of Holcroft's *Anna St. Ives* (1792), is the least interesting. Though not himself a savage, he is early associated with the wilds, and he looks to the natives for the principles of his Godwinian and natural-reason moral philosophy. The hero of Robert Bage's *Hermsprong, or Man as He Is Not* (1796) is far more interesting, and the novel itself has considerable literary merit.[4] He appears suddenly from nowhere on the scene of the story and a great mystery is made of his origins, but it finally appears that he was born in America of a German merchant and raised among the Nawdoessie Indians in the village of Michillimakinac. As is common with Children of Nature, Hermsprong is much given to long walks in the open country—up to forty miles in a day—and to simple meals of two pounds of cold roast beef "seasoned with a quart or two of good spring water." He is also given to sudden and unpremeditated acts of benevolence, for which he apologizes that "It was an impulse; and it was irresistible." His naïveté is shown not only in his lack of polish or his outlandish table manners, but in his notable lack of tact in dealing with people whom he considers arrogant or hypocritical, including, unfortunately, the father of the woman whom he wishes to court. But of course his heart is good and his instincts are sound, thanks to the unpretentious moral training which he received in youth from the Indians of Michillimakinac. This novel has an additional interest, however, in that a clear contrast is set up between the hero, who is a Child of Nature, and the narrator, who is a Man of Feeling. Glen, the narrator, although poor, is a gentleman of education and sensibility; unhappily, he is also of a meek and passive nature, resigned after an early unfortunate love affair to a life of retired bachelorhood: he admires from afar the beauty which the more vital and aggressive Hermsprong wins with ease.

With the Child of Nature of William Godwin's *Fleetwood* we arrive at the truly Romantic stage of our hero's transformation. The hero has by this time been further sentimentalized: instead of meals of roast beef, forty-mile walks, feats of daring (Belcour engages in a duel and Hermsprong stops a carriage on the very edge of a cliff), or sententious philosophical comparisons between civilization and noble savagery, the fully romanticized Child is more inclined to solitary brooding and dreaming, to music, and to the writing of poetry. Even so, the greatest change is not so much in the character of the hero as in the Nature of which he is the child. Nature is no longer the construction (or the conglomeration) of abstract principles that formed the neoclassic world or the world of Godwinian reason (*Political Justice*). Nature has become warm, living, and even mystical – it has become organic. Godwin wrote *Fleetwood* (1805) in the last stage of his gradual transformation from the abstract eighteenth-century empiricism of *Political Justice* to his nineteenth-century full-blown Romanticism, and his hero shows the change. Born in the solitary savagery of Merionethshire, in North Wales, Fleetwood early imbibes his goodness of heart and cultivates his innate sensibilities in the wildness of nature. He shows his benevolence not only in countless acts of kindness to the simple peasantry, but in his refusal to persecute dumb animals by hunting or fishing. Even when he goes up to Oxford he is accompanied by his favorite dog (one is reminded of Byron at Cambridge). But here begins his period of dissipation, as in all such *Bildungsromane*, a dissipation which he continues later in Paris. There he is disillusioned in love and flies in desperation to the Alps, like Byron in rather different circumstances, and in Switzerland he also is restored by the wild mountain scenery, by the simple life of the Swiss peasantry, and by the advice of the perennial didactic solitary. The novel indeed goes on for another two volumes, but the type is already clear, and the parallels both with Wordsworth and with *Childe Harold* are certainly obvious.

Appropriately enough, the account of this hero closes with the Wordsworth of the *Prelude*. Here we have the fully developed Child of Nature of Romanticism. His solitude, his daydreaming, his sensibility, his love of music and poetry, and above all his love of Nature, are familiar to everyone. And it is equally clear that in the *Prelude* Wordsworth has passed far beyond the principles of rational simplicity, the common reason of the golden age, or the mere goodness of heart of the sentimentalized Child of Nature. The difference lies very largely in Wordsworth's conception of the universe, which is as different from that of Swift's Houyhnhnms or of the early Godwin as either conception is different from our own.

But Wordsworth is the only great poet of the Romantic Movement proper who makes much use of the Child of Nature. This hero in all his manifestations was essentially an eighteenth-century figure, and he was on the decline in the Romantic Movement. Speaking more particularly of the Noble Savage, Professor Fairchild writes that "those poets born well before the close of the eighteenth century, and who began to write about 1790, are most likely to feel the noble savage idea . . . I have a strong opinion that the noble savage was dead as a significant figure by 1810."[5] There are elements of the Child of Nature in the person of Childe Harold, to be sure, but I believe this is his last significant appearance not only in Byron's works, but in Romantic poetry in general, and even Childe Harold is far more than, and not even predominantly, a Child of Nature.

III THE HERO OF SENSIBILITY: Man of Feeling or Gloomy Egoist

THE Hero of Sensibility was more of a novelty in the eighteenth century than the Child of Nature, and, in spite of his always much less robust constitution, he proved to have far greater survival power in the literature of the times and of the succeeding age. By the Hero of Sensibility I mean to denote the hero who is distinguished not by daring exploits or superior intelligence, but quite simply by his capacities for feeling, mostly for the tender emotions – gentle and tearful love, nostalgia, and a pervasive melancholy that ranges from autumnal musing to "grave-yard" moralizing, with occasional lapses into charnel-house sensationalism. The two eighteenth-century forms of this type – the Man of Feeling and the Gloomy Egoist – reached their peak of importance before 1780, but the Hero of Sensibility, with feelings deepened to genuine *Weltschmerz* or *Sehnsucht nach Unendliche*, remained a dominant figure all though the Romantic Movement. Closer to the Child of Nature than the Gloomy Egoist, the Man of Feeling is probably the more important of the two for the Romantic Movement.

As most of his critics have pointed out, the Man of Feeling was newborn in the eighteenth century, a natural product of that great spring thaw of sentiment which affected most of western Europe, but especially England, in the beginning of this period. Most historians agree that the Man of Feeling shares a common philosophical background with the Child of Nature in the two basic assumptions of what is called eighteenth-century optimism: the belief in the moral goodness of the "natural man," and the egalitarian conception of a common reasonableness, both in man and in the natural universe. But when attempting anything more specific as to his origins, almost every literary historian has held to his own theory, or at least implanted his own emphasis.[1]

Most philosophical-theological theorists trace the Man of Feeling to the "father" of eighteenth-century sentimentalism, the third earl of Shaftesbury, and to his disciple and popularizer, Francis Hutcheson. Certainly Shaftesbury became the most famous philosophical exponent of "natural goodness," and in his *Characteristics* (1711), he coined the term "moral sense." Moreover his theories found a grateful audience among literate men all though the century: Adam Smith pays him tribute, and, as recent historians of philosophy have shown, even the hardheaded skeptic David Hume was considerably in his debt for his ethics. Other theorists have pointed out that latitudinarian Anglicans, influenced (as was Shaftesbury) by the Cambridge Platonists, were preaching doctrines of natural benevolence as far back as the end of the seventeenth century. Certainly also the low-church elements and the dissenting sects, with their emphasis on the emotions and on self-analysis – what Leslie Stephen, with some bias, called "mildewed Christianity"– are partly responsible for the rise of sentiment.

Sociologically oriented theorists have been inclined to point to the rise of a new reading public in the commercial middle classes – many of them low-church or dissenting. These were the readers to whom the *Tatler* and the *Spectator* appealed, for instance, and there is certainly abundant evidence both of moralism and of sentimentalism in many of these papers, some of which were in print even before the publication of Shaftesbury's *Characteristics*.

Finally, as antisentimental, orthodox Anglican divines were quick to recognize even at the time, much of the new sentiment was an importation from France. The sentimental novel of adventure, beginning with Mme. de La Fayette's *La Princesse de Clèves* (1678), had been flourishing in France for at least fifty years before Richardson emerged, and a good many of these novels had reached England, in translation and in the original language. Although Richardson could not read French, there is enough similarity between Marivaux's *Vie de Marianne* (1731–41) and *Clarissa* for some critics to maintain that he must have heard of the Frenchman's story. The Abbé Prevost, however, forms the most direct link between the two countries. He helped popularize English sentiment in France, particularly with his condensed and adapted version of *Clarissa*, but the influence was by no means one way. His sentimental novels had a great vogue in England, beginning with his pseudohistorical *Cleveland* (trans. 1731–32), the hero of which has some right to be called the first Man of Feeling, and a modern critic has called Prevost the "originator of the novel of introspection." [2] Certainly Patrice, a secondary but important figure in Prevost's *Dean of Coleraine* (trans. 1742–43), one of Sterne's favorite novels, is as much a Man of Feeling, especially of suffering, as most of his English counterparts.

Whatever his origins, however, the Man of Feeling was firmly established in the English literary scene by the middle of the century. But in the latter half of the century a considerable change took place in his personality. Just as the earlier morally upright and stoically sententious Noble Savage gave way to the later romanticized and often wayward Child of Nature, so the early, moral Man of Feeling, inordinately pious and devout, and given to interrupting the story with long edifying discourses, began to yield place to a new type which one can call, by contrast, the esthetic Man of Feeling. Perhaps this shift can be attributed to the increasing secularization in what the Victorians were to call the "godless" eighteenth century, for, as we shall see, a parallel development took place with the Gloomy Egoist.

In any case, there is a radical difference, not just of degree, but even of kind, between Bevil, the hero of Steele's *Conscious Lovers* (1722), Prevost's Cleveland (1731), and Richardson's Sir Charles Grandison (1754), on the one hand, and Sterne's Parson Yorick (1768) on the other, but that the difference is more than the addition of a sense of humor is often overlooked. Yorick still uses the accepted moral arguments as a justification for his adventures in sensibility, but it is surely obvious that for him these arguments are a mere rationalization. Yorick is an epicure of feeling, an esthete of sensibility. At one point in *A Sentimental Journal*, for instance, he offers a humorous apology for his going out of his way to pay a return visit to the poor mad Maria: "'Tis going, I own, like the Knight of the Woeful Countenance, in quest of melancholy adventures; . . . but I am never so perfectly conscious of the existence of a soul within me, as when I am entangled in them." [3] This *patior, ergo sum*, in parody of Descartes' *cogito*, points up the basic change of attitude in the age of sentiment, but more than that, it is an egocentric assertion of personality, not primarily a social or a moral assertion as it would have been with Grandison. And I believe it was this frankly esthetic attitude toward sensibility, not Sterne's doubtful jokes, which called forth the anger of moralists who had read Richardson's rape scenes in *Pamela* or *Clarissa* without a murmur of disapproval.

This type reached a climax of sentimentality and absurdity in a short novel by Henry Mackenzie which gives our hero his name: *The Man of Feeling* (1771). The influence of Sterne is obvious not only in the personality of the hero, Harley, but also in the whimsical and episodic structure of the plot. The story is briefly told: Harley, a poor young man of the country gentry, goes off to London to attempt to recoup the family fortunes. This short and of course unsuccessful trip provides most of the vignettes of the novel. Among other things he is duped and robbed by a couple of London sharpers, he rescues a fallen woman from a brothel and restores her to her forgiving father, and he picks up and takes home a broken-down discharged army captain, setting him up on a neighboring farm with his long-lost grandchildren. When he returns home, Harley meets again Miss Emily Walton, but, intimidated by her fortune, is unable to declare his love, and through the last chapters of the novel he gradually pines away and dies of nothing more or less than an excess of sensibility. Beyond this, sentimentality could not go, and the novel has left its name for the hero of an age.

The major characteristics of the Man of Feeling are by now clear.

He shares his goodness of heart and his benevolence with the Child of Nature, but in the remainder of his characteristics he is indeed quite different. The Man of Feeling belongs generally to the middle classes or to the lower gentry; he is not often an aristocrat, but on the other hand he never shares the peasant and humble origins of the Child of Nature. He is quite well educated, even if, as is the case with Harley, his education comes from the charitable tutoring of the local parson (but one remembers that another Man of Feeling, Captain Booth of Fielding's *Amelia*, has all of his author's classical learning, which was considerable). In physique and appearance he is also very different from the Child of Nature. He is not necessarily handsome, and he is never robust; usually he is pale and inclined to fevers, especially "brain fevers" brought about by fits of melancholy. Sometimes he is distinctly effeminate. He also has the temperament to match his appearance: he is timid sometimes to the point of cowardice. When Belcour is called a coward, for instance, he challenges his antagonist, albeit he is a friend, to a duel; but when Harley is called a coward, "the blood ran quicker to his cheek – his pulse beat one – no more – and regained the temperament of humanity!" Then, too, as further testimony of his timidity, we are early informed that Harley has the bashfulness not of a booby, but of a "consciousness which the most delicate feelings produce and the most extensive knowledge cannot always remove."[4] Harley is benevolent, to be sure – his quixotic adventures testify to this – but the benevolent acts are usually sporadic and ineffectual. There is far more in him of the esthetics of feeling. He is a victim of his sensibilities, but often he deliberately places himself in these sensitive situations; as Yorick says, he "goes in quest of melancholy adventure." Finally, he is always something of a solitary in the sense that he is set off from the general run of men by his very sensitivity. In this self-imposed isolation we have indeed the very antithesis of the moralistic Man of Feeling's emphasis on social sympathy, and it is not a very long step from this solitary of supersensibilities to the isolated poetic personality of Romanticism – as, for instance, Childe Harold.

But before we leave the Man of Feeling there are two foreign heroes, of great importance, who deserve some attention: Rousseau's Saint-Preux and Goethe's Werther. Oddly enough both of these heroes were to an extent products of English sentimentalism, but when they came again to English shores they brought with them depths of thought and feeling, expressions of the greater genius of their authors, which were quite new to the nascent English Romanticism.

It is common knowledge that Rousseau's *La Nouvelle Héloïse* owes much to Richardson in its epistolary form and in the plot of seduction and its tearful consequences (although in other respects it owes more to Prevost), but although Julie may bear some slight resemblance to Clarissa, Saint-Preux is certainly no Lovelace. Lovelace was by and large a Restoration rake; Saint-Preux is an eighteenth-century Man of Feeling. Like Harley or Yorick he is a gentleman; although poor, he is well educated and cultured (he is tutor to Julie), and he has a very delicate constitution (the final parting from Julie throws him into an almost fatal "fever"). But as is not the case with the English heroes, Saint-Preux's love is no mere dalliance with feelings: here we come far closer to the true Romantic passion of Byron's heroes. Rousseau writes that he decided to pattern his hero on himself, or rather on his conception of himself, and it is certain that Saint-Preux shows much of the self-exacerbating passion of his author.[5]

Rousseau had already an English reputation based on his *Discourses*, but it was the publication of this novel in 1760 that resulted in the first pronounced widening of his fame in England. Though more orthodox critics disapproved of the moral influence of the novel, all granted its emotional and rhetorical appeal, and it even found champions in such English men of letters as Richard Hurd and James Beattie, who used its doctrines of natural goodness to criticize Hobbes and Hume.[6] The French Revolution was to cause a considerable dampening of Rousseau's reputation in England, but one remembers that it was *La Nouvelle Héloïse* which Shelley introduced to Byron in Geneva in 1816, and which the two poets carried about with them on the trips around the lake that inspired the memorable tribute to Rousseau in *Childe Harold*.

Werther is of greater importance for this discussion than Saint-Preux, not only because he enjoyed a far less equivocal reception in England, but also because he represents that added breadth and profundity which transformed eighteenth-century sentimentalism into genuine Romantic *Weltschmerz.*

Werther owed much of its genesis to English sentimentalism. Goethe himself testifies to this when in *Dichtung und Wahrheit* he attempts to explain the novel's immediate and astonishing popularity among German youth. He outlines current and for the most part traditional causes for melancholy, and then goes on to say that these would not have been sufficient had there not been another "outside inducement" driving German youth toward the same end. "This came about under the influence of English literature, especially poetry, the excellences of which were accompanied by a grave melancholy, which everyone shared who had any dealings with it," he writes. The poets he mentions by name are Milton (for the "L'Allegro" and "Il Penseroso"), Edward Young (for his *Night Thoughts*), Goldsmith (for "The Deserted Village"), Gray (for the "Elegy"), Joseph Warton, and above all Ossian, who furnished "a perfectly becoming locale" for these musings, with his "ultimate Thule" of endless heaths under a Scottish Highlands moon.[7] In another passage he credits the influence of "Yorick-Sterne" in the creation of a sentimentality which, he admits, Germans like himself lacked the wit to control.[8]

Of course the same influences which prepared a welcome for Werther in Germany prepared a welcome almost as enthusiastic when he made his appearance in England. In 1779 the novel was first published in English, and six more translations appeared before 1810. By 1786, at the height of its popularity, over a score of English imitations had been published, a tragedy was being produced on the London stage, and "there were more Werther poems . . . in English than in any other language, including German." [9] Scenes from the novel appeared on ladies' fans and even on china, and prints of "Lotte" cutting bread for the children or mourning over Werther's tomb were to be found even in farmers' cottages.

Werther does of course fit the qualifications of the "esthetic"

Man of Feeling. He is a gentleman of liberal education, and well acquainted with Homer and the classics, even if he comes eventually to prefer Ossian. His sensibilities are fully as acute as Yorick's or Harley's: he is frequently overcome with Charlotte's songs played on the harpsichord, and he shares her enthusiasm for Klopstock's poetry as well as for *The Vicar of Wakefield.* He also has Yorick's passive or gently "esthetic" attitude toward sentimental situations. As he himself puts it: "And I indulge my heart as an ailing child; its every wish is granted." [10]

He is not merely an esthetic Man of Feeling, however, as were his eighteenth-century English counterparts, and herein lies his peculiar importance: however much he was popularly misunderstood at the time, he definitely points forward to Romantic Heroes of Sensibility such as Childe Harold. In the first place his feelings and his speculations have a passionate intensity which English Men of Feeling were never able to muster: one need only compare Harley's supine fading away into death with Werther's exit in suicide to see the difference. And except for the family scenes, Werther's social sympathy has also been deemphasized: he is primarily a solitary Romantic; as he puts it: "Solitude is the most precious balm of my heart," and again, "I turn in on myself, and find a world!" [11] Then, too, he is not merely a dabbler in the arts; he is like many of his Romantic counterparts an artist by profession, and much of his speculation turns upon the artist and his private vision. Finally, he is the first full victim of Romantic *Weltschmerz*; his sorrows are not merely those of unrequited love, they have taken on something of cosmic significance. Expressions like the following are among the first of the *Sehnsucht nach Unendliche* which was to be a constant theme with the Romantic Hero of Sensibility:

A great twilight All rests before our soul, our feeling dissolves in it as do our eyes, and we long, Oh! to surrender our whole being, so that we might be filled with all the ecstasy of a single magnificent consciousness – But Oh! when we hurry toward it, when the Far-off becomes the Here and Now, everything is as before, and we stand in our poverty, in our own narrowness, and our soul languishes for the refreshment which has eluded our grasp.[12]

Paradoxically enough, in another situation Werther expresses also that peculiar fear of the premature drying up of the sensibilities which was to become so characteristic of the early Byronic Hero as to be almost his trademark (see, for instance, the opening of *Childe Harold* III): "If you could but see me, my dearest, in this deluge of distractions! How parched my sensibilities are becoming; not one moment of real feeling, not a single blest hour!" [13]

But in naming the Englishmen who were so influential in creating a receptive atmosphere for *Werther* Goethe mentions not only the sentimentalists, but also and primarily the English poets of melancholy – the poets of English "spleen" who gave England in the eighteenth century of reason an international reputation as a nation of melancholics and suicides. For the second of the Heroes of Sensibility of the eighteenth century, the Gloomy Egoist, was almost as famous as the Man of Feeling. Edward Young, for instance, had an international reputation second only in importance to the reputations of Richardson and Sterne. The three influences which contributed most to the fostering and the development of the Gloomy Egoist were certain classic precedents popular in the Augustan age, the minor poems of Milton, specifically "L'Allegro" and "Il Penseroso," and a religious melancholy particularly popular among the dissenters of the period.

It is important to note that the Gloomy Egoist did have a classical sanction of sorts, as the Man of Feeling did not. The themes of withdrawal from life and of rural retirement, as represented in Horace or in the ever popular Vergilian Bucolics or Georgics, were closely allied to themes of the Gloomy Egoist, and Pomfret's *The Choice* (1700) remained for a long time one of the most popular poems of the century. More specifically, the third book of *De Rerum Natura*, in which Lucretius attempts to banish fears of death by a long "complaint of life," was quite popular, and had many imitators, including Dryden.

But Milton was the most important English poet for the eighteenth century, and his "Il Penseroso" undoubtedly exerted the single greatest influence for gloomy egoism. Milton had made melancholy respectable, associating it with beauty, with saintliness, with wisdom, and with a delight in solitary reflection in natural scenes. "Il Penseroso" provided not only a standard metric but also a standard paraphernalia for a host of gently melancholy poems, from Parnell's "Night-Piece on Death" (1721), through the Wartons and Collins, to Gray's "Elegy" (1750) and beyond, in countless imitations. Still, all the poems of this tradition remained largely "classical," in the loose sense of the term; they were restrained, in a sense impersonal, full of traditional personifications, stock references, and half-remembered "tags" from Milton and from the Greek and Latin classics. True Gloomy Egoism, with the emphasis on egoism, developed from more personal religious melancholy.

In the development of the Gloomy Egoist from the religious melancholic one can see a transformation parallel to that which occurred in the Child of Nature or the Man of Feeling. As the rather stiff moral savage developed into the Romantic Child, and as the upright moral Man of Feeling developed into an esthetic dabbler in sensibilities, so the true religious melancholy lost its motive and developed into a pose, into the exploitation of feeling for its own sake, and the cultivation of either fashionable melancholy (and this merged with the Miltonic tradition, although it remained more personal), or the more vulgar sensationalism of charnel-house horrors.

Around the turn of the century a flood of pious poems on the four last things (death, judgment, heaven, and hell) was turned out by a host of long-forgotten poets, including such men as Flatman, Baxter, and Nahum Tate. Some graveyard sensationalism emerges in this poetry, but the motives nonetheless appear to be essentially religious: the theme of a traditionally Christian (and medieval) preoccupation with death as a close and ever present reality and as a threat to move men to repentance, intensified in the late seventeenth century by visions of the awful and somewhat vindictive God of Puritan and dissenting theology. So also there seems little reason to doubt the religious purpose of the enormously popular "Day of Judgment" or "Death and Eternity" from Isaac Watts's *Horae Lyricae* (1706), or even of "The Last Day" (1713), the first considerable poetic effort of the youthful Edward Young.

But when we come to the popular works of the great triumvirate of purveyors of gloom during the "melancholy 'forties"– Edward Young, Robert Blair, and James Hervey – we do, I think, have reason to doubt the sufficiency of religious motives. Edward Young's *Night Thoughts* (1742–45) enjoyed a popularity throughout the eighteenth century, especially on the Continent (note the passage from Goethe quoted above), which was out of all proportion to its literary merit. Young's blank verse is heavy and pompous, attempting to be epigrammatic in the manner of the Augustans, but only occasionally succeeding (Johnson writes in his *Life* of Young that in his lyrics he "is always labouring to be great, and at last is only turgid"), and it is the poet's complete egocentricity and self-absorption which impress the reader most. The poem is full of self-dramatization and self-analysis; only once in all its vast length does the poet attempt to universalize his sorrows (I, 238). In Robert Blair's *The Grave*, on the other hand, we have a more Jacobean blank verse, with little of Young's turgidity. Blair uses all the well-worn properties of graveyard verse – the "sickly taper" in the "night, dark night"; the "trusty yew . . . / Midst skulls and coffins, epitaphs and worms." But what is especially striking is the occasional sensationalism which points directly ahead to the terrors of Gothic Romanticism. When we find that the "misty vaults" are "Furred round with mouldy damps and ropy slimes," or that on Beauty's "damask cheek, / The high-fed worm, in lazy volumes rolled, / Riots unscared," we have a type of morbid sensationalism out of all proportion to the professed religious motive of the verse; such details are worthy of M. G. Lewis at his best (or worst), as in the charnel-vault rape scene in *The Monk*. After Young's egocentric gloom and Blair's sensationalism James Hervey's "A Meditation among the Tombs" could not add much, but the continuing popularity of this poem and its companion pieces in *Meditations and Contemplations* (1746–47) testifies to the well-established position of the Gloomy and introspective Egoist among our galaxy of heroes.

With the waning of the fashion for puritanic and dissenting pessimism which gave him birth, the Gloomy Egoist faded away into the gentler melancholy of the countless minor imitators of Collins or of

Gray, but he left to the Romantic Hero of Sensibility the important bequest of a pose, a storehouse of stock images, and a collection of poetical themes.

The Gloomy Egoist by the very nature of things could only be a persona or a pose, not a protagonist. The Child of Nature could be initiated into adult society; the Man of Feeling could go through endless tender and soulful adventures; but the Gloomy Egoist, surfeited with life, could only meditate on death, and death is unfortunately a static subject.

But the wealth of graveyard images – a bit shopworn, to be sure, though still useful – could be counted on for stock emotional responses all through the Romantic Movement. The images of this sort – everything from the far-off sounds of evening, or midnight gloom and spectral moonlight, through Gothic ruins to charnel-house worms and skeletons – are too familiar to need cataloguing here. The more sensationalistic effects were put to good use in the new terror-Romanticism, and the gentler ones suited the moods of the new Romantic Hero of Sensibility: even Wordsworth and Coleridge could use ruined abbeys or desolate moors, and Childe Harold's fondness for ruins and moonlight are too familiar to need comment.

In addition to the stock images, the Gloomy Egoist bequeathed to the Romantic Hero of Sensibility a collection of Gothic themes. These were for the most part shorn of their specifically religious significance, but many of them, borrowed as they were originally from the secular classical tradition, remained essentially the same. The complaint of life theme, the *sic transit gloria mundi*, the meditation on the omnipotence of King Death – all remained the property of the Hero of Sensibility, and are familiar to any reader of *Childe Harold*. The intense concern with personal grief, the long pessimistic self-analyses, the nature imagery so subjective as almost to amount to pathetic fallacy, particularly in the work of Edward Young, seem to be especially close to the moods and attitudes of Byron's Childe.

There is one more eighteenth-century poet in the Gloomy Egoist tradition who served as a kind of bridge between Young and the

Romantic Hero of Sensibility. The influence of Ossian (or rather of Macpherson) was exceedingly important for Romanticism, both in England and on the Continent (it is worth noting that in Baldensperger's *Bibliography of Comparative Literature* Ossian is the only poet of the eighteenth century given a separate chapter with a full page of listings). Most of the English Romantics made youthful attempts to versify songs or episodes from Ossian; three such poems are among Byron's *juvenilia.* But Ossian was also an especial favorite of Goethe's, and one can do no better than quote in full the passage from *Dichtung und Wahrheit* already alluded to, to show what Ossian meant to the Hero of Sensibility (Werther, in this case):

> . . . so Ossian charmed us into that ultimate Thule, where we wandered on sombre endless heaths, among settled tombstones overgrown with moss, the grass about us bowing to an unearthly wind, and over us a heavily clouded sky. Not till then did this Caledonian night become like day with moonlight; long-since departed heroes and faded maidens hovered around us, until at the last we could actually believe we had caught sight of the fearful countenance of the ghost of Loda.[14]

It is difficult for a twentieth-century reader to recapture quite this enthusiasm, but it is obvious that for a Hero of Sensibility like Werther the long periods of Ossian were heart-stirring music indeed.

That the Gloomy Egoist was in a sense merged with the Man of Feeling to produce the Romantic Hero of Sensibility perhaps needs no further proof. However, it is well to remember that these sensibilities – for the tearful and for the "Gothic" – were never far apart. One finds Clarissa after her rape spending long weeks writing letters in the solitude of her room, using her coffin for a writing table; Mrs. Radcliffe's heroines (as well as her young heroes) have a great taste for Gothic ruins, for wild moonlit landscapes, and for languishing over loved-one's tombs; and Jane Austen's redoubtable Catherine and Isabella in *Northanger Abbey* take equal delight in sentimental novels and in tales of horror. Admittedly there seems to be no important Hero of Sensibility in English who combined the characteristics of the Man of Feeling and of the Gloomy Egoist until *Childe Harold*, but that the public was ripe for such a combination seems abundantly obvious from the immediate and immense popularity of that first famous Byronic Hero.

Before going on to the great villain of the eighteenth century, it seems worthwhile to pass our heroes briefly in review by considering an especially important poem which combines in a peculiar way the characteristics of all of them – the Child of Nature, the Man of Feeling, and the Gloomy Egoist. James Beattie's *The Minstrel* (1771–74) is usually considered important in any study of pre-Romanticism, since, as an "autobiographical" poem of the soul of a poet written in Spenserian stanzas, it is in a sense a precursor of both *The Prelude* and of *Childe Harold* (Byron of course acknowledges the debt in the preface to Books I and II). But *The Minstrel* is an inconsistent poem: Edwin begins as a Child of Nature and develops into a Man of Feeling (with some characteristics of the Gloomy Egoist), but then after being disillusioned by a didactic old hermit, he ends as an Augustan man-of-reason moralist (Pope or Swift), who hails the progress of science (James Thomson). The latter development comes only in the second book, and since this book is never anthologized, perhaps there is a reason why this reversion is never noticed.

Edwin is clearly first of all a Child of Nature, although of the later, more sentimentalized type. He is of humble origin, his father being

> A shepherd swain, a man of low degree;
> Whose sires, perchance, in Fairyland might dwell,
> Sicilian groves, or vales of Arcady. (Book I, stanza xi) [15]

Edwin's grandsires *might* have dwelt in "vales of Arcady" had this been the neoclassical golden age, but as a matter of fact Edwin's father "was of the north countrie; / A nation famed for song, and beauty's charms" (xi). And as with all of these Children, Nature herself is Edwin's mentor: the author's persona (presumably a Scottish Minstrel, but Beattie is not consistent) advises Edwin that "[Nature's] charms shall work thy soul's eternal health, / And love, and gentleness, and joy impart" (x). Edwin's father himself had sought "No subtle or superfluous lore . . . / Nor ever wished his Edwin to pursue" (xxviii). Finally, Edwin is also born a natural solitary: we are told that even when he was a child some of the neighbors "deemed him wondrous wise, and some believed him mad" (xvi). "Concourse, and noise and toil he ever fled" (xvii); instead, he takes long walks alone in the Highlands. He is especially fond of the more sublime aspects of nature, and in one particularly Wordsworthian stanza we find that

> oft the craggy cliff he loved to climb,
> When all in mist the world below was lost.
> What dreadful pleasure! there to stand sublime,
> Like shipwrecked mariner on desert coast,
> And view the enormous waste of vapour, tost
> In billows, lengthening to th' horizon round . . . (xxi)

Yet he is a young Man of Feeling, too. We find that from birth he eschewed all toys, "Save one short pipe of rudest minstrelsy" (xvi), and one of his favorite preoccupations is to compose poetry while on his wanderings: "Song was his favourite and first pursuit" (lvii). Furthermore, he is not interested in exploits of "strength, dexterity, or speed," and although a Child of Nature, he refuses to hunt or trap, since "His heart . . . would bleed / To work the woe of any living thing" (xvii). Finally, he spends most of his waking hours in day-dreaming, the subjects of his imaginings ranging from fairyland, to medieval knights, to troops of dancing "dames from myrtle bowers," and he is moved alternately to delight and to tears by his Beldam's ballads of knightly feats of arms or of the Babes in the Wood. There is also a touch of the Gloomy Egoist in him, since sometimes on evenings when the curfew "loaded with loud lament the lonely gale," he would

> dream of graves, and corses pale;
> And ghosts that to the charnel-dungeon throng,
> And drag a length of clanking chain, and wail,
> Till silenced by the owl's terrific song
> Or blast that shrieks by fits the shuddering aisles along. (xxxii)

So far Beattie the Romantic Minstrel, but the second book introduces the neoclassic poet, after a few stanzas of fair warning:

> So I, obsequious to Truth's dread command,
> Shall here without reluctance change my lay,

> And smite the Gothic Lyre with harsher hand . . .
> Edwin, though loved of Heaven, must not aspire
> To bliss, which mortals never knew before . . .
> Vigour from toil, from trouble patience grows. (iii–v)

Edwin, now grown a man, takes a longer walk one day than usual, and in the course of it he meets a hermit, disillusioned with society, who introduces him to the spirit of philosophy. The sage teaches the young poet that his dreams of a golden age are but the visions of Fancy; the truth is that "The mind untaught / Is a dark waste, where fiends and tempests howl" (xliv). (This seems a particularly harsh judgment to pass on the evidence of one brief Gothic nightmare.) Contrary to the teaching of Book I, we now find that Nature as a teacher is not enough; indeed, the sage goes so far as to say, "As Phoebus to the world, is science to the soul" (xlvi). The remainder of the poem passes in a Thomsonian paean in praise of reason and scientific progress, and as the poem closes we find that Edwin himself, a Romantic poet *manqué* if there ever was one, must learn to regulate his art according to the precepts of Aristotle's *Poetics* and the *Discourses* of Sir Joshua Reynolds. The next logical step after Book I would have been *The Prelude* or possibly even *Childe Harold* (Byron also spent part of his boyhood in the Highlands), but Beattie is too much of the Scottish moral philosopher and true child of the eighteenth century to venture so far. England had to wait another thirty years for the Romantic Movement.

IV THE GOTHIC VILLAIN

BY THE beginning of the Romantic Movement the Child of Nature as a poetic hero was on the wane, as we have seen, and in general the same is true of the eighteenth-century Man of Feeling. Never very robust of constitution, he seems to have died partly of a kind of emotional anemia, partly as a victim of wit and humor (parodies of and satires on the excesses of sentimentalism had begun to appear even before the end of the century), and partly because he was eclipsed by more robust Romantic heroes.

This decline is vividly illustrated in the young heroes of two of Mrs. Radcliffe's most famous novels. Valancourt is the ostensible hero of *The Mysteries of Udolpho*, since he is Emily's love throughout the novel and the man she marries at the end, and Valancourt is also a Man of Feeling. He first wins Emily's heart, as a matter of fact, because he can discuss her favorite poets and novelists, teach her new songs while he accompanies her on the lute, and share her enthusiasm for the rugged scenery of the Pyrenees. But Valancourt is at best a weak and passive hero. He is never around when Emily needs him most, and during the period of her imprisonment in Udolpho he is off in Paris, getting involved in gambling debts (although, to be sure, they turn out to have been debts incurred for the sake of friends). Vincentio di Vivaldi of *The Italian* is also a Man of Feeling. He falls in love at first sight, and the mere thought of a second sight so overcomes him that "he [is] obliged to rest for a few moments to recover breath and composure." He, too, is fond of music, and especially of serenading Ellena with his "exquisite" tenor. At one time when she is imprisoned in a convent, he serenades her while "perched on the point of a cliff" below her lattice window, and we are told that "the liquid cadence, as it trembled and sunk away, seemed to tell the dejection of no vulgar feelings, and the exquisite taste, with which the complaining notes were again swelled, almost convinced her that the musician was Vivaldi." [1] As, indeed, it was. Although Vivaldi is more active in attempting a rescue of his beloved than is Valancourt, he also is on the whole inept and ineffectual, and he finally succeeds only in getting himself locked up in the dungeon of the Inquisition along with the villain, so that he must be rescued through the influence of his noble father.

The truth is that Mrs. Radcliffe's Men of Feeling were not only by nature weak and passive, they were also completely eclipsed in their world of the Gothic novel by a relatively new and far more powerful personality – the Gothic Villain. Mrs. Radcliffe's villains, with their depth of mystery, their ingenious minds, their indomitable wills, and their unmitigated evil, are by far her greatest creations, and, by contrast, her heroes as well as her heroines are bound to seem somewhat dull.

To include the Gothic Villain in a list of heroes may seem to be stretching terms somewhat, but if he was not a hero at first, he was shortly to become one in the later dramas, and in combination with the Noble Outlaw, he becomes eventually (with Scott and Byron) a true Romantic rebel. The Gothic Villain made his first appearance in a novel, Walpole's *Castle of Otranto* (1761), but within ten years he appeared also on the stage, and his development in the two media was significantly different. He remained an unregenerate villain in the novel, but on the stage he became gradually more sympathetic, until at last he appeared as half-villain, half Hero of Sensibility. Since he became a personality first in the novel, however, and since it is in this form that he is comparatively well known, it seems reasonable to discuss the villain of the novel first.

The origins of the Gothic Villain of the novel are not far to seek. Villains we have always with us, and they are especially necessary in novels the prime purpose of which is to provide vicarious thrills for largely feminine audiences through the agonized sensibilities of persecuted young heroines. Insofar as this villain is peculiar, he derives especially from the flood of subliterary pseudohistorical "romances" (as distinguished from "novels"), which were popular all through the century, both in France and in England, and which received a new lease on life with the influence of German *Schauerromane* at the close of the century. Even the villainous monks of Mrs. Radcliffe and Lewis are natural developments of the anticlerical and "wicked-Jesuit" romances so popular in protestant countries and even in France all through the Age of Enlightenment.[2]

In any case, it is not so important to search for the origins of the Gothic Villain, since he has after all no psychological, much less philosophical complexity. It seems simple enough, if often overlooked, that although the Gothic Villain is the protagonist of the novels in which he appears in the sense that he is the major character, he is nevertheless always a villain, not a Romantic rebel-hero. He fits into the morality of the age: unlike the Romantic hero, he acknowledges the moral codes of society and his own wickedness in violating those codes, and he therefore never engages our sympathies with his rebellion.

The major characteristics of the Gothic Villain are so familiar that only a brief review seems necessary here, especially to point out the relationships between the Gothic Villain and the Noble Outlaw of Scott and Byron. There are of course countless numbers of the type, but they are for the most part standard enough, and the villains of the four most famous pre-Byronic Gothic novels can be considered representative: Manfred of Horace Walpole's *Castle of Otranto*, Montoni of Mrs. Radcliffe's *The Mysteries of Udolpho*, Schedoni of *The Italian*, and Ambrosio of M. G. Lewis's *The Monk*.[3]

In appearance the Gothic Villain is always striking, and frequently handsome. Of about middle age or somewhat younger, he has a tall, manly, stalwart physique, with dark hair and brows frequently set off by a pale and ascetic complexion. Aside from this, the most noticeable of his physical characteristics are his eyes; Schedoni, for instance, has "large melancholy eyes" which "were so piercing that they seemed to penetrate, at a single glance, into the hearts of men, and to read their most secret thoughts; few persons could support their scrutiny, or even endure to meet them twice." [4]

By birth the Gothic Villain was always of the aristocracy, partly for the sense of power which his nobility confers, and partly for the air of the fallen angel, the air of Satanic greatness perverted. Frequently, also, there is some mystery connected with his birth or his upbringing. We do not find out until near the end of the novel, for instance, that Schedoni is a count and the uncle of the heroine, and we are first told of Lewis's Ambrosio that "the late superior of the Capuchins found him while yet an infant at the abbey-door: all attempts to discover who had left him there were vain, and the child himself could give no account of his parents." [5]

The sense of mystery is apparent not only in the origins and in the general appearance of the Gothic Villain, but in his entire personality. An air of mystery is his dominant trait, and characteristic of all his acts. Frequently it is increased by an aura of past secret sins: either family sins, as is the case with Walpole's Manfred, or more frequently, personal sins, as is the case with Schedoni, who, we eventually discover, has committed fratricide and seduced his widowed sister-in-law before the novel opens.

Of the rest of their personalities there is really little to say; they are, after all, pasteboard characters. They do have great strength of will; in the novel, they persevere in evil to the end – all four of these villains, at least, spurning any death-bed repentance. They have also forceful and ingenious minds; they are obliged to have, since they must devise the endless machinations of evil which make up the intricate plots of three-volume novels. But as with Iago, their motives seem inadequate to the torrents of evil unleashed in their personalities. Manfred's interest is in restoring his family honor, a peculiar motive in view of the fact that he works the total destruction of his line; Montoni and Schedoni are both motivated by cupidity, by the desire for wealth and luxury, which seems much too ordinary a motive for such depths of sadistic villainy; Ambrosio, the most villainous of all, is activated by plain and simple bodily lust.

It should be noted, moreover, that they are misogynists all. They take great delight in persecuting women, partly from the exigencies of the plot, since these are all novels of female sensibility; but they go much farther in this persecution than would be necessary to further their particular ends. Montoni, for instance, hounds his rather simple-minded wife to death in order to get her to sign over her property, and takes a fiendish delight in persecuting his wife's niece. Schedoni almost ruins his scheme by calling his patroness and the hero's mother weak and contemptible ("as are all women") when she has qualms of conscience about the proposed murder of the heroine. Although later he has a moment of weakness himself and fails to carry out the murder when he finds that the heroine is his daughter, he quickly recovers his equanimity, and within a matter of hours he is planning to marry her advantageously to the man he has up to this time been attempting to ruin. Ambrosio, of course, reaches the depths of misogynistic sadism: in a convent charnel house, with rotting corpses all around, he drugs and then rapes his own sister.

According to the sentiments of the age, of course, any act of cruelty or even of unkindness and disrespect for women was unforgivable; it is this characteristic misogyny which makes the villain of the novel completely unregenerate, and Byron and Scott take advantage of this fact when portraying their Noble Outlaws. Make your protagonist a Hero of Sensibility in his regard for women, and this characteristic alone will mitigate all of his other crimes, no matter how Gothic. This is obviously what Scott has done with his outlaws: their "courtesie" and their patriotism are really their only redeeming characteristics, and yet they die more than half-sympathetic figures. And of course a Romantic love for his mistress and a courteous attitude toward women in general is the "one virtue" amidst a "thousand crimes" which makes Conrad, hero of Byron's *Corsair*, a character over whose death readers could weep.

So much for the general characteristics of the Gothic Villain, but two of these villains – Montoni and Schedoni – deserve more particular attention, since they show noteworthy connections with the heroic Noble Outlaw of Scott or of Byron.

Of Mrs. Radcliffe's Montoni one could almost go so far as to say that he *is* a "noble" outlaw, since like Karl Moor or Conrad-Lara he is a renegade aristocrat who leads a group of banditti from the fastnesses of Udolpho to prey on the villas of the neighboring rich. The resemblance goes no further, however; Mrs. Radcliffe had no intention of associating her villain with Robin Hood, and we find that Montoni's brigands are a villainous bunch of thieves and cut-throats, squabbling with one another on the slightest provocation. Montoni maintains his ascendancy by pure force and fear; there is none of that "organic" relationship between the leader and his faithful followers which is so indispensable a part of the picture of the Noble Outlaw, and which in the latter case never fails to engage the reader's sympathies.

It has long been evident to critics that Mrs. Radcliffe's Schedoni bears a general physical resemblance to Byron's Lara, but Mario Praz has pointed out passages in the description of each in which the parallel seems even verbal, and the passages are worth quoting in full to show the close connection between the appearance and mystery of the Gothic Villain and of the Noble Outlaw. First Mrs. Radcliffe's Schedoni:

> the *livid* paleness of his face . . . There was something in his physiognomy extremely singular, and *that cannot easily be defined*. It bore the traces of many *passions*, which seemed to have *fixed* the features they no longer animated. . . . His eyes were so piercing, that they seemed to penetrate, at a *single glance*, into the hearts of men, and to read their most secret *thoughts*.

And then Lara:

> That brow in furrow'd lines had *fix'd* at last,
> And spoke of *passions*, but of passions past:
> The pride, but not the fire, of early days,
> Coldness of mien, and carelessness of praise;
> A high demeanour, and a *glance* that took
> Their thoughts from others by a *single* look . . .
> And some deep feeling *it were vain to trace*
> At moments lighten'd o'er his *livid face*.[6]

The passages are certainly close, but before the reader accepts Praz's conclusion that the imitation is "slavish," it would be well to consider that the resemblance is, after all, only in appearances, and only in selected aspects of that. Schedoni's figure was striking, "but not so from grace; he was tall, and, though extremely thin, his limbs were large and uncouth"– certainly not Byronic characteristics. In any case, *pace* Mr. Praz, there is little or no resemblance in character, and it is the character of the Byronic Hero even more than his appearance which makes him unforgettable.

One can readily see that the Gothic Villain of the novel was in somewhat the same situation as was Satan before he was romanticized by Blake and Shelley. He has attractive characteristics, including his striking appearance, his air of the fallen angel, and his romantic mystery, but he is not yet a Romantic rebel. To become a Romantic hero he must take on some of the characteristics of the Hero of Sensibility, and he must be able to enlist at least a portion of our sympathies in his rebellion against society.

On an even lower level of literature – that of the Gothic drama – one finds that the Gothic Villain had already progressed far along the road to becoming a hero, while Byron was still in his nonage, and even before Scott began his series of metrical romances. This transformation had come about by the shifting of emphasis from unmitigated wickedness on the part of the villain of the novel to a deep and agonized remorse for past sins on the part of the villain of the dramas. In the throes of this remorse the villain becomes as egocentrically analytic of his emotions as the Man of Feeling, although of course with far greater intensity, and by his very agony he can gain something of the sympathies of the audience. This villain turned remorseful hero is of primary importance in the development of such a protagonist as Byron's Manfred.

Bertrand Evans, the only scholar who has made a thorough study of the Gothic drama, points out that this transformation began almost with the first Gothic dramas in English, and it shows a significant divergence from the development of the Gothic Villain in the novel.[7] The earliest remorseful villains whom Professor Evans discusses, in the last decades of the eighteenth century, are not of course full-fledged sympathetic characters. Each drama has still a weak Man of Feeling for a hero, and in each case the villain still performs his function of persecuting helpless females with threats of murder, rape, or abduction. These villains do approach the sympathetic in the intensity of their remorse when they finally repent, however, and by the turn of the century this development of the stage villain had gone so far that a number of dramatists felt free to dispense with the usual weak and sentimental hero and make their villains fill both roles. The plays of three of the more notable of these dramatists illustrate the trend: Joanna Baillie, "Monk" Lewis, and William Sotheby.

Joanna Baillie, although unread today, won impressive champions in her time. Scott thought very highly of her and became in a way a patron; Byron called her "our only dramatist since Otway and Southerne" (although this in a courtship letter to Annabella Milbanke, who was another of Joanna's patrons: *LJ*, III, 399). Following theories of the eighteenth-century "ruling passion," or the psychology of Elizabethan humours, Mrs. Baillie's major dramatic effort was a group of thirteen *Plays on the Passions*. In a number of these the villain becomes a hero, but the most famous of them, and the only one staged, even if unsuccessfully, can serve to illustrate the transformation: *De Montfort, a Tragedy on Hatred* (1801).

De Montfort has many of the characteristics of the typical Gothic villain:

> Th' indignant risings of abhorrent nature;
> The stern contraction of . . . scowling brows,
> That like the plant whose closing leaves do shrink
> At hostile touch, still knit at [his enemy's] approach;
> The crooked curving lip, by instinct taught,
> In imitation of disgustful things,
> To pout and swell . . .[8]

Gloomy, haughtily reserved, and inordinately proud, he is given to "tossing his arms," clenching his fists, and gnashing his teeth in a half-suppressed rage which he relieves in near-apoplectic soliloquies.

Yet he has also many of the characteristics of the Man of Feeling. Even his enemy, the unfortunate victim of his "ruling passion," supposes that de Montfort was always

formed with such antipathy, by nature,
To all affliction of corporeal pain,
To wounding life, e'en to the sight of blood (IV, i)

that he could never bring himself to murder, even if he would (although this of course turns out to be tragic irony, since eventually de Montfort does murder his enemy, in a Gothic forest near a funereal convent chapel). Although he often abuses his servants quite unreasonably, still, as one of them testifies, he has

with all his faults . . .
Such bursts of natural goodness from his heart,
As might engage a harder churl than I
To serve him still. (I, i)

He will frequently curse a servant roundly for intruding on a soliloquy, and then call the vassal back to ask him about his wife or to give him a jeweled ring. Finally, he is as much moved by remorse as by hatred (as Professor Evans remarks), and when he has committed his villainous murder his agony knows no bounds:

Come, madness! come to me, senseless death!
I cannot suffer thus! Here, rocky wall,
Scatter these brains, or dull them!
[*Runs furiously, and dashing his head against the wall, falls upon the floor.*] (V, ii)

After expiring tearfully in his sister's arms, he earns this epitaph from the monk who shrove him:

He is with *Him* who made him; *Him* who knows
The soul of man: before whose awful presence
Th' unsceptred tyrant stands despoiled and helpless,
Like an unclothed babe. (V, v)

Mrs. Baillie was not the only dramatist to produce such villains become Gothic heroes; Matthew "Monk" Lewis, that inveterate Gothic sensationalist, also wrote two dramas which deserve mention. *Adelmorn, the Outlaw* (1801), is especially peculiar in that he begins as a hero, but since he believes himself guilty of the murder of his uncle, he takes on the guilt of a Gothic Villain. Lewis was thus able to have a remorseful hero and at the same time claim the sympathy of the audience because of the hero's real innocence.

Even Osmond, in that most violent and vulgar of Gothic tragedies, *The Castle Spectre* (1797), has some admirable qualities, with almost a superfluity of remorse, and, as Professor Evans remarks, "it is perfectly plain that . . . Lewis intended him to invite sympathy."[9]

But Lewis's Gothic dramas were ventures in undisguised commercialism, and although their popular success was phenomenal (especially that of *The Castle Spectre*), their literary merit is nil. The same cannot quite be said of the Reverend William Sotheby's *Julian and Agnes* (1801), and this drama also centers on a Gothic Villain turned hero in the person of Alfonso (alias Julian). Professor Evans calls this "the strangest and perhaps the best Gothic play," and the most likely link between the Gothic Villain and the Byronic Hero of *Manfred*.[10] In all probability Byron had read the play after it was published as *The Confession* (in *Five Unpublished Tragedies*, 1814), since in the next year he was engaged in an attempt to bring another of Sotheby's plays onto the stage at Drury Lane. Byron, however, was never really enthusiastic about Sotheby's dramas, partly, perhaps, because he considered the clergyman himself a dreadful bore (see *LJ*, V, 433; Sotheby is also satirized as "Botherby" in *The Blues*).

Alfonso is nevertheless an interesting example of a Gothic Villain turned Hero of Sensibility. His secret sin, divulged in the third act, is that he had lived in a bigamous relationship with Agnes and the young Ellen, and that when Ellen's brother returned to accuse him, Alfonso slew the young soldier in a sudden fit of anger. He then retired in the usual agony of remorse to a monastery in the Alps (providing Alpine scenes which, as Professor Evans notes, anticipate *Manfred*), from whence he now ventures out to rescue lost travelers. In one of these remorseful expeditions he comes upon Agnes and the invalid Ellen, who have been beset by bandits, and succeeds in rescuing them by force of arms, although he is himself mortally wounded in the engagement. Then in a long repentance scene both women tearfully forgive the villain-hero, and he expires in the good graces of God and man.

One could cite other dramas to illustrate this transformation of the Gothic Villain into a remorseful Hero of Sensibility, but perhaps this has been sojourn enough in these largely subliterary regions. The point, in any case, has been made. In the novel, the Gothic Villain remains unregenerate, but in the drama, as he nears the Romantic Age, his remorse is ever more emphasized at the expense of his villainy, and he begins to take on many of the characteristics of the Hero of Sensibility. As Professor Evans was the first to note, the connection between these remorseful villains and the Byronic Hero, particularly Manfred, is very close indeed.

This relationship could, however, be overemphasized: Adelmorn, Alfonso, and de Montfort are not yet Romantic rebels. These Gothic agonizers gained the sympathy of the audience at the expense of their postures of defiance; they become sympathetic by submitting to the judgments not only of their consciences, but also of traditional morality and of orthodox religion. There is still a considerable development between de Montfort, who accepts the comforts of the church and dies in the arms of his sister and of God, and Byron's Manfred, who spurns the comforts of society just as he scorns the invitations of the demons, and whose dying answer to the Abbot (who represents the church) is only: "Old man! 'tis not so difficult to die!"

This pre-Byronic sentimentalizing of the Gothic Villain does, however, illustrate the transformation from villain to hero which will be a major theme of the next chapters – especially with the figures of Cain-Ahasuerus and Satan-Prometheus. These heroes became true Romantic rebels: remorseful, perhaps, but largely under the judgment of their own consciences – and defiance toward traditional social codes and morals and toward orthodox theology becomes their dominant characteristic.

☙ PART TWO. ROMANTIC HERO TYPES

V THE NOBLE OUTLAW

THE eighteenth-century hero types – the Child of Nature, the Gloomy Egoist, and the Man of Feeling – are not, as their Romantic successors are, full-blown solitaries or social or theological rebels. They are distinctive in society, to be sure: the Child of Nature because of the peculiarities of his breeding; the Gloomy Egoist and the Man of Feeling because of their peculiar sensibilities. They are even critics of society, as we have seen, either implicitly, giving the lie to social hypocrisy by their lives of simple virtue, or explicitly, given to somewhat sententious moral analyses of the people around them. But in their criticism they accept, by and large, the professed social or theological codes of the society of which they are a part; there was a large body of shared values to which they could appeal as common ground. Indeed, for a good many of these heroes – including Tom Jones, Belcour, or Beattie's Edwin – a gradual adjustment to social standards becomes the story of their lives. The pre-Byronic Gothic Villain, on the other hand, is a rebel, both against society and sometimes even against God, but he is never a hero in that he never succeeds in gaining our sympathy with his rebellion. In the novels, he has his role to play in the struggle of sensibility versus villainy, and it would confuse and spoil the story if he had anything in him on the side of the angels. When he does succeed in gaining some of our sympathy in such dramas as Sotheby's *Julian and Agnes*, it is for the most part not because we sympathize with him in his villainy (his rebelling against the injustices of society), but because of the very agony of his remorse when he comes to accept the justice of his punishment.

The Romantic hero types, on the other hand – the Noble Outlaw, Faust, Cain or Ahasuerus, Satan or Prometheus – are invariably solitaries, and are fundamentally and heroically rebellious, at first against society only, and later against the natural universe or against God himself.

They are solitaries in the sense that the eighteenth-century types are – by birth, by nature, or by breeding; because of the acuteness of their minds and sensibilities – but most of them are solitaries also because of conscious moral choice, and this fateful decision, with Faust, Cain, Satan, or Prometheus, is dramatized as the climactic event of their tragedies. In any case, adjustment to society as it exists, is impossible for them; they either go down to glorious defeat, cursing God and dying, or they commit their lives to transforming the world.

Finally, it is important to note that most of these heroes are in one sense transformed eighteenth-century villains: the Gothic Villain becomes sentimental or becomes the sympathetic Noble Outlaw; the Cain of biblical story or of Gessner's drama becomes the hero of Byron's tragedy; the Satan of Milton's epic is transformed into a Prometheus figure in the works of Blake and Shelley. This transformation characterizes the basic shift of values in the Romantic Movement: from conformism in large social patterns of conduct or thought, to radical individualism; from humble right reason, common sense, and the proper study of mankind, to a thirst to know and experience all things, to encompass infinities; from acquiescence before God and the social order, to heroism and *hubris*.

The Noble Outlaw is, roughly speaking, the first of the Romantic heroes in point of time. Goethe began his literary career with Götz, and Schiller launched his with Karl Moor;[1] Wordsworth's *The Borderers* preceded even the *Lyrical Ballads* (although the drama was not published for almost fifty years); and Scott's first great successes were his verse romances. In a way the Noble Outlaw is first not only in time, but in importance: he was certainly the single most popular hero of the Romantic Movement. Karl Moor gained a wide and profound reputation in England when Faust was still being ostracized; the vast popularity of Scott's dark heroes is undisputed; and the dark figure who is the hero of Byron's romances ruled the domain of popular poetry almost until his creator's death.

The Noble Outlaw is also probably the most hybrid figure among these Romantic types. One could summarize his ancestry in England by saying that he was born of a merging of the popular ballad outlaw with the Gothic Villain, but he bears characteristics also of Satan, and later of Prometheus, and he certainly received an infusion of Teutonic blood from Götz and Karl Moor.

Outlaws noble by birth or in heart have always been with us, to be sure, on the literary and on the popular and subliterary level. Ulysses shows something of the outlaw in some of his sea adventures; and all through the Middle Ages, Norse pirates, while they were cursed, were probably also admired. Noble Outlaws have always been particularly popular among oppressed people, and Robin Hood, in some versions a renegade Earl of Huntingdon, is a prototype of most of the modern outlaws in the English-speaking world.

Eighteenth-century England, too, had its glamorous or tender-hearted criminals of popular fancy, of street ballads and song. The portrait of Macheath is more than a satire on Walpole; it is also a caricature of the popular figure of the glamorous highwayman with his little band of loyal thieves. Somewhat later Magistrate Fielding took the threat to law and order in this sentimentalizing of criminals very seriously, as witness his heavy-handed satire on the philosophy of the "Great Man" in *Jonathan Wild*. But Macheath, in spite of his glamour, is a comic figure, and Wild, seen through the irony, is of course a villain. Eighteenth-century English readers could not have tolerated a Marmion, or perhaps they could not have taken him seriously.

At the close of the century, however, the French Revolution produced a host of living and historical Noble Outlaws – radicals and democrats who were aristocratic rebels against their hereditary class, like Byron's later heroes in his romances and dramas. Robespierre was once something of a hero for both Wordsworth and

Coleridge; the Duke of Orleans, a leader in the early stages of the Revolution, was called *Philippe Égalité*; and of course the Marquis de Lafayette was celebrated both for his part in the American Revolution and for his abortive role in Paris: in 1794 Coleridge honored him with a sonnet on his imprisonment. One remembers that Byron pictured himself in just such a role as aristocrat turned rebel leader when he thought England near rebellion in 1817, and that at one time he meant to have Don Juan "finish as *Anacharsis Cloots* in the French Revolution," as he wrote to John Murray (*LJ*, IV, 48; V, 242).

Although these actual outlaws furnished some immediate inspiration, in general the Romantic poets turned to literary precedents for their Noble Outlaws – to the close of the Middle Ages, to the robber barons of Germany, or the border outlaws of England and Scotland. They turned to the last fading days of little "organic" societies, to the days of personal loyalties, personal justice, and personal heroism, before the rise of the new nationalistic states with their ever increasing bureaucracy. As Sir Walter Scott put it, in discussing the days of the robber barons in fifteenth-century Germany, "Amid the obvious mischiefs attending such a state of society, it must be allowed that it was frequently the means of calling into exercise the highest heroic virtues. Men daily exposed to danger, and living by the constant exertion of their courage, acquired the virtues as well as the vices of a savage state; and among many instances of cruelty and rapine, occur not a few of the most exalted valour and generosity." [2]

So much for the origins of the heroic outlaw as a literary figure, but before going on to discuss a few of his more important pre-Byronic incarnations, perhaps it would be best to pause in order to review his major characteristics.

First, and perhaps most important, the Noble Outlaw is invariably fiery, passionate, and heroic; he is in the true sense bigger than the life around him. He always pre-empts the stage in the productions in which he appears, even when, as sometimes happens (in Scott's *Rokeby*, for instance), there are others of the *dramatis personae* who have more lines, more action, and ostensibly more sympathetic characteristics. In all of his appearances the Noble Outlaw personified the Romantic nostalgia for the days of personal heroism, for the age when it was still possible for a leader to dominate his group of followers by sheer physical courage, strength of will, and personal magnetism.

Of course such *Führerschaft* was possible pre-eminently in the small organic group of the robber band: hence the Noble Outlaw usually appears as the leader of a group of comrades of undying loyalty. Within this society in miniature he is a "natural" leader, owing his position neither to hereditary rank alone nor, of course, to popular election; his authority is unquestioned, and is as integral a part of his person as his commanding voice or his all-seeing, dark, and terrifying eyes. (In spite of the obvious differences of situation and character, I am sure that the relationship between this hero and his band and Abbot Samson and his loyal brethren, or indeed Carlyle's Romantic conception of the political "hero" in general, is close and direct.) Then, too, in such a society justice is swift, personal, and real, as both Götz and Karl Moor demonstrate; there is nothing of "the law's delay" that Romantic poets found in the bureaucracy of judiciary systems – of the Chancery in England, for instance, or of the Imperial Court in which the young Goethe worked.

The Noble Outlaw is also largely a sympathetic character. He is figured as having been wronged either by intimate personal friends, or by society in general, and his rebellion is thus always given a plausible motive. And no matter what his outlawry may seem on the surface, he is never by nature cruel or sadistic, as was his cousin, the Gothic Villain. He is also invariably courteous toward women; one can forgive a Byronic Hero such as Conrad-Lara a multitude of sins when he risks his life to save a woman in distress, or when we see him followed about by a sensitive, frail beauty in page's costume, in whom he has inspired an undying love and faithfulness.

Most of these qualities, however, can be found in the noble outlaw of any age; what particularly distinguishes the fully-developed Romantic Noble Outlaw, after Götz and the ballad heroes, is his cloak of mystery and his air of the sublime. Gone are the cheerful green glades of Sherwood or of Ettrick Forest; they are replaced by

Gothic castles, bleak windswept shores, or lonely and deserted moors. The hero is dogged eternally by secret sins (usually, however, more than half-forgiven by the indulgent reader), and he is filled with a high-souled and hidden remorse which flashes forth in occasional quick bursts of temper, or of kindness. Finally, the sublimity, the air of the fallen angel, or of the noble and generous nature coarsened by rough pirate life, is borrowed either directly from Milton's Satan (as in Karl Moor), or at second hand from the Gothic Villain.

These are the essential characteristics, in the abstract, of the pre-Byronic Noble Outlaw. He appeared, of course, in a host of long since forgotten dramas and verse tales, but his characteristics and his gradual transformation can be illustrated most conveniently in a group of major Romantic dramas and poems, all remarkably closely related, and all influential, directly or indirectly, on the early Byron: Goethe's *Götz von Berlichingen* (1771); Schiller's *Die Räuber* (1781); Wordsworth's *The Borderers* (1795–96); and Scott's three first and most successful romances: *The Lay of the Last Minstrel* (1805), *Marmion* (1808), and *Rokeby* (1813).

Götz von Berlichingen, a historical figure of Luther's Germany, was discovered accidentally by the young Goethe, who, bored by his legal apprenticeship to a court worse than England's Chancery (the Imperial Court was ten years behind on cases, and falling more behind each year), was digging about in the musty records of the old empire. His imagination fired by Herder's interpretation of Shakespeare, Goethe attempted to do in this play for Germany what Shakespeare had done for England in the history plays: he wanted to recapture for the German theater the world of the early Renaissance Empire, and his play shows many general influences of Shakespeare besides the choice of subject.

In the play, as in life, Götz is one of the last of the many robber barons in the reign of Maximilian I. He held a small feudal seigniory outside of Nürnberg in the days when the more important peers, the city states, and the prelates were organizing under the Emperor to abolish the costly local warfare among rival barons and establish stronger central control in the empire. As the play opens,

Götz is the victim of a plot on the part of the Bishop of Bamberg and a group of his henchmen who are out to destroy the warrior knight and seize his land. Götz is treacherously betrayed by a former intimate friend (who had once sworn loyalty on his knightly honor), and a large force of imperial troops are sent out to conquer and capture him. He defends himself manfully, with the aid of his little band of loyal retainers, defeating far larger forces of the empire, but at last he is hopelessly besieged, and to spare his wife and followers, he allows himself to be taken prisoner. He gains a temporary respite and is released on "house arrest," since Maximilian too is fond of the "knight of the iron hand," albeit he is a robber, and hopes to use him in the wars against the Turks. But fate plays Götz a final trick, and while he is on parole in his castle a local but very bloody uprising of boorish peasants breaks out. Götz, although he has little sympathy with their cause, is half-forced, half-persuaded to be their leader in hope that he might be able in turn to persuade them to stop their senseless slaughter and their desolation of the countryside. He is immediately seized by the imperial army, and since the nobility refuse to credit his motives for taking the lead of the peasants, he is imprisoned and sentenced to death. He languishes for some time in his Gothic dungeon, and when given a last-minute reprieve, he is too far gone to recover, borne down as he is by grief, dishonor, and the death of his favorite squire. He dies in the prison courtyard in the arms of his loving wife, his last vision being of the "heavenly sky," and his last words, "Freedom! Freedom!" But the age of heroes and the age of freedom is past; as it is expressed in the closing lines of the play: "Woe to this age that has lost thee! . . . And woe to the future, that cannot know thee!" (V, x, close)

There are of course individual villains in the drama – Götz's treacherous friend Weislingen, or the Bishop of Bamberg – but the real villain of the piece is nothing more than "bureaucracy." The Emperor himself is a sympathetic character (one is reminded of Robin Hood and Richard Coeur de Lion), but his good intentions are constantly frustrated by the corruption and inefficiency of the courts, and above all the shortsightedness and selfishness of the petty princes who come between the Emperor and his just decrees

There is also a vivid contrast all through the play between the disloyalty and defection of the imperial troops, on the one hand, and the unflinching courage and undying loyalty of Götz's little band of retainers on the other.

Götz's character is, largely speaking, that of the typical Noble Outlaw. His courage and personal dignity are never questioned, even by his enemies. He is much engaged in robbery, of course, especially of messengers for the greater nobles (as for instance the Bishop of Bamberg), but his goodness of heart is always evident: in a deed of kindness to a wandering friar, in his gentle treatment of his wife and his sister, and in his loyalty and love for his squires and servants.

Although there are touches of the Gothic in the drama, there is little or nothing of Gothic gloom in the character of the hero. The castles and dungeons are Gothic, to be sure, and there is even a scene with a secret court, or *Vehmgericht* (which probably accounted for Scott's first interest in that quaint medieval Ku Klux Klan); but Götz himself is free and open in character, with no mystery about him and no secret sins. If he is sublime, it is only in his courage and in his passionate love of freedom (in spite of the empire), not in the sense of being a fallen angel. And there are no questionable complications in his love life; he is happily and loyally married to a valiant and quite unsentimental woman who is as free and open in character as himself.

The general influence of Goethe's drama and of his hero on English Romanticism is problematical, but of his influence on Scott there can be no doubt. Scott translated the drama in 1799 as one of the first fruits of his interest in German literature. Although the problem of particular influences of detail or incident on Scott's verse romances is doubtful, there is no question but that the drama stimulated his interest not only in historical narrative but in outlaw heroes in general. And of course anything which influenced Scott necessarily influenced Byron, if only indirectly.

One important incident in the drama, however, leads me to think that Byron may have read the play (in Scott's translation, most likely) and been influenced directly. Götz, one remembers, is finally seized and sentenced to death because, however unwillingly, he has taken the leadership in a peasant revolt and in this way turned against his fellow aristocrats. So Lara also accepts the leadership of a peasant revolt (although in his case willingly and by instigation), and is mercilessly destroyed by his fellow nobles. The similarity may of course be coincidental, but I can think of no other romance of the time with a like catastrophe, and although Byron never mentions Götz, his avid reading of Scott's works would certainly suggest that he must have read this translation.

However that may be, there can be no doubt of Goethe's influence on the next Noble Outlaw, Schiller's Karl Moor (*Die Räuber*, 1781), nor of the influence of Karl Moor on English romanticism. Like *Götz*, *Die Räuber* also shows evidence of the popularity of Shakespeare among the young *Stürmer und Dränger*, although not in setting or incident so much as in verbal reminiscence.

The main lines of the plot are relatively simple. As the play opens the young Karl Moor is off at school, taking the lead in student pranks which get him into trouble with the local magistrates. But far more serious trouble is brewing for him at home. His younger brother, Franz, an Iago-like character who seems also to have read and profited from the soliloquies of Richard III, and Edmund in *Lear*, turns his father against the rightful heir, partly (as does Edmund) by means of a forged letter. As a result of this treachery, the old Count disinherits and disowns Karl, his older son and heir (as Gloucester, in *Lear*, disowns Edgar).

When Karl hears through his brother of his father's action, not knowing of the real reason, he vows vengeance on all mankind, and goes off to organize a band of robbers in the forests of Bohemia. Many years later, after a particularly daring pillage of a city, the band is at last hopelessly surrounded by a vastly superior force of the army. When a delegate of the law offers amnesty to all if they agree to turn over Karl, they refuse, and in a valiant fight most of the band manages to escape. After this they return to Moor's ancestral estate, and there Moor (in disguise) discovers the treachery of his brother, and discovers also his father, who has been incarcerated in a very Gothic prison and kept alive for ten years on bread and water. The band of course avenges Karl, and Franz dies a suicide, remaining (like Iago) defiant unto death.

After talking to his father Karl repents his life of crime, and when Amelia, his long-lost love, refuses to leave him even after he confesses his trade in the most gruesome terms, he slays her in a fit of frenzy, and then in a touching closing speech he turns himself over to justice – so that a poor laborer with eleven children can claim the reward.[3]

Karl Moor is frequently called the first of the misanthropic Romantic heroes, even by so astute a critic as Eino Railo, but to say this without qualification is to do his character a serious injustice. It is true that in his fit of frenzy upon being disowned by his father he says, "Then away with all sympathy and human forbearance! I have no longer a father; I have no longer affections, and blood and death shall teach me to forget that anything was ever dear to me!"[4] But in reality we find that he has a heart of gold; as one of the two villains in his band puts it: "He does not slay for the sake of plunder as do we – he appears to care nothing for the money . . . and even the third of the loot which is rightfully his he gives away to orphans, or to poor but capable students" (II, iii). He is a man of sensibility under his rough exterior; he loves flowers, the woods, and fields in the autumn sunset, and frequently when out of sorts he goes off to console himself with his lute and a song. And of course he is faithful first and last to Amelia; even when he stabs her at the close he does so in a fit of madness, and obeying her supplications.

He is not only a sympathetic figure however; he also represents a definite step forward from Götz in the evolution of the Noble Outlaw in that he displays a full set of the characteristics of the fallen angel. In the preface to the published text Schiller compares Karl to Brutus and Catiline, to Don Quixote (in that we both admire and pity him), and to Richard III, but he also compares him to the Satan of *Paradise Lost* and to Adramelech in Klopstock's *Messiah*, and in the "Advertisement" he calls him "the very picture of a great soul gone wrong – furnished with all of the capacities for greatness, and with all his gifts – lost . . . such a man we must mourn for and hate, abhor and love." During the course of the play he is compared to Abaddon and to the devil, and he himself (in lines dropped in a later revision) draws the parallel with the Satan of *Paradise Lost*, "that extraordinary genius [*Genie*] who could not bear to have a superior."[5] Finally, when Amelia is shocked by the confession of his crimes, she calls out "Murderer! Devil! I cannot leave you, my *angel!*" (V, ii)

One soliloquy is particularly interesting in this connection since it contains not only a verbal echo of a famous speech of Milton's Satan, but because part of it is echoed by Manfred. Moor is feeling despondent, a song with his lute has failed to console him, and he begins a long speech in contemplation of suicide (obviously reminiscent of *Hamlet*). He meditates on time and eternity, and then bursts out: "Be as you will, nameless Beyond, so long as my Self remains true to me! Be as you will, if I can but take my Self with me – External forms are only the appearances of the man – I am my heaven and my hell!" (As Milton's Satan had put it: "The mind is its own place, and in itself / Can make a Heav'n of Hell, a Hell of Heaven"; and these lines are also echoed in *Manfred*, III, iv, 129–32.) The close of Moor's soliloquy sounds like the defiant close of *Manfred*: "Shall I concede the victory to misery? – No! I will endure it. Let the torment yield to my pride! My destiny shall be fulfilled!" (IV, v)

Die Räuber was Schiller's first bid for literary fame, and the influence of his early works (especially of this drama) on the older English Romantics was profound and lasting. Wordsworth and Coleridge both esteemed Schiller far above Goethe; it is to Schiller as the author of *Die Räuber* that Coleridge dedicates his complimentary sonnet. On his first reading of the play Coleridge not only compared Moor to Milton's Satan, but rated him above the devil for sublimity.[6] And twenty-five years after Hazlitt's first reading, he still recalled with ecstasy the "hurricane of passion and eloquence" in the robber's speech. Scott was of course familiar with the drama (he had attempted a translation of the *Fiesco* early in the 1790's), and may have been influenced by it in his descriptions of Marmion. Byron notes in a letter that he had read the drama in translation in

1814 – after he had written *The Giaour* and *The Corsair*, and as he was writing *Lara*.

But Karl Moor, for all his fallen-angel sublimity, is not really a full-fledged Noble Outlaw such as we find in Scott or Byron. He moves too much in the light; his motives and his past are all in the open; he has no secret sins, no real cloak of mystery. Then, too, like the Gothic Villain, he nowhere denies the validity of traditional Christian morality; he repents his life of rebellion at the end of the play. Schiller admits in the Preface his concern that Karl might be taken as a sympathetic character even in his flouting of traditional morality, although of course Schiller laid himself open to such misinterpretation when he made the true villain of the piece, the brother Franz, a very personification of evil.

Wordsworth must also have shared Coleridge's enthusiasm for Karl Moor, to some extent, since he wrote his tragedy *The Borderers* under the influence of Schiller's drama. Wordsworth's play, written in 1795–96, during the time of the poet's disillusionment with the French Revolution and with Godwin's intellectualism, was kept a well-hidden secret for fifty years, even from close friends, and when finally published in 1842 it was too late to influence any of the Romantic generation. The drama is interesting not only in that it shows the influence of *Die Räuber*, but in proving that even Wordsworth, usually considered far removed from the violent and rebellious aspects of Romanticism represented by the Noble Outlaw, was in his youth infected with the same enthusiasm.

The drama is set in the time after the first Crusade, and the hero, Marmaduke, has collected a band of "outlaws" for the noble purpose of protecting the innocent, and restoring the rights of the harassed, "Along the confines of the Esk and Tweed"– where Scott's outlaws were to rove. The outlaw life is one in which "Souls are self-defended, free to grow / Like mountain oaks rocked by the stormy wind," and in which justice is personal and sure, since "Men alone are Umpires."[7] There are really two protagonists in the drama: one, Oswald, who is given all the mystery and the secret sins, the strength of will, and the villainy; the other, Marmaduke, is given the chieftainship, the loyalty of the band, and the tenderness of heart.

But beyond these outward similarities Wordsworth's drama is not really in the line of development of the Noble Outlaw. Wordsworth's characterization is not in any way consistent or successful: he seems to have been far more interested in the philosophy of moral conduct than in character or plot. Oswald, the villain, represents the perversion of Godwinian "naked-reason" revolutionary principles, and Marmaduke, the hero, represents the noble soul of sentiment seduced. The play thus illustrates an important stage in the development of Wordsworth as a poet, but not in the development of the Noble Outlaw as a hero.[8]

It was Scott, feeling the full influence of the ballad outlaw, the Gothic Villain (both in his English and German manifestations), and the Teutonic outlaws Götz and Moor, who developed the Noble Outlaw to his last stage before Byron. Scott records the strong impression of his first reading of Percy's *Reliques* in his thirteenth year, but the tales of outlawry in the border ballads of his native country made an impression on his young mind fully as early, and the influence lasted fully as late. Aside from his translations, his first considerable literary work was his two-volume edition of the *Border Minstrelsy* (1802–3), in which he collected such ballads as "The Song of the Outlaw Murray," a renegade chief of the Ettrick forests who dared to defy the king; or the story of the bold and brave "Johnnie Armstrang," tricked by a treacherous King James V into submitting to a truce, only to be ignominiously hanged with his leading comrades, while men sighed and women wept.

Even had he not been well acquainted with the Noble Outlaw of the *Sturm und Drang*, then, it would not be surprising to see that a border outlaw figures in Scott's first considerable original work, the enormously popular *Lay of the Last Minstrel* (1805; Scott noted in the 1830 Preface that in all it sold thirty thousand copies). Among Lady Branksome's knights is Sir William of Deloraine: "A stark moss-trooping Scot was he / As e'er couched Border lance by knee," and we find that he has also the dubious distinction of having been "Five times outlawed . . . / By England's king and Scotland's

Queen."[9] But Deloraine is still a ballad outlaw, not the romanticized figure of the later Scott or of Byron. He shows little respect for religion, it is true:

> For mass or prayer can I rarely tarry,
> Save to patter an Ave Mary,
> When I ride on a border foray (II, ii),

although he has no mystery and no secret sins. Moreover, he has no soul of sensibility; the ruins of Melrose Abbey in the "pale moonlight," for instance, fail to move him: "Little recked he of the scene so fair" (II, vi). A good deal of Gothic gloom pervades the tale, but it has not yet colored the picture of the Noble Outlaw.

This is distinctly not the case with the hero of Scott's next verse romance, the equally popular *Marmion* (1808; thirty-six thousand copies were sold between 1808 and 1825, as Scott noted in the 1830 Preface). In this poem for the first time the Noble Outlaw takes the center of the stage, and for that reason Scott achieves something of the focus and the concentration of force and interest of Byron's heroic romances. This is the hero Byron chose to describe in *English Bards and Scots Reviewers*, in a passage the youthful poet was later to regret, as he regretted most of his rash criticisms in this early satire:

> Next view in state, proud prancing on his roan,
> The golden-crested haughty Marmion,
> Now forging scrolls, now foremost in the fight,
> Not quite a Felon, yet but half a Knight,
> The gibbet or the field prepared to grace;
> A mighty mixture of the great and base. (165–170)

Marmion has indeed all the features of the complete Noble Outlaw. He has first of all the physical characteristics, the "thick mustache," the "curly hair, / Coal-black," and above all the "eyebrow dark, and eye of fire, / [Which] show'd spirit proud, and prompt to ire" (I, v). He is equipped also with a secret sin, in this case having forged a letter in order to taint with treason the name of his rival De Wilton so that he might gain for himself the hand of the Lady Clare. Of course, as Byron noted in the passage just quoted and as Scott admitted in the 1830 Preface to the poem, forgery is a particularly "unknightly" sin, and not one calculated to gain the sympathy of many readers. In spite of his somewhat shady character and his tendency toward mystery and laconic speech, Marmion too has the wholehearted loyalty of his retainers, not merely because of his bravery and his instinctive sense of command, but because although among men of his own rank he was the "proudest of the proud," "Yet, train'd in camps, he knew the art / To win the soldier's hardy heart" (III, iv). He calls himself a skeptic, and it is said of him that "he scarce received / For gospel, what the church believed," but he is nevertheless superstitious enough to be frightened almost to madness by ghosts and portents, as are all of Scott's Noble Outlaws. His relations with women are somewhat equivocal, and not very courteous. He entices the nun Constance to perjure herself so that she might follow him about in page's costume (one is reminded of the similar practice of Gulnare in *Lara*), and he then deserts her in order to woo Lady Clare, whose estates he covets. On the other hand, the fact that Constance is walled up alive in the convent crypt is no fault of his. Indeed, when he finds the murder out, he gives vent to a vivid curse on all altars, monks, and priests, and contemplates dire revenge. Then, too, our minstrel avers that to the end, "If e'er he loved, 'twas her alone, / Who died within that vault of stone," and on the battlefield when he is mortally wounded he refuses to take the time to be shriven because he wants time to be able to clear Constance's name with the Lady Clare (V, xxviii, xxi). Finally, to his other sympathetic qualities is added that of patriotism. When dying on Flodden Field his last thoughts are of Constance and of England, and after death he is accorded a patriot's epitaph: " 'He died a gallant knight, / With sword in hand, for England's right' " (VI, xxxvii).

Deepen the passion and the mystery that surrounds Marmion, provide him with a more complex and enigmatic character, give him a more "honorable" secret sin, and remove the taint on his courtesy toward women, and you have a true Byronic Noble Outlaw.

Scott's *Rokeby* (1813) was far less popular than its predecessors for a number of reasons, foremost among them being the fact that Byron had by this time appeared on the scene and was beginning to "take the wind out of my sails," as Scott put it in the 1830 Preface to the poem. *Childe Harold* I and II had appeared in 1812, *The Giaour* (1813) was ready for the press, and in the next year *The Bride of Abydos*, *The Corsair*, and *Lara* appeared in rapid order.

Rokeby is, however, a regular treasure trove of Romantic hero types. There is a Gothic Villain in the person of Oswald, a character of endless guile, utterly devoid of sympathetic qualities, who makes the Noble Outlaws of the poem appear even more noble by comparison. Of the two young heroes of the piece, one is a Man of Feeling, and the other a Child of Nature. Wilfred, the young Man of Feeling, is oddly enough the son of the Gothic Villain, but we learn that in contrast with his father, he had "A heart too soft from early life / To hold with fortune needful strife." He was from birth a "sickly boy," and "No touch of childhood's frolic mood / Showed the elastic spring of blood." Instead, he spent his time with poetry; he was wont to "muse with Hamlet," and often he would "weep himself to soft repose / O'er gentle Desdemona's woes" (I, xxiv). He also lacks all skill in arms, but, as might be predicted, makes up for this loss by his skill with the minstrel's harp, "The art unteachable, untaught" (I, xxvi). Wilfred's rival in love is a rude Child of Nature named Redmond. In reality the son of the noble Mortham, he was kidnapped to Ireland as an infant by the wild chieftain O'Neale, and raised in that barbaric land until the age of sixteen. He is brave and bold of heart, skilled in arms, candid and outspoken, contrasting at every point with Wilfred except in that both have been somewhat sentimentalized, and both are in love with the poem's young heroine. The conflict is resolved, not surprisingly, by the dramatic expiration of Wilfred in the heroine's arms, so that she is free to marry the more virile Redmond. (It is interesting to note that Children of Nature seem always to win out over Men of Feeling in contests of love. So also in Bage's novel, for instance, Hermsprong easily overcomes Glen in winning the heroine's hand.)

But the poem's major interest centers in not one but two Noble Outlaws: Mortham and Bertram. An important innovation in the poem is that these are not only border outlaws; they have been comrades in arms in a "daring crew and dread" of English privateers on the Spanish Main. From this poem Byron may very well have taken the idea of making his Noble Outlaws contemporary pirates in the Mediterranean. The relationship seems especially close in that both Scott's Mortham and Byron's Lara are returned pirates, the former from the Spanish Indies, the latter from the eastern Mediterranean.

Mortham is the more noble of the two outlaws, both by birth and by disposition. Although a man of wealth and title, he has been driven to buccaneering by remorse for his secret sin: he has in a fit of jealousy, instigated by Gothic-Villain Oswald, killed his innocent wife. Bertram also reports that when among the pirates Mortham was "a moody man . . . / Desperate and dark, whom no one knew," but still fierce and brave: "On each adventure rash he roved, / As danger for itself he loved" (III, xxii). Nevertheless he is really gentle of heart and spirit; he scorns his portion of the spoil of their pirate victories, and takes even in battle the liberty of preaching to his comrades of "mercy and humanity." But Mortham has supposedly been murdered by his former associate Bertram before the story opens, and hence he appears only twice in the poem. His story is reported in the speeches of Bertram and in a long last will and testament.

At the center of the plot is Mortham's former associate in piracy, Bertram. He lacks the sensitivity and mystery of the older Mortham, but otherwise has all the characteristics of the Noble Outlaw. In physical appearance he is fearful enough, with his face darkened by the Indian sun, his "sable hair," his "lip of pride" and his "eye of flame / . . . that seemed to scorn the world" and that "knew not pain or woe" (I, viii). He also shares with Schedoni and Lara the peculiarly Byronic traces of burnt-out passions: it is said of his "swart brow and callous face" that "Evil passions cherished long / Had ploughed them with impressions strong" (I, ix). He is unique among Scott's Noble Outlaws in that when he is with his robber band, the minstrel-narrator compares him with the Satan of *Paradise Lost*: "While Bertram showed amid the crew / The Master-fiend that Milton drew" (III, xiv). He is also unique in that he is the first of Scott's Noble Outlaws to have a trace of Satan's sardonic smile in his "full-drawn lip that upward curled" (I, viii). Bertram's secret sin is that, as the poem opens, he has just attempted to murder his former dear comrade and associate in piracy, the noble Mortham, and throughout the poem he is half defiant, half remorseful. Then, too, Bertram is a skeptic, with nothing but contempt for the church and for religion. He even dies unrepentant: we are told that his "parting groan / Had more of laughter than of moan" (VI, xxviii). Still, from childhood on he has been "trained in the mystic and the wild" (II, xiii). As a result he is almost childishly superstitious, as when he easily persuades himself that the nameless antagonist with whom he duels over a tomb is Mortham's ghost, when actually, of course, it is Mortham himself (we remember that Marmion also duelled with what he believed to be a ghost who turned out to be his "murdered" foe).

Nevertheless, Bertram shows many sympathetic qualities. His secret sin is palliated if not excused by his feeling he has been betrayed by Mortham; when they were pirates together Bertram "loved him well"– he three times saved Mortham's life in battle or in shipwreck – and now that they have returned, Mortham has undergone a change of heart and has spurned his old comrade in arms. Bertram's last act is to give up his life in order to kill the villain and save Mortham's son from hanging. Like Marmion, Bertram too earns a soldier's epitaph from his enemies: "Fell as he was in act and mind, / He left no bolder heart behind" (VI, xxxiii). Finally, although Bertram has little of Mortham's sensibility, he takes part in one gentle scene which does much to redeem him in the reader's eyes. He has told the story of his life, and of his final resolve to die for Mortham's sake, to a sensitive young fellow robber named Edmund. Upon hearing the story, Edmund cannot but "drop a tear" in tribute to Bertram's courage. And when Bertram notices Edmund's tears, the poet tells us, "It almost touched his iron heart: / 'I did not think there lived,' he said, / 'One who would tear for Bertram shed.'" In appreciation of Edmund's sympathy, the Noble Outlaw takes from his baldric a "buckle broad of massive gold" which he bids Edmund "wear for Bertram's sake" (VI, xxii). One such touch of simple pathos is enough to win from the heart of the sternest moralist some sympathy for the hero, and Scott knew it.

Rokeby was the last of Scott's verse romances to become truly popular, and by his own admission Scott lost out in this field to the youthful Byron. Part of his decline in popularity was of course due to the adventitious factor of the younger poet's personal notoriety. Part of it was also due, as Scott generously admits, to Byron's verse having both more passion and more facility than Scott could muster. A final reason lies in the fact that Byron's heroes are far more skillfully characterized than Scott's. Marmion is certainly mysterious and forceful, but, to put it in Romantic terms, he doesn't have "soul" enough, and he finally fails to hold our sympathies. Bertram is more sympathetic, it is true, but has about him a bit too much of the "big bad boy"; there is something almost pathetic about his simple hearted superstition and his adolescent swagger. Scott's minstrel-narrator may compare him with Satan, but the comparison is ill balanced; Bertram is too simple, both of mind and of heart, to merit comparison with such a Titanic rebel.

With the Noble Outlaws of Byron's romances and dramas it is another matter. Byron dropped Scott's medieval setting and with it most of the older poet's Gothicism, but (following Southey and Moore) he gave his tales the exoticism and the luxury of the Middle East, a region with which he was personally well acquainted. He also gave his Noble Outlaws a depth of mystery and a passionate force which make Scott's Marmion seem pallid by comparison.

Although Byron had many eminent predecessors in this type of composition, he was followed by no eminent successors, at least in England. This is partly due to the changing temper of the times, of course, to the failure in the beginning of the Victorian age of the rebellious ardor which characterized the Romantic Movement. Moreover, this type of hero took Byron's name and became almost his personal property; for a poet to attempt to write of another Noble Outlaw would have been to invite comparison with Byron, to challenge the master on his own grounds.

VI FAUST

FAUST is of course much more than a Romantic hero. Since his first literary appearance in the *Urfaust* of 1587 he has come to typify man's eternal quest for knowledge – not only of scientific truths, but of Absolutes. His tragedy in its broadest sense is one which has been with us since the dawn of intellectual history: the tragedy of epistemology. As a popular literary hero, however, Faust certainly owes his revival to the Romantic Movement, particularly in Germany. But partly because he is a German figure, Faust has been the subject of an endless number of scholarly monographs and dissertations since his inception, and it would be a work of supererogation on my part to try to add to that list: he already shares with Hamlet the distinction of possessing a longer bibliography than any other figure in Western literature. All I would like to do here is to analyze briefly his major characteristics and the circumstances of his revival, and then to relate him to his fellow Romantic heroes.

In his first appearance in the German and the English Faust books of the sixteenth century Faust was neither more nor less than a typical medieval magician. As a matter of fact, the *Urfaustbuch* was compiled in honor and about the person of a rather obscure German-Swiss charlatan named Helmstatter, who, with "Faustus" as an alias, had practiced his art with fair profit for a number of years in and around the city of Basel. The book consisted of a collection of traditional medieval stories about magicians and necromancers, given focus and narrative line by being attributed to one central figure. In spite of these humble origins, Faust even in this earliest manifestation can be seen to stand for the aggressive, analytic side of man's nature, the eternal thirst for knowledge which will not stop at *hubris*, and which is perhaps for that reason essentially and inevitably antireligious. Since the authors of the early Faust books and the audience for whom they were written were quite pious, Faust is therefore depicted as a fearful villain at "best," and at his lowest, as something of a criminal buffoon.

It was Marlowe who raised Faust's stature to that of a tragic hero. His motives are clarified and his character ennobled, and the seeming injustice of an eternal punishment for a temporal and very human failing gives the tragedy the proper elements for a classical catharsis. This transformation of the hero is seen most clearly in the Helen episode, which in its new form is Marlowe's most important addition to the story. In the Faust books the hero's desire for Helen was a degrading lust for an unattractive demon; in Marlowe's tragedy this desire becomes symbolic of the Renaissance obsession with beauty in its purest, most attractive, and most human form. In general, perhaps nothing shows more clearly the basic similarity between the spirit of the Renaissance and the spirit of the Romantic Movement than this comparison: Faust in Marlowe's drama is a Renaissance hero struggling out from under the repression of medieval orthodoxy; and Faust in Goethe's drama is a Romantic hero emerging from the dead certainties of the eighteenth-century enlightenment.

After his incarnation in Marlowe's drama at the very height of the English Renaissance, Faust went into a decline from which he was not to revive for almost two hundred years. Both in England and in Germany he survived largely as a popular folk figure in subliterary puppet dramas. These were no longer intellectual tragedies, to be sure, but they nevertheless kept something of the poetic force of the popular concern with the sin of magic from which the *Urfaust* had sprung. On the literary level, however, the degradation was complete, and Faust became a clown, an object of ridicule along with the magic he represented; the true tragedy of epistemology was disregarded. He made two appearances on the English stage, for instance, once in the Restoration and once in the age of Pope. The titles of the pieces tell the story: *The Life and Death of Doctor Faustus, made into a Farce* (by W. Mountfort, 1684), and *Harlequin Doctor Faustus* (by J. Thurmond, 1724), a ballet-pantomime.

For his resurrection Faust had to wait for the German *Sturm und Drang*, the period of "Great Men" par excellence, and the age which gave rise also to Götz and to Karl Moor. Lessing had attempted a Faust drama, but caught in the dilemma of having to make a tragedy of a search after truth and knowledge in an enlightened age which was quite sure it had both, Lessing had given up, and scholars suspect that it was perhaps not with feelings of unmixed regret that he reported the loss of his manuscript on a coach trip from Dresden to Leipzig. But Lessing's idea fell on the more sympathetic soil of the *Sturm und Drang*, and soon Fausts were springing up under every bush and tree. Goethe's Faust so much overshadows his innumerable lesser brethren that one sometimes comes to think of him as standing alone, though almost every author of the period tried his hand at a creation of his own, until by 1808, when the whole of *Faust I* appeared, the magician had become the most popular literary figure in Germany. Of these authors one might mention three whose works are fairly typical: "Maler" Müller, who is of interest because he also produced a Cain, wrote *Fausts Leben dramatisiert* (1778), perhaps the most stormy of the *Sturm und Drang* Fausts; Friedrich von Klinger, whose earlier drama gave the movement its name, wrote a full-length novel called *Fausts Leben, Thaten, und Höllenfahrt* (1791), which while more intellectual than Müller's drama, is also far more pessimistic (toward the close it reminds one at times of *Manfred* or *Cain*); Chamisso, who was later to give birth to the story of poor Peter Schlemihl, created in his *Faust: Ein Versuch* (1804), a figure peculiarly characteristic of mature German Romanticism. This Faust combines the traditional religious idea of the guilt inherent in the desire for knowledge of Absolutes, with the Kantian idea of the utter impossibility of knowing any ultimate reality outside the mind.

Of course Goethe's Faust is much more than a typical Romantic hero or a typical Renaissance "man," and in the second part of the drama Goethe reached toward a personal solution to the Faustian dilemma which in its balance, its skepticism, and its broad humanism transcends completely the limits of the narrowly Romantic or of the narrowly Classic. But the Faust of Part One is symbolic of much in the Romantic Movement; his defining characteristics are his thirst for absolute knowledge and his lust for experience. There is no hint in his nature of the medieval Faust's cupidity, of his yearning for wealth and luxury, nor is there much of the Marlovian longing for knowledge partly for the sake of power. Faust does retain the Titanism of Marlowe's hero, to be sure; he is the "Great Man" who is not as other men, he is isolated as are all of the heroes of Romanticism, but he is so rather as an aristocrat of suffering than as a hero of action.

It is perhaps by now fairly easy to see where this argument is leading. I believe that the Romantic Faust lies in the line of descent of the Hero of Sensibility: the author of *Faust* is also the author of *The Sorrows of Werther*. I developed in a previous chapter the argument that the combined sensibilities of the Man of Feeling and of the Gloomy Egoist produced the Romantic Hero of Sensibility, with his characteristic affliction of *Weltschmerz*. The main line of descent of the Romantic Hero of Sensibility thus stretches from Yorick through Werther to Childe Harold and Manfred. In Harley or Yorick this dabbling in the sensibilities of sorrow is still somewhat detached, esthetic, and definitely egocentric. But with the crumbling of the eighteenth-century certainties of the enlightenment, and with the spread of the "English" melancholy of the Gloomy Egoist, this sensibility begins to take on a cosmic significance, apparent already in *Werther*. Finally, with the deep disillusionment caused by the failure of the French Revolution, and with the increasing religious skepticism on the metaphysical or theological level, this sensibility becomes true *Weltschmerz*, the prevailing attitude of the Romantic Hero of Sensibility, best typified in England in *Childe Harold* or *Manfred*.

Of the many attempts to define *Weltschmerz*, that much used and much abused term in Romantic criticism, few have been wholly satisfactory. One scholarly authority on the literature of both England and Germany defines it as "the psychic state which ensues when there is a sharp contrast between a man's ideals and his material environment, and his temperament is such as to eliminate the possibility of any sort of reconciliation between the two." Professor Rose goes on to say that it is not a philosophy, but a "state of mind"; essentially passive, it usually leads to the building up of an imaginary world with a distinctively erotic and even masochistic coloring.[1] Now this definition, in spite of the qualifications, is still rather general, so Rose narrows it further by reference to psychology: only those states of mind which are distinctly pathological will be called *Weltschmerz.*

To me, this definition remains vague in its assignment of origins (almost any kind of human unhappiness, almost any attitude of disaffection with the world, arises from such a disparity between "ideals" and "environment"), and at the same time the somewhat arbitrary limitation by reference to the pathological seems (in spite of Goethe's concurrence) particularly dangerous in the field of literary criticism. But Rose's argument that *Weltschmerz* is a state of mind, that it is essentially passive, and that it arises from the discomfort of an irreconcilable dilemma, is well taken, and his further point that the attitude is really more often "*Ichschmerz*" than *Weltschmerz* is convincing, although the very passion of the egoism of the *Weltschmerzler* usually makes him involve the whole world in his peculiar plight.

For the purposes of this study, however, I would like to redefine *Weltschmerz* in slightly different terms. Those afflicted with this Romantic disease appear to suffer from an almost irreconcilable conflict between two opposing forces in their personalities: forces not peculiar to the Romantic psyche, of course, but made especially acute in that age because of its increasing skepticism of the solutions of the Enlightenment and because of its ever present sense of rebellious individualism. The one force or drive is to lose oneself in some vision of the Absolute; a longing for some intellectual and moral certainty, ranging from positive commitment to an orthodox creed, to a mystic conception of oneself as a part of a living organic universe. The twin and opposing force in the personality is toward a positive and passionate assertion of oneself as an individual, a self-assertion which makes impossible any wholehearted commitment to dogmas or to absolutes outside oneself, and which usually takes the form of a lust for violent emotional experience, even for suffering – any psychic activity which will heighten and make more acute a sense of self-awareness and self-identity. For some Romantics the first drive wins out, and they become wholly committed to a vision of an organic and mystic Nature, as was Wordsworth, or to an equally mystic conception of a Kingdom of Love, as was Shelley. (This definition of course begs the metaphysical question as to whether or not those conceptions of the universe are more than mere visions, are more than metaphysical projections of the very egos which committed themselves, but that is another matter indeed, and it must be sufficient to say here that these Romantics did not themselves think of their Absolutes as empty dreams.) For other Romantics, however, as for the Goethe of *Werther* or of the early *Faust*, or for Byron in all of his works, such commitment was impossible; for these poets a sense of life, of individuality, of a skeptical self was too strong; they remained to the end detached, insulated, and passionately individual.

This unresolved tension, I believe, constitutes the basis of Romantic *Weltschmerz* in all of its various guises, and this is the characteristic attitude of the Romantic Hero of Sensibility. It is easy to see that this "state of mind" is closely related to that described by modern existentialism: man caught between the realization of the relativity of all values ("If God is dead, all things are possible," as Ivan Karamazov says), and the necessity for a positive self-assertion in this realm of relativistic chaos, this realm of the "absurd," in Camus' expression. If any escape from this tragic dilemma is possible (other than in a commitment to absolutes outside the self), I suppose it must lie in the solution of modern humanism: a realization of the limits of the human mind and a cultivation of one's own values in an assertion of a community of selves in an ultimately unknown and unknowable universe. This is Goethe's ultimate solution in *Faust II*, and I believe it is also the solution toward which

Byron pointed in *Manfred* and in *Cain*, and which he perhaps achieved in the narrator-persona (if not the person) of *Don Juan*.

To return then for another look at the Hero of Sensibility as seen in this light: he is always isolated, set off from the rest of mankind; he is essentially passive, since uncommitted; he is egocentric and self-consciously introspective, sometimes passionately, sometimes even morbidly aware of his own identity in a world of ever shifting and ever amorphous values.

When he is so defined, one can easily trace his development in the heroes of the Romantic Movement and beyond. First there is Yorick, with his *Patior, ergo sum*, but with a largely esthetic attitude toward sorrows and sensibility. In Werther the suffering takes on cosmic overtones, and eventually it becomes too much to bear. Wordsworth's Oswald tells us that

> Action is transitory – a step, a blow,
> The motion of a muscle – this way or that –
> 'Tis done, and in the after-vacancy
> We wonder at ourselves like men betrayed;
> Suffering is permanent, obscure and dark,
> And shares the nature of infinity.
>
> (*The Borderers*, III, 1539–44)

Faust is already from the beginning of the drama disillusioned with the abstract studies in which he has spent his life searching for truth; he makes great fun of the self-certainties of the Enlightenment in the figure of his pupil Wagner. But when Mephistopheles finally tempts him to indulge his sensual appetites, he spurns the suggestion: it is not vulgar sensual pleasure that interests him:

> But thou hast heard, 'tis not of joy we're talking.
> I take the wildering whirl, enjoyment's keenest pain,
> Enamoured hate, exhilarant disdain.
> My bosom, of its thirst for knowledge sated,
> Shall not, henceforth, from any pang be wrested,
> And all of life for all mankind created
> Shall be within mine inmost being tested:
> The highest, lowest forms my soul shall borrow,
> Shall heap upon itself their bliss and sorrow,
> *And thus, my own sole self to all their selves expanded*,
> I too, at last, shall with them all be stranded.[2]

It is the same passionate self-assertion which motivates Byron to write that "the great object of life is sensation – to feel that we exist, even though in pain;"[3] this is also essentially the doctrine with which *Childe Harold* closes, and it is the final position of Manfred and of Cain. It is this same passionate and uncommitted Hero of Sensibility who continues through the Victorian age: in the person of Teufelsdröckh before his baptism of fire and his commitment to a conception of an organic universe, borrowed from German idealism; in the person of Arnold's Empedocles, with his isolation and his impassioned skepticism; or Clough's Dipsychus, the "little Victorian Faust," who finds commitment to any principle outside himself impossible. At the close of the century one finds a return to estheticism in such a person as Marius the Epicurean, who longs for commitment to Apuleius's Neoplatonism, or to the Stoic doctrine of the state, or to the new Christianity, but for whom any such commitment is impossible, since it means loss of self and of esthetic distance and moral detchment. This is after all not so far from the estheticism of Sterne's Yorick, though somehow harder and more humorless, without the essential optimism of the amiable parson. On the other hand, if it is harder in its intransigent skepticism, it is softer in its *fin de siècle* tone. One feels that the passionate intensity of Faust or of Manfred, or even of *Empedocles on Aetna*, has long since died down to a small, blue, if gem-like, flame.

With Faust so placed in this tradition of sensibility and *Weltschmerz*, it becomes easier to see why Byron was the only poet of the English Romantic Movement who was deeply influenced by Goethe's drama (even in translation), and why Byron's heroes (especially Manfred and Cain) won Goethe's full approval. Crabb Robinson could never interest Wordsworth in *Faust*, perhaps because the poet had read part of *Wilhelm Meister* and thought it indecent. Coleridge too was offended with *Faust*, and consistently rated Schiller above Goethe. Shelley was interested enough to translate part of *Faust I*, and perhaps it was he more than "Monk" Lewis who introduced Byron to the poem. Aside from Shelley and Byron, Faust had to await Carlyle before he could gain any considerable reputation in England.

VII CAIN AND AHASUERUS

THE Noble Outlaw, although often compared to Satan or Prometheus, was still *menschliche*, even *allzumenschliche*; and his rebellion, for the most part, was against the laws of society, not against the laws of God. Faust, although he dabbled in magic and the supernatural, was still very human in his feelings and in his failings, but his rebellion, being inward even if intense, was against God, not merely society, and was of course unsuccessful. The next two Romantic heroes, Cain and Ahasuerus, although human to begin with, take on superhuman qualities in the course of their tragedies and become at last figures of fantasy and allegory rather than merely men. Their rebellion, however, is also most certainly against God and his decrees, and quite personally so. The last two of our heroes, Satan and Prometheus, are supernatural from the beginning, and their rebellion, also against God, is perhaps only equivocally unsuccessful.

Cain and Ahasuerus are obviously twin figures in legend and in literature. It is very likely, in fact, that the eternal Jew owes something of his origins to his older counterpart. In any case, the similarity of their crimes and of their fates early associated them in the popular and in the literary mind, and the figures they represent for the Romantic poet – the outcast from God and society, the eternal wanderer, the man of fate or of destiny, and the wisher for death – are so intimately associated that it often seems a matter of chance that a poet chose to write of one figure rather than the other.

Cain is the simpler of the two heroes, both in origin and development, and it is perhaps because his story is thus capable of fewer variations that he has also been the less popular of the two. As a matter of fact, although Cain has made occasional or casual entrances in poems or dramas through many hundreds of years, Byron himself is the only major Romantic poet to have used him as a protagonist in an important work.

Cain makes his first appearance, of course, in Genesis, and the story there given is familiar and simple enough. Cain is Adam's older son and a tiller of the soil; Abel is the younger son and a shepherd. These facts alone immediately associate Cain with sweat and toil, and Abel with pleasant pastorals. Then we are told that Cain's sacrifice is not acceptable to God, while Abel's is, and that this made Cain exceedingly wroth. Later, meeting Abel in the fields, Cain becomes angry again (for what reason we are not told), and slays his brother. For this crime God seeks him out, asks him where Abel is, receives Cain's famous reply, and then curses him to eternal wandering and penance. When Cain complains that the punishment is more than he can bear and that everyone who meets him will attempt to slay him, God gives him a protective mark as a sign that he is to be spared, and that anyone who harms him will in turn be cursed of God.

It is important to note that no real motive for the murder is given, and this is a loophole in the story of which the Romantics took advantage. Jealousy is implied, perhaps, but no more than implied: God warns Cain only of the possible "sin at his door" when he becomes angry at the rejection of his sacrifice.

One must also note that although we hear no more of Cain, we do hear more of his children, and we learn that they were both wicked and inventive, a common pairing of attributes in religious narrative. Then, too, although it is not explicitly stated that it was the siren daughters of Cain who married the pious and upright "Sons of God," the association was made early in Christian tradition (Milton follows this tradition in Adam's vision in *Paradise Lost*). It seems to me that this gives interesting evidence of a fact that in the Prometheus legend becomes exceedingly important: in the religious mind ambition and inventiveness, attributes which demonstrate an aggressive and analytic attitude toward the universe, are associated with rebellion against God. One remembers that in the biblical narrative the children of Cain are credited not only with the invention of the harp and the organ and with the first cultivation of cattle, but that Tubal-Cain was the "instructor of every artificer in brass and iron," and that Cain and his children were the first of the builders of cities. Milton elaborated the point in *Paradise Lost.* Adam has seen in his vision the industrious children of Cain, and is agreeably impressed, but Michael warns him:

> Those Tents thou sawst so pleasant, were the Tents
> Of wickedness, wherein shall dwell his Race
> Who slew his Brother; studious they appere
> Of Arts that polish life, Inventers rare,
> Unmindful of their Maker, though his Spirit
> Taught them, but they his gifts acknowledg'd none.
> (XI, 607–612)

There is surely a parallel here with the inventiveness and creativity of Prometheus, and there is a clear implication of *hubris* in both legends.[1]

So much for the biblical story. It has of course been used in countless allusions in the literature of Christian tradition, but like Faust or Ahasuerus, Cain made his first appearance as an imaginary figure in the folk literature of the Middle Ages, although this time not in *Volksbücher*, but in Mystery plays, including several of the cycles in England. Cain in these works is never a hero, however, nor is he even vaguely sentimentalized. He is treated as a thorough villain, second in wickedness only to Satan or to Judas, although occasionally he is allowed, like them, a bit of coarse or cynical humor.

For his first incarnation in formal and serious literature Cain had to await Gessner's eighteenth-century *Der Tod Abels*, a lyrical prose "rhapsody," which, interestingly enough, is obviously an imitation of and a sequel to *Paradise Lost.*[2] The details of Adam's story and his long moralizing speeches are certainly borrowed; the prose is full of awkward epic similes; like Eve in Milton's poem, Cain is here tempted by an evil spirit in a dream which gives him a panoramic vision of the future (like the vision Michael gives Adam at the close of Book XI); and finally, the poem closes with another banishment, this time of Cain and his wife Mehala, in a passage echoing almost verbally the dying fall of Milton's semitragic close.

The plot of the poem needs no summary. Gessner adds little to the biblical narrative except an immense amount of pastoral detail and long moralizing speeches on the part of Adam and Abel. The central contrast, of course, is between the pious blond shepherd Abel and the dark and moody Cain, although we are not given much reason for the latter's moodiness beyond his (not quite unreasonable) envy of his brother's pastoral ease compared with his sweat and toil in the fields. But as the drama is a product of the sentimental movement, so the character of Cain is also sentimentalized; he is shown as devoted to his wife and children, and his motive for the murder is developed far beyond the cryptic account given in Genesis. Cain is angry at the rejection of his sacrifice, but this is not his final motive for killing his brother. A particularly malicious devil gives him a vision of a future in which his sons and daughters are persecuted and enslaved by the children of Abel, and upon waking, while his frenzy is still on him, he commits the murder. He is immediately repentant, and the rest of the poem is divided between the pathos of Abel's interment and the pathos of Cain's remorse.

The main critical point to be made about the rhapsody is that, as its early date and its pious author's reputation might indicate, it is sentimental, but not Romantic. Adam and Abel are eighteenth-century moral Men of Feeling, and the moods of Cain himself seem more like school-boy sulks than titanic rebellion. Gessner's fame rests on his lyrical and pastoral prose – his *Idyllen* was the most popular German book in Europe before *Werther* – but in treating the Cain legend he was plainly beyond his depth. The rhapsody is full of irrelevant "idylls" and is cloyingly sentimental, and these faults were accentuated in its abominable English translations. To say, as a good many critics have, that any of the major English Romantics were influenced by more than the theme and the subject matter is to insult far greater talents than Gessner's.[3]

When one considers the poem's literary merit, especially in its translations, its immense popularity in England in any period but the sentimental close of the eighteenth century would be unbelievable. Still, popular it most certainly was. The poem was translated almost immediately by a Mrs. Colyers in 1761, whose version went through more than eighteen editions in the next forty years, and there were five other translations before 1811. The *Quarterly Review* reports in 1814 that

> No book of foreign growth has ever become so popular in England as the *Death of Abel.* Those publishers whose market lies among that portion of the people who are below what is called the public . . . include it regularly among their 'sacred classics'; . . . it is found at country fairs, and in the little shops of remote towns almost as certainly as the *Pilgrim's Progress* and *Robinson Crusoe.*[4]

Considering the vast popular appeal of the poem, we could reasonably expect it to have been read, if not always kindly remembered, by the English Romantics, and so it was.

Wordsworth mentions in Book VII of the *Prelude* (551f.) that the "comely bachelor" parson, "Fresh from a toilette of two hours," whom the poet listened to in London, used Gessner's drama (along with Shakespeare, Milton, and Ossian) for "ornaments and flowers" for his sermons. The simple and affecting close of Wordsworth's drama *The Borderers* obviously echoes the story of Cain, if not necessarily in Gessner's version. Marmaduke feels himself damned for his murder of an innocent, and tells us that

> a wanderer *must I* go . . .
> No human ear shall ever hear me speak;
> No human dwelling ever give me food,
> Or sleep, or rest: but over waste and wild,
> In search of nothing that this earth can give,
> But expiation, will I wander on –
> A Man by pain and thought compelled to live,
> Yet loathing life – till anger is appeased
> In Heaven, and Mercy gives me leave to die. (V, close)

Gessner's story was to have a more profound effect on Wordsworth's companion of those years, the youthful Coleridge. In a preface to his fragment called "The Wanderings of Cain" Coleridge tells of the abortive scheme of collaboration in which he and

Wordsworth engaged one evening during those fruitful months the poets spent together at Nether Stowey.[5] Coleridge drew up the plan of a prose poem in three cantos which was to "imitate the *Death of Abel.*" While Wordsworth began the first canto, Coleridge began the second, and whichever finished first was to write the third. Coleridge finished his "at full finger-speed," but Wordsworth could only sit and stare at his blank paper, and shortly thereafter the whole scheme was abandoned as a joke. In response to the urging of friends, Coleridge published his lyrical prose fragment in 1828. It is impossible to tell from the fragment what Coleridge really intended with the poem, except that Cain is distinctly sentimentalized (even given a little son to lead him), and that there is also more than a hint of Manichaeism in the story. It features a return of Abel, who reports that the "God of death" is not in the least friendly toward him, as was the God of life, and when Cain quite understandably becomes anxious to hear more of this God, Abel agrees to show him – and the fragment ends. There is a *Todessehnsucht* speech which is interesting in that it illustrates one of the recurrent Cain themes, but otherwise the Ossianic prose of the poem doesn't evidence enough of the Coleridgean genius to make one wish that the project had been completed.

The important point to note here is that, as Coleridge put it, "the whole scheme . . . broke up in a laugh: and the *Ancient Mariner* was written instead," and from the similarities in the stories of Cain and of the Mariner – the crime against innocence, the curse, the eternal and compulsive wandering – one could guess the probability of influence even had its actuality not been so carefully documented by John Livingston Lowes in *The Road to Xanadu.* But Cain is not the only progenitor of the Mariner; the influence of the similar story of the Wandering Jew was, as Professor Lowes has shown, far more important for the genesis of that Romantic masterpiece.

Wordsworth and Coleridge both abandoned Cain, and Byron remains the only important Romantic poet who used Cain as the protagonist in a major work of art. Byron acknowledges the influence of Gessner in the preface to his drama, writing that he had read the German poem with his tutor when he was eight years old, and not since. He also records that "the general impression on my recollection is delight; but of the contents I remember only that Cain's wife was called Mehala, and Abel's, Thirza," names which he did not use. He concludes: "Whether, then, a coincidence of subject may have caused the same in expression, I know nothing, and care as little" (*Works*, V, 208–9). That he did remember a few other details, such as the scattering by a whirlwind of Cain's sacrifice, and that he may possibly have been influenced by the sentimentally moral characters of Adam and Abel, may be granted. Beyond that the influence seems minor, indeed. Gessner's Cain is weak, sulky, and a bit adolescent; Byron's Cain, one of the poet's most striking characters, is not only a Cain type – as cursed, and as a wanderer – but he has been given the characteristics of a Titan, of a Faust, and even of a Prometheus.

The Wandering Jew is peculiar among these Romantic heroes in two respects: he is the only one who did not reach his majority in the Romantic Movement, having to wait until the 1830's for the period of his greatest flourishing; and, although many poets projected plans for epics or tragedies about this hero, he remains the only one of this group who has never been featured in a poem or a novel of the first rank (unless one is to overrate Eugene Sue's *Le Juif errant*). He has been vastly popular in literature, however, especially in Germany, where he has probably been the subject of more minor dramas and epics than any other hero except Faust.

Since there is no real basis in biblical story for Ahasuerus, his earliest origins are of course harder to trace than those of Cain. The slim biblical foundation for the story is probably found in the verse in Matthew's Gospel in which Christ tells his disciples that there will be some of them who "will not taste of death, until they see the Son of man coming in his kingdom" (6.28). There are also the legendary eternal life of the apostle St. John, the story of Cain, and an early Christian legend of John Buttadeus (the "striker of God"). There is even a Far Eastern analogue in the story of Buddha and his disciple Pindola (for whatever the parallel may be worth), and the name of the Wanderer, "Ahasuerus," is for some unknown reason taken from that of a Persian king of the Old Testament (Esther

1.17). However confused its origins, the legend appeared finally in its medieval form in chronicles of the thirteenth century, in which the wanderer is represented as a Jew who chid Christ into hurrying on the way to the crucifixion. Christ thereupon turned to him and told him "I will go, but thou shalt tarry here until I return."

Ahasuerus, like Faust, makes his first formal appearance in literature in a *Volksbuch* in northern Germany called the *Kurtze Beschreibung und Erzehlung von einem Judem mit Namen Ahasverus* (1604). By this time he is a Protestant, ragged and old, the father of a family, and a shoemaker by profession (perhaps, as one critic suggests, because he must have worn through a good deal of leather in his wanderings). It is this *Volksbuch* which is the basis for his treatment in several ballads, notably (in England) one in the Roxburghe collections, and one in Percy's *Reliques*. In the latter form the story may have influenced some of the English Romantics, but none of them mentions it.

It is important to note that in its medieval presentation the story had a distinctly religious motive. Ahasuerus is represented as neither a hero nor a villain, but rather as a pious and tired old man, who, having been converted and baptized, wanders about Europe witnessing to the mercy and justice of God. He can of course also serve in the role of a persona, of a teller of religious tales, since his age and experiences have given him a truly encyclopedic knowledge of the history of the world since Christ.

Ahasuerus receives his first "Romantic" treatment in a "lyrical rhapsody" by the Christian poet C. F. D. Schubart, "Der Ewige Jude" (1783). Schubart got his information from an expanded French version of the *Volksbuch* story, but his *ewige Jude* bears little relationship to his meek ancestor in medieval folklore. Schubart's rhapsody, a fragment of a projected drama, is in the form of a long soliloquy in which Ahasuerus expresses his longing for death and recounts some of his many attempts at suicide by fire, water, or the sword. He has even made an Empedoclean attempt to throw himself into Aetna, but all to no avail: he is saved each time by divine intervention; he cannot die. The poem then concludes somewhat inconsequently with God's taking pity on the poor accursed and sending a ministering angel to put him into a deep sleep until the second coming. The most important thing to note about the poem is that Schubart's *ewige Jude* is no decrepit German shoemaker; he is a very Titan, and the force of his passionate longing for death gives him tragic stature.

Goethe also planned a long work on *dem ewige Jude*, this time an epic, in which the ambitious young poet intended to include a comprehensive history of Christianity and of the church. Perhaps fortunately, *Faust* took precedence, and only a few fragments of Hans Sachsian verse remain of the projected epic. But the conception of Ahasuerus in Goethe's fragment is not at all typically Romantic: since the poem was to be humorous and satirical, the Jew was to be not only goodhearted, but also something of a hardheaded man of affairs. Still, the fragment is at least of interest in showing that even the greatest of Romantic poets could get so excited about the idea of the Wandering Jew that he could write:

> Around about midnight I first begin,
> I spring like a lunatic out of my bed:
> Never before was my soul so thrilled
> To sing the tale of the well-travelled man.[6]

Schiller, too, has left his *ewige Jude* fragment, although his is in the form of an unfinished novel, *Der Geisterseher* (1789). Here Ahasuerus appears as a figure in the "Sicilian's Tale," a protracted story which lends the novel most of its Gothic air of mystery. He has much of the Gothic Villain in his appearance: the stunning look from dark eyes under heavy brows, the deep and persistent melancholy, even the traces of burnt-out passions under a surface calm — the feature of the Gothic Villain which was to become so important for the Byronic Hero of the romances. But Schiller adds several other characteristics peculiar to his account: Ahasuerus is invested with the capacity to change persons or disguises (although he usually appears as a fake Armenian), and for some mysterious reason he is obliged to go into a deathlike trance once every twenty-four hours, between midnight and one o'clock. He usually manages this in private, but needless to say he is once "caught out," to the considerable consternation of the assembled company. This enigmatic figure is nowhere called Ahasuerus, but rather "der Unergrundliche," or simply "the Armenian," but that it is the Jew that Schiller had in mind is fairly obvious. He has most of the Jew's characteristics, and Schiller even makes him impervious to death in some of the same trials which Schubart had given the hero in his lyrical rhapsody. It is impossible to say just what Schiller meant to do with his Ahasuerus, since he abandoned the novel unfinished, apparently in disgust at its Gothicism. Fragmentary as it was, however, it was translated into English twice before 1800, and it was in this form that the Romanticized Wandering Jew first reached England.

England had had eighteenth-century Wandering Jews, not only in the medieval figure of the Percy ballad, but also in the encyclopedic traveler who appears in an early popular drama called *The Turkish Spy* (1746) and as a buffoon in a melodrama called *The Wandering Jew or Love's Masquerade* (performed at Drury Lane in 1797). But the first Romanticized Wandering Jew appeared in that potpourri of German *Schauerromane*, Lewis's *The Monk* (1796). Ahasuerus here appears only in an episode in which he does a favor for one of the novel's young cavaliers, but even in this episodic appearance he manages to display all of the characteristics Lewis had found in his German reading, particularly of Schubart and Schiller. "Monk" Lewis's Jew has the same "romantic" appearance, the same melancholy eye, the *Todessehnsucht* and the Schubartian trials of death, and he has in addition one characteristic which can be traced eventually (wherever Lewis got it immediately) to the Ahasuerus of Spanish legend: the mark of a flaming cross on his brow, obviously borrowed originally from Cain.

Coleridge had reviewed Lewis's novel for *The Critical Review* in 1797, and that he had read Schiller's *Der Geisterseher* (probably in translation) is proven from the fact that in the same year he was using the remainder of the Sicilian's story for the basic plot of his tragedy *Osorio* (produced in 1813 as *Remorse*). Coleridge wrote no fragment on the Wandering Jew, but that he planned such an epic one learns from his notebooks. What is far more important, of course, is that the figure of the Ancient Mariner owes many of his most basic characteristics to Ahasuerus as he appeared in *The Monk* and in *Der Geisterseher*.[7]

Wordsworth left no fragment, but he did leave a short lyric called "Song: For the Wandering Jew," written in 1800. The poem is composed of six ballad stanzas each with a natural object or animal and its "home" (a somewhat heterogeneous collection, to be sure: torrents, clouds, a chamois, a sea horse, a raven, and an ostrich), and a seventh stanza in which the wanderer speaks of his own longing for a home – the goal of death.

It was Shelley who of all the English Romantics made the most use of this wandering hero. Ahasuerus makes his first appearance in the violently youthful and atheistic *Queen Mab*, and in a long note to the scene Shelley includes a translation of the poem he used as a source – a poem he says he found in Lincoln's Inn Fields, and the author of which he was unable to identify. As his translation shows, his "German work" was none other than Schubart's rhapsody, but in Shelley's drama "der ewige Jude" undergoes a considerable transformation from the figure drawn by the pious German. Shelley's Ahasuerus is also a Titan, to be sure, but this time in the original sense of the term: he is a rebel against God. Shelley first of all changes the story, so that we have Ahasuerus mocking Christ on the cross, giving as his reason the fact that "No pain assailed His unterrestrial sense; / And yet He groaned." In resentment at this insult Christ curses him to eternal wandering, and at the same time slays all of his kindred. Instead of searching for death, however, as did the Jew of Schubart's poem, Shelley's Ahasuerus tells us that

> my soul,
> From sight and sense of the polluting woe
> Of tyranny, had long learned to prefer
> Hell's freedom to the servitude of Heaven.
> Therefore I rose, and dauntlessly began
> My lonely and unending pilgrimage,
> Resolved to wage unweariable war
> With my almighty Tyrant . . . (VII, 192–9) [8]

and much more to the same effect. The fourth line of this passage is almost a verbal echo of Satan's famous "Better to reign in hell than serve in heaven," and it would take very little revision of the last two lines to fit them into Shelley's greatest drama, his *Prometheus Unbound.*

Shelley also left three fragments of a projected drama on the Wandering Jew. One is a single-stanza "Song" on a dying maiden, and another merely carries out a simile used earlier in *Queen Mab*, that of a lightning-scathed tree which refused to die under God's curse. In the third fragment, "The Wandering Jew's Soliloquy," Ahasuerus again calls defiantly for God's thunder, reminding Him of the curses He has cast on others. The list includes one curse which again reminds the reader of Milton (showing, I think, the association in Shelley's mind), and which raises clearly the problem of fate versus free will:

> . . . the Angel's two-edged sword of fire that urged
> Our primal parents from their bower of bliss
> (Reared by Thine hand) for errors not their own
> By Thine omniscient mind foredoomed, foreknown.

The Jew makes one more appearance in Shelley's works, this time in the late drama on Greek independence, *Hellas* (1821). In order to get his advice for the future, the hero of the drama, the sultan Mahmud, has called up Ahasuerus from "where he dwells in a sea-cavern / 'Mid the Demonesi, less accessible / Than . . . God" (163–5). In this appearance, however, although still a Titan and a prophet, he has now become reconciled with God, but of course this god is no longer his old Hebraic enemy of *Queen Mab*; this god is the Neoplatonic Essence of Shelley's later years, the "Fathomless," "the One, / The unborn and undying," the eternal Will and Idea (768, 806) – the same pantheistic Spirit with which Shelley in *Adonais* hopes to be reunited in death.

Finally, Byron must also have been familiar with the Ahasuerus legend, since he used the wedding-feast plot of Schiller's "Sicilian's tale" as the basis for his Ossianic *juvenilium*, "Oscar and Alva," and since he later records the strong impression which a youthful reading of *Der Geisterseher* had left on his mind. He had also read the novel of his friend "Monk" Lewis, and of course Shelley's *Queen Mab*, and very likely he discussed the Wanderer with his poet-friend. So, even though Byron makes no more than allusive reference to the hero in any of his works, I think it is fair to conclude that the stories of Cain and of Ahasuerus – those death-wishing outcast wanderers, cursed of God – made a deep impression on Byron's mind. The themes are repeated many times in his poetry, especially in *Childe Harold*, in *Manfred*, and in *Cain*.

It remains, then, but to add a note on the characteristics of these two heroes which made them so popular with the poets of Romanticism. Both of these heroes, it should be remembered, are indigenous products of the Romantic Movement – they bear very little relationship indeed to their medieval forebears – and they are also among the most characteristic products of that movement. The Wandering Jew is in a sense the most Protean of Romantic heroes; later in the century he was to become almost all things to all men – including the lover of Herodias's daughter, a nationalist, a heretic, and a patriot-savior – but during the Romantic Movement proper he was still limited very largely to those characteristics which he shares with his brother outcast, the murderer Cain.

The most prominent role of this twin hero is that of the eternal wanderer. In this role he is of course associated with all kinds of other wandering heroes, from medieval pilgrims and crusaders to flying Dutchmen, but Cain-Ahasuerus is particularly attractive to the Romantic imagination in that he has lived for almost an eternity and can therefore add to the attraction of far-off places the attraction of long-past ages.

He is a wanderer not from curiosity or from a cheerful wanderlust, but (like Childe Harold) because he is an outcast from society and accursed of God. It was in this role, I am sure, that he was particularly close to the soul of the Romantic poet, because it was in this role that the Romantic poet most often conceived himself. They are both almost from birth, it seems, fated to live their lives outside the society of companionable men, ostracized and isolated because they have been cursed by God with a private vision which must be eternally misunderstood by the world around them. And as Ahasuerus and the Ancient Mariner are compulsive tellers of tales, so are also the Romantic poets. It is quite true, as Yvor Winters has said, that there is something deterministic about Romantic esthetics; a poem is an organic growth, it comes from the poet sometimes without plan or control, like lava from a volcano, as Byron put it, and sometimes even in spite of his conscious will. As the Ancient Mariner tells his tale from a compulsion neurosis, so Byron tells us that he writes poetry because he must, because otherwise he would go mad.

Finally, although no critic has developed the idea, it seems to me that among the most obvious of the characteristics of Cain-Ahasuerus is the death wish. The following passage from Schubart's rhapsody is typical, and it seems to me to represent this *Todessehnsucht* eloquently:

> Oh! Unable to die! Unable to die!
> Unable to rest after the toils of the flesh!
> Bearing this spiritless body of dust,
> Its cadaverous hues, its smell of the grave!
> That I must behold for ages to come
> That yawning monster *Sameness*!
> And that lewd hungry Time,
> Forever bearing, forever devouring her children!
> Oh! Unable to die! [9]

But here a necessary qualification: to recognize the existence of this peculiar attitude and even to call it by name the "death wish" is not necessarily to subscribe to the particular *Weltanschauung* of late-Freudian psychoanalysis. The phenomenon as an end-result is there and to be dealt with in a great deal of the world's poetry, whatever may be its cause or its origin.

It must also be remembered that in the Romantic Movement (as particularly with Cain and Ahasuerus) longing for death is most certainly not a longing for the bliss of heaven. When Bach's fellow parishioners sang "Komm süsser Tod" they looked upon death as a gateway to life eternal, even if the emphasis in medieval or Reformation hymnology seems more often to have been on escaping the burdens of this vale of tears than on being rewarded in heaven. But when Keats sings "for many a time / I have been half in love with easeful Death"; or "Now more than ever it seems rich to die, / To cease upon the midnight with no pain," there is certainly no hint in the context that Keats is thinking of bliss to come, and the same must be said of a hundred passages in the poetry of Novalis, or of Shelley, or even occasionally of Byron.

For my part, I am inclined to associate this typical death wish of Ahasuerus with the *Weltschmerz* of the Romantic Hero of Sensibility. I attempted above to define this *Weltschmerz* in terms of two contradictory and opposing drives in the Hero of Sensibility: one toward egoistic and skeptical self-assertion, a passionate holding-fast to the feeling of self as a separate and individual identity; the other an equally passionate longing for commitment to absolutes outside the self – in its most intense expression, perhaps, the longing which Shelley's personae express for some sort of Neoplatonic absorption into "the One" (such as Ahasuerus expresses in the passage referred to from *Hellas*). Now this latter drive, in its passionate denial of self and of all individuality, seems to me very closely associated with the death wish, and this intellectual and emotional realization of the intimate association shared by certainty, eternity, security, and death seems to me basic to much Romantic poetry. It supplies the central agony of two of Keats's greatest odes, for instance – that to the Nightingale and that on the Grecian Urn – the realization that all that is certain, absolute, and eternal, is also lifeless and cold. Keats's attempted solution, that of grasping the eternal in the creation of things of beauty, is oddly enough also Schopenhauer's solution in *The World as Will and Idea*, and it was this philosopher who formulated the death wish which now bears Freud's name. Finally, lest this association of mystic commitment with the death wish seem too eccentric, one can recall the words of Zarathustra, in a curious answer to Kierkegaard (especially so in that Nietzsche had never read him): "Weariness, that with one leap wishes to reach the ultimate, with one last death-leap; a poor unknowing weariness, that wills no more to assert itself: this creates all gods and other-worlds." [10]

Whatever reasons one assigns for the death wish – and whether or not one is willing to associate it in a Freudian or Nietzschean way with self-commitment to mystical absolutes – it remains an important theme especially of Romantic poetry, and it is most obviously represented by the Cain-Ahasuerus figure. More than that, it also associates the Cain-Ahasuerus hero with the Romantic Hero of Sensibility, who has the same concern with time and eternity, frequently the same concern with the tediousness of life in its seemingly endless rhythmical recurrences ("Das gähnende Ungeheuer Einerlei" of Schubart's Jew), and who so often expresses a longing to be relieved of this life which has become more of a burden than a joy.

In some ways, then, the Cain-Ahasuerus hero is the most typical of all of the Romantic heroes. In his different manifestations in Romantic literature, he combines elements of all the others: he is by definition an outlaw; he becomes in Byron's poetry, at least, something of a Faust; and in many of his appearances, but especially in Shelley's poetry, he is a Promethean rebel. To these characteristics he adds others, also in their very essence Romantic: the characteristics of the wanderer, of the social outcast, of the cursed and "marked" of God.

Cain-Ahasuerus also shows most clearly the transformation a typical hero undergoes when he is caught up by the spirit of Romanticism. The Noble Outlaw was always a hero, and the Romantics transformed him largely by making him darker and more Gothic; Faust was of course a hero of the Renaissance long before he was given a Romantic revival; Satan was first made heroic, if not a hero, by Milton; and Prometheus was both heroic and a hero in Aeschylus. But Cain, the lubberly villain of medieval Mysteries who was too cowardly to admit his crime ("Am I my brother's keeper?"), was first sentimentalized by Gessner in Germany, and then Prometheanized by Byron. The change in Ahasuerus is even more extreme: from his humble origins in the *Volksbuch* as a pious, poverty-stricken, white-bearded cobbler, he grows in stature and in mind, in suffering and in dignity, until in the nineteenth century he can challenge Jehovah, and put Christ Himself to shame. No contrast could be more striking; no transformation more dramatic and typically Romantic.

VIII SATAN AND PROMETHEUS

SATAN and Prometheus represent the Romantic Hero apotheosized; in these figures he reaches the ultimate in sublimity, in dignity, and in rebellion. All of the Romantic heroes have to a certain extent taken on titanic characteristics: the Noble Outlaw fought against the injustices of society; Faust and Ahasuerus in their symbolic suffering sometimes stood for all mankind; but it was Prometheus who became symbolic, through all the Romantic Movement, of man in his fight for liberty against oppression in all its forms: he combines in his person those two most prominent and not always compatible concerns of Romanticism – the concern for individual liberty, and the concern for society, the brotherhood of man.

Prometheus's counterpart in Christian legend, the Satan of *Paradise Lost*, shares the distinction with Cain of being the only one of these Romantic heroes who does not owe his origin to the German *Sturm und Drang*: the Noble Outlaw, Faust, and Ahasuerus all appeared first in Romantic form in the novels, plays, and poems of this "Great Man" movement of German literature. Even the Hero of Sensibility probably first appeared as Werther, who was more than merely an English Man of Feeling. Satan the Sublime, however, appeared first as heroic, if not as a hero, in an English epic.[1]

In German literature, for the most part, Satan remained Mephistopheles, and there is nothing titanic about this devil. In most of the Faust stories, for instance, he is the orthodox Christian and medieval personification of evil, and the fact that he is also "Lucifer" seems almost to have been lost sight of. He has undergone a considerable transformation in Goethe's drama, it is true, but he is still no Titan. He has become witty, personable, and eminently sophisticated, but he remains even here and perhaps pre-eminently here negative and cynical, the eternal nay-sayer – a far cry both from Milton's ever hopeful militant and also from any *Sturm und Drang* conception of the "Great Man." Of course Milton's epic was widely read in Germany – Lessing in *The Laocoön* places it first among modern epics – and the sublimity of his Satan was recognized by the new generation of writers. We have seen that Schiller in *Die Räuber* lists Satan among the compeers of Karl Moor, and the only important exceptions to this generalization about Germanic devils are found in a work obviously written as a kind of sequel to *Paradise Lost.* Klopstock's *Der Messias* has evil angels who approach the sublimity (or perhaps one should say attempt the sublimity) of Milton's Satan, especially Adramelech, whom Schiller mentions also in the preface to *Die Räuber*.

Of course it was a Romantic interpretation which made a hero of the Satan of *Paradise Lost*; in a way he demonstrates in his development the same transformation already seen in the Gothic Villain and in Cain: he becomes gradually more and more sympathetic, and his sins are more and more easily forgiven on the grounds of his sublimity, until at last with Blake and Shelley he emerges as no longer a villain, but a hero.

One need not go so far as to say that even in *Paradise Lost* Satan is a hero, but one must admit that he is at least heroic. The tide of endless controversy over the putative hero of Milton's epic has in this anti-Romantic age run in favor of the anti-Satanists, but any unbiased reader (by which I mean anyone who has not started out with "a good morning's hate" of Satan) must admit that Satan has most of the heroic action, and that in the first three books, at least, he has most of the commendable sentiments, expressed in the poem's most powerful language.[2] The subsequent "degradation" of Satan does not seem to me to erase the impression created by the heroic figure of the first books. Above all, it is clear that Satan stands for basically humanist sentiments, and that here, at least, he is in sympathy with those Arminian tendencies in Milton which caused him to despise a "cloistered and a sheltered virtue" and to "de-emphasize" such uncongenial doctrines as that of the vicarious atonement. Satan is, after all, an aggressive and inventive spirit, and he thus becomes I think inevitably associated with the aggressive, inventive spirit of man, that proud self-assertion which is the basis of all heresy and *hubris*, but which is also the basis of Romantic and humanist self-reliance. All through Christian tradition, but especially in Gnostic and Manichaean sects – which Milton would take seriously even if he did not agree (one remembers his sonnet on the slaughter of the Albigensians) – Satan has at various times been held responsible for the arts, for human reason, and even for the creation of the world.[3]

Whatever his status in Milton's epic, however, Satan began in the eighteenth century a slow and gradual rise in the esteem of critics and estheticians, a rise due partly to the waning of Christian orthodoxy in an age when devils were likely to be relegated to the level of other "superstitions," partly among the pre-Romantics to the recognition of his sublimity, and partly among the sentimentalists to an increased emphasis on his "humanity."

Dryden, in his preface to the *Aeneid*, was really the first to call Satan the hero of *Paradise Lost*, and he was echoed or answered by Addison in the *Spectator*.[4] Dryden wrote that Milton's poem would have been a great epic "if the Devil had not been his hero, instead of Adam," and "if the giant had not foiled the knight, and driven him out of his stronghold, to wander through the world with his lady errant" (Dryden had just been discussing *The Faerie Queene*). Dryden, however, was of course no Romantic, and his judgment that Satan was the hero was based on his interpretation of neoclassical rules for the epic; the hero must be active, he must be successful, and on these grounds Adam could not qualify.

Even then, however, Satan had begun to grow in the favor of critics and estheticians.[5] Dennis had already in 1704 noted and praised the sublimity in the conception of the fallen angel, and Thyer, in his notes to Newton's edition of the poem, is perhaps the first to compare him with Prometheus. By 1783 the revaluation had begun in earnest: James Beattie, in his "Illustrations on Sublimity," places heavy emphasis on the dignity of Satan's character, and attempts a rather lame "poetic" excuse for his "humanity"; and in the same year the popular Hugh Blair, in his *Lectures on Rhetoric*, notes at such length Satan's "good points" that his discussion comes almost to sound like an apology for the devil.

Still, it comes as something of a surprise when at the end of the century Blake writes: "Note: The reason Milton wrote in fetters when he wrote of Angels and God, and at liberty when of Devils and Hell, is because he was a true poet and of the Devil's party without knowing it." As usual, in this passage from *The Marriage of Heaven and Hell* Blake has anticipated the full flood of Romanticism as it was to come in Shelley or Byron. Blake's was truly a voice crying in a wilderness of indifference to his works and thoughts; his identification of traditional Christianity with all that is repressive of man's best energy and passion, with a morality of slaves, anticipates not merely Romanticism but even more clearly Nietzsche, Shaw, or D. H. Lawrence.

Shelley is less eccentric and perhaps more characteristic of the Romantic age when he writes of *Paradise Lost* in the *Defence of Poetry* and in the Preface to *Prometheus Unbound.* In the Preface he is comparing Satan and Prometheus, to the latter's advantage, but the association is none the less clear: "The only imaginary being resembling in any degree Prometheus, is Satan." In the *Defence of Poetry* he is more specific, and states most clearly the Romantic contention:

> Nothing can exceed the energy and the magnificence of the character of Satan as expressed in *Paradise Lost.* It is a mistake to suppose that he could ever have been intended for the popular personification of evil . . . Milton's Devil as a moral being is as far superior to his God as one who perseveres in some purpose which he has conceived to be excellent in spite of adversity and torture is to one who in the cold security of undoubted triumph inflicts the most horrible revenge upon his enemy, not from any mistaken notion of inducing him to repent . . . but with the alleged design of exasperating him to deserve new torments.[6]

This is no mere eighteenth-century recognition of Satan's sublimity. Shelley sees and pays tribute to this aspect of Satan's character, to be sure, but he sees much more: he recognizes that Satan clearly has a humanist moral dignity (he is, of course, speaking of the Satan of the first books); he recognizes that Milton has entangled himself in the ancient and thorny problem of theodicy (an omnipotent God must somehow eventually be held responsible for Satan's rebellion); and he recognizes the inadequacy of Milton's presentation of God the Father, although he blames this inadequacy on the difficulties in Milton's story. Shelley makes these points even more clear in the witty "Essay on the Devil and Devils," an unpublished work from which he quotes for his *Defence of Poetry*.[7]

Still, Shelley used Ahasuerus or Prometheus instead of Satan for the rebels in his poetry, and we come again finally to Byron. It is easy to see that in spite of the influence of *Faust* on Byron's *Cain*, the character of Lucifer is largely in the English tradition of the Satan of *Paradise Lost*, rather than in the tradition of the Mephistopheles of the Germans. Byron's devil has more wit and sophistication than Milton's Satan, although he shares the latter's sublimity, defiance, and courage. He is, above all, a Titan, a yea-sayer, not merely a cynic or destructively negative like Goethe's Mephistopheles. But the influence of Milton's Satan is more pervasive in Byron's poetry than in the drama in which his namesake appears. Many of Byron's heroes echo Satan's sentiments of defiance, of love of individual freedom, and of self-reliance. Milton's "The mind is its own place" speech was especially popular with the Romantics – we have already seen that Schiller's Karl Moor remembers it – and Manfred also echoes it in one of the more famous passages from that play:

> The Mind which is immortal makes itself
> Requital for its good or evil thoughts,–
> Is its own origin of ill and end –
> And its own place and time . . . (III, iv, 129–132)

We come at last to Prometheus, certainly the most sublime of all the Romantic Heroes, and at the same time the most refined. Since he is the Romantic Hero apotheosized, he is pure allegory; there is nothing in him of the Gothic, nothing of the dark mystery or taint of sin of the other Romantic heroes. It is worth noticing, too, that although Prometheus lends "Promethean" characteristics to all the rest of these heroes, he borrows nothing from them.

Prometheus as hero and savior of men owes his character almost entirely to Aeschylus in the *Prometheus Bound.* He had appeared earlier in Hesiod, but there he was something of a scamp and a wily cheat, one who tricked Zeus in a sacrifice and stole fire from heaven. In Aeschylus he becomes completely transformed into a titanic hero and a savior of man, and it is in this form that he has captured the minds of poets ever since. He is not only the bringer of light and fire to man (there is of course a parallel here with Satan in the person of "Lucifer"), but a benefactor in many other ways: he has taught man the sciences of astronomy and mathematics and the rudiments of physics. He has initiated the culture of the soil and the building of cities; he has taught man the means of locomotion on land and on sea, and he has even introduced the art of music.

In doing all this for man, however, he has incurred the wrath of Zeus, and for this he is to suffer eternal punishment. In his condemnation one sees again the parallel with Cain's children and with the legend of Lucifer: in the religious mind any deviation from the norm of God-dependence is deprecated; human self-assertion, aggression, and inventiveness exist in perpetual danger of *hubris* and the consequent calling down of the wrath of the gods.

Aeschylus's drama was probably only the first part of a trilogy, however, and since almost all the text of the later two plays is lost, there can be no sure knowledge as to what Aeschylus intended to do with his hero. That Prometheus became reconciled with Zeus and was eventually freed from bondage is sure, but how this came about has been a subject of much controversy among classical scholars. Some critics have theorized that since a reconciliation between Prometheus and the malicious Zeus depicted in the extant tragedy would be dramatically impossible, Aeschylus must have in the later plays introduced a Zeus who with the passing of time had matured in understanding and human sympathy, and therefore come closer in outlook to his noble opponent.[8] This interpretation is lent some force since it is repeatedly emphasized in the first play that Zeus has only recently acceded by revolution to the throne of the gods, and since the Zeus who appears in Aeschylus's other dramas is certainly mature and sympathetic. In this view, then, Zeus became not the god of arbitrary authority and tyranny, as he is pictured in *Prometheus Bound*, but a god of order and justice, and as such a god to whom Prometheus could submit in true religious piety.

There are of course other and variant legends of Prometheus in antiquity, in one of which (mentioned by Horace, Propertius, and Ovid) Prometheus is not only the savior of man, but his creator. This version of the legend is important, since, as we shall see, it was this story to which Shaftesbury referred and which thereupon became particularly important for the German *Sturm und Drang*.

The Aeschylean legend of Prometheus survived through the Middle Ages as a subject for allusion and reference, but as might have been expected, the identification was not made between Prometheus and Satan, but between Prometheus and God the Father or Christ. Jehovah and Prometheus were similar in one respect in that, according to the variant Prometheus legend, they had each created man, but the most frequently noted parallel was between the "vicarious" sufferings of Prometheus and the passion of Christ.[9]

The first modern treatment of the Prometheus legend is in Calderon's *Estatua de Prometeo* (1679). Calderon had evidently not seen the Aeschylean drama, and got his information about the legend from Boccaccio's *De Genealogia Deorum.* Consequently his treatment of the legend is in a way an odd mixture of the major Prometheus legend with the Pandora legend. For the pious Spaniard, however, the entire story became Christian allegory; it is interesting here only in that in his allegorical treatment he makes the gift of fire equivalent to the gift of the spirit (this was of course incipient in Aeschylus's drama) and in that his treatment may have been an influence on Shelley. In Calderon's drama Prometheus is neither a god-defying Titan nor a true Romantic rebel.

As is the case with most of these rebellious heroes, Prometheus owes his first Romantic treatment to the period of the German *Sturm und Drang*.[10] Oddly enough, however, the initial impetus for the Germans' interest in the legend came from their reading of that ubiquitous English pre-Romantic philosopher, the Earl of Shaftesbury. In an essay entitled "Soliloquy, or Advice to an Author," Shaftesbury had written of an ideal artist as "the man, who truly and in a just sense deserves the name of poet, and who as a real master, or architect in the kind, can describe both men and manners. Such a poet is indeed a second maker; a just Prometheus under Jove. Like that sovereign artist of universal plastick nature, he forms a whole, coherent and proportion'd in itself . . ."[11] The young Germans seized upon this comparison to symbolize the idea that the artist is not merely an imitator of Nature, but a creator in his own right of worlds of the imagination. So Aeschylus's Prometheus, in an indirect manner, to be sure, became an inspiration for the new Romantic Movement: as Ahasuerus can symbolize the Romantic poet in the sense of his isolation, his eternal and private message, and his compulsive telling of tales, so Prometheus became a symbol of the poet as a creator – first "under" Jove, and later in the face of Jove.

It was this conception of Prometheus, as the creator and patron of Man and as the rebel against God, that the youthful Goethe embodied in his fragmentary *Prometheus* (1773). Goethe was not at this time acquainted with the Aeschylean drama, and the plot of the first two acts of his fragment came from two popular German guides to Greek mythology.[12] He makes Prometheus the son of Jove, but a rebellious son who finds his joy in creating clay images (men) which he hopes to bring to life. Jove sends a message offering to give life to his figures if he will submit, but Prometheus disdainfully refuses. Then Minerva, who loves him, tells him the secret of the Fountain of Life so that he may vitalize his human beings without Jove's help. He then teaches and guides his creatures, giving them all gifts with which to build a humanist civilization, and the last of these is the gift of death. So far the first two acts. The third act consists only of a soliloquy which Goethe had written and published separately, and which he added as Act III when he prepared the entire fragment for publication in 1830. It is a long and eloquent hymn of defiance in which Prometheus recounts his benefits to man and declares himself and the men he has created independent of the power of any Jove.

Goethe's Prometheus is a Titan, a creator, and a rebel against

God, but he does not suffer the punishment of divine wrath which Aeschylus's hero had undergone, and which was to become of primary importance for Shelley and Byron. Goethe's drama does have this in common with Aeschylus's, however: both Titans appeal to Fate or to Time as a higher power than Jove's, and one which consequently can give them the final victory.[13]

It was Shelley who seized upon the legend to embody his most cherished beliefs, and who "wrote it up" finally for the whole Romantic movement. He returns to the picture of Prometheus in the Aeschylean drama, and his story of Prometheus's revolt and of his punishment are the same as in his Greek source. But as Shelley tells us in the Preface, he could not accept the idea of an eventual reconciliation between Jupiter and Prometheus: "I was averse from a catastrophe so feeble as that of reconciling the Champion with the Oppressor of mankind . . . The moral interest of the fable . . . would be annihilated if we could conceive of him as unsaying his high language and quailing before his successful and perfidious adversary." [14] Consequently, Shelley has Jupiter overthrown by Demogorgon, and the freeing of Prometheus which follows initiates the reign of the kingdom of Love.

Shelley's drama, written partly under the influence of his current reading of Calderon (he had learned to read Spanish in order to read the religious allegorist), and partly under the influence of his enthusiastic study of Plato and Plotinus, is allegorical in the extreme, and consequently very difficult of interpretation. It is generally conceded that Prometheus himself represents the mind of man, and that Jupiter represents either the gods of traditional religions, or, perhaps more accurately, man's conceptions of the gods of these religions. This explains the fact that in the drama Prometheus calls himself the creator of Jove and the sole cause for his power. This interpretation, however, leaves the question of any ultimate order in the universe something of a mystery.

In any case, Shelley's conception of the hero of his drama is traditional in that Prometheus is the benefactor of man, a Titan, a sufferer, and a rebel against God. Shelley adds in addition the Christ-like attribute of mercy, that capacity to forgive one's enemies which the poet says in the Preface makes Prometheus superior to Milton's Satan, and the capacity which makes Prometheus repent of his curse against Jove, saying, "I wish no living thing to suffer pain" (I, i, 305). According to one interpretation, at least, it is this transformation in the character of Prometheus which represents man's *Selbstüberwindung*, and which prepares the way for his ultimate victory over the vindictive God of his own creation.[15]

By this time the general conception of Prometheus as a Romantic Hero is I suppose clear enough, but before one can classify him as the Romantic rebel epitomized, one must be sure of what he is rebelling against, and this is not on the surface at all clear, either in Aeschylus's drama or in the redactions of Goethe or Shelley. In order to define his character fully, then, I think it is necessary to take up briefly the question of the order – moral, amoral, or immoral – of the universe in which he appears.

Let me first outline my conclusions, and then I can proceed to give my evidence. I believe that the myth tends in its Romantic development toward a vision of a *naturalistic* universe colored by a *humanist* faith. By a naturalistic universe I mean an amoral universe, one which is morally indifferent but which is nevertheless ordered, but ordered so that what is strong is also successful; in other words, I mean the universe as it is generally presented to us by the evidence of modern science. By a humanist faith I mean the belief that the heart or the soul of man is so constituted that given the conditioning of a moral and reasonable environment, and given a normal hereditary endowment, he will most of the time choose the good. And what establishes the good? It has no supernatural sanction, obviously, and therefore it is also obviously relative to time and place, but in general it exists for us, as for these dramatists and poets, in those values admired in Western secular culture – those values, for instance, for which Prometheus stands: the value of art (however interpreted), the value of efficiency and progress (in the sense of overcoming nature for the sake of man's comfort and leisure), and the value of mercy, sympathy, and kindness toward one's fellowmen. This faith is humanist since the only values are those which individual men choose, and they are values only because men choose them; and since this vision of value is essentially relativistic, it also gives man a "dreadful freedom": man is in a sense his own creation, and the value structure of any society is a collective product of individually free men. Finally, it must be admitted that this is not a typically Romantic universe. Most of the great Romantics (the young Goethe and Byron were among the exceptions) subscribed to an organic universe with a moral order divinely ordained – the world of the German idealists, of Coleridge, or of Carlyle, or, in a different and less systematic sense, the moral Nature of the poetry of Wordsworth.

It is difficult to theorize about the ultimate order of the Aeschylean universe, since only the first drama of the trilogy remains, and in this fragment, at least, the order is confused, perhaps deliberately. There is first of all the Promethean level, a realm of humanist values, since Prometheus is the patron and guide of man, and his gifts (noted above) are the things man values. Then there is the realm in which Zeus reigns: a vindictive and cruel order, irrational and capricious, at least in the terms of the play. It is possibly true, as some critics say, that this order represents the rule of the gods as presented in early Greek myth – as for instance in Homer's epics – really a view of the world as ruled by individual caprice and whim, and hardly worthy of the title of rational order at all. Finally, there is the order of Fate to which Prometheus appeals in his opening soliloquy, and which is obviously conceived as being above both Prometheus and Jove. We cannot know for certain how Aeschylus reconciled these three levels of order, since his concluding dramas are lost, but it would seem probable that his final reconciliation was a religious one, that is, one in which Zeus aspires to the third and ultimate level: he becomes omnipotent, but at the same time he also develops in wisdom and justice so that he comes to embody that later Greek vision of a universe in which moral order and natural law are ultimately synonymous.

Goethe in his drama retains the basic conception of three separate "orders," and since his play is also fragmentary, his reconciliation is also unknown. Prometheus appeals to Fate, Time, or Chance, saying that Jupiter is also a slave of these – but these are, after all, the essential elements of a naturalistic universe (taking Fate to mean no more than simple deterministic laws of science). And Goethe, even more than Aeschylus, celebrates the basic Promethean values of simple humanism. At one point in the drama, when Zeus has offered Prometheus a place in Olympus and the rule of earth, and the Titan has already proudly refused, Epimetheus asks him what then remains for him to rule? And he answers:

> The realm which my effects fulfill!
> Nothing beyond and nothing below!
> What authority over me
> Have the stars above
> That gape on me?

Epimetheus then points out to him that in his lonely defiance he is denying himself the consolations of religion:

> *Epimetheus:* You stand alone!
> Your obstinate will forgoes that bliss
> When the gods, and you,
> Your works, the world, and the heavens all
> Feel a blessed inner wholeness.

Prometheus disdains such consolation, and answers somewhat condescendingly: "I know that well! / I beg you, brother dear, / Do as you will, and leave me."[16]

He has already in the opening interchange with Mercury denied his own divinity ("I am no God, / And form for myself as much a one as another"), and in this short interchange with his brother Epimetheus he sums up the proud faith of the artist and of the humanist: he asks for no absolutes, no certainties beyond that of a naturalistic universe in which he can fulfill his own human and finite destiny in freedom and in peace.

The order in Shelley's Promethean universe is also on three levels, since as the play opens we have Prometheus, who stands for humanist values (although admittedly with the significant addition of the quality of mercy which is absent in both Aeschylus and Goethe); Jupiter or Jove, who is as capricious and cruel as in the two previous dramas; and finally, "Demogorgon's mighty law" to which all spirits are apparently subject. But if Jupiter is in reality only a conception in the mind of man (as seems reasonable, since he owes his existence to Prometheus), then we are left only with the Promethean humanist level and the rule of Demogorgon. It is not really clear in the drama what this latter and ultimate order is; when Asia presses Demogorgon for an answer he is cryptic and oracular, and finally states that "the deep truth is imageless" (II, iv, 116). Still, he also says that all spirits, including Jupiter and Prometheus, are subject to "Fate, Time, Occasion, Chance, and Change," and these are also of course the elements in a naturalistic order of the universe. Then, at the close of the third act, when the universe has been freed from the tyrannical rule of Jupiter, we find that man is now lord of all things except "chance, and death, and mutability" (III, iv, 201), another way of describing the determined natural laws of the universe.

It seems fair to say, then, that Shelley's drama can also be seen as a vision of a humanist faith existing in a naturalistic universe. The universe is not necessarily morally ordered; the fact that Jupiter is dethroned is due to the basic goodness in the heart of man, and in the closing lines of the play Demogorgon gives us to understand that this idyllic state of affairs is somewhat precarious: there may in the dim future be a time when another Jove may rise to plague the earth.

Still, for all his atheism and his humanism, Shelley was also in his own way a deeply religious poet, and although his play may be interpreted as I have described it here, such an interpretation is still open to qualification. Demogorgon also says that although all spirits are subject to "Fate, Time, Occasion," etc., there is an exception: "All things are subject but eternal Love" (II, iv, 120). Shelley would seem in such a statement to be reintroducing, almost in an aside, a moral and "religious" order in the universe, and how this can be made to consort with the idea of man as ultimately subject only to "chance, and death, and mutability," or with the idea of a possible return of tyranny and disorder, I must confess I cannot see. Perhaps there is a basic inconsistency in the drama, born of an imperfect amalgamation in Shelley's mind of a humanist and naturalistic legend with a religious Neoplatonic world picture which includes the idea of an ineffable and indefinable "God" of Love.

In Byron's brief lyric poem there is no such inconsistency. The picture which he presents of Prometheus, or rather of Prometheus as representative of man, is the same proud vision of humanist values in an alien and amoral universe which Goethe had presented in his fragmentary drama. In the first forty-four lines of the poem Byron presents the Prometheus of Aeschylus's drama, and the many echoes of the Greek text show how familiar Byron must have been with his source. The picture he presents is that of a proud rebel, triumphant even in his eternal punishment:

Titan! to thee the strife was given
Between the suffering and the will,
Which torture where they cannot kill;
And the inexorable Heaven,
And the deaf tyranny of Fate . . .
The wretched gift Eternity
Was thine – and thou hast borne it well.

And of course the cause of his suffering is his love for humankind:

Thy Godlike crime was to be kind,
To render with thy precepts less
The sum of human wretchedness,
And strengthen Man with his own mind . . .

In the last fifteen lines of the poem Byron presents what he considers the "mighty lesson" which we as men inherit from our titanic forebear:

Thou art a symbol and a sign
To Mortals of their fate and force;
Like thee, Man is in part divine,
A troubled stream from a pure source;
And Man in portions can foresee
His own funereal destiny;
His wretchedness, and his resistance,
And his sad unallied existence:
To which his Spirit may oppose
Itself – an equal to all woes –
And a firm will, and a deep sense,
Which even in torture can descry

Its own concentered recompense,
Triumphant where it dares defy,
And making Death a Victory. (*Works*, IV, 49–51)

There is no hint here of an ultimate moral order in the universe: man's existence is "sad unallied." There is, however, the proud humanist vision of man "in part divine," who creates in a world he did not make his own "concentred recompense," taking even death as a victory. The last line, curiously enough, echoes the very sentiment of the close of Goethe's fragment, although there could of course be no question of influence.

I have dwelt on this point at such length because I feel that it is important not only for the study of the Romantic hero in general, but of the Byronic Hero in particular, especially in *Manfred* and *Cain*. The Byronic Hero of *Childe Harold* I and II is attractive, but only because he is a potpourri of heroic characteristics: he has no final consistency of character or of outlook. In the Byronic romances the hero appears as Gothic, dark, and remorseful. In the more mature *Childe Harold* III and IV he appears as one who has dallied with the vision of an ultimate morally ordered and mystic universe as in Wordsworth or Shelley, but who has rejected it, preferring to keep intact his sense of a skeptical self, his sense of reason and freedom. Finally, in the dramas, there appears this Promethean vision of man not fated, but free; defending his essential dignity and his chosen values in a naturalistic and alien universe.

It was the nobility of this vision which captured the minds and hearts of such men as Georg Brandes and Nietzsche, and prompted their perhaps eccentric evaluations of Byron's genius. Brandes ranked Byron's *Manfred* and *Cain* as almost equal in style to Goethe, and as surpassing the German in their central vision of man, and Nietzsche rated *Manfred* far above *Faust* in the sublimity of its conception.[17]

Such a conception of man as hero, however, is perhaps not fashionable in our later antiheroic age. The humanist faith which it implies – a faith in "Man as in part divine"– is for some too sanguine a vision for our latter-day "imagination of disaster," darkened as our minds have been with the shadows of two world wars and the pseudo-*Führerschaft* of Fascism. The entire heroic tradition offends not only our sense of realism, but probably also our sense of the democratic, of the commonness of everyman. Still, one must admit that the idealism of this tradition, the sense of the largeness and importance of man's role in the universe, is attractive yet; we can admire the hero's bravado, his self-certainty, and his unconscious assurance of his own identity, even if at the same time we deny the possibility of his present-day existence.

There is something very modern in the other side of this picture, however: the concept of the universe as naturalistic, as morally indifferent, as alien to all our dearest hopes and ideals. In this sense Byron is closer to us than any other of the English Romantics. Wordsworth's vision of an organic and morally-centered universe suffered from a long Victorian disillusionment, and seems now as distant from us as the idyllic pastorals of his Northumberland dales; Shelley's vision of a divine "kingdom of love," for all its spiritual nobility, seems almost pathetically utopian; and we can no longer see with Coleridge or Carlyle the natural universe as the garment of God. But Byron's skeptical vision of an alienated universe which takes no reckoning of man or of his hopes and infirmities is a universe in which we can, I think, feel quite uncomfortably at home.

Prometheus, then, is the Byronic Hero at his noblest, and set in a typically Byronic universe, and that the poet owed much of his conception both of his hero and of his universe to Aeschylus is abundantly evident. A fragment of his first English exercise at Harrow, a translation of a chorus from the *Prometheus*, is still extant in his published works, and he himself writes, in reference to *Manfred*: "The *Prometheus*, if not exactly in my plan, has always been so much in my head, that I can easily conceive its influence over all or any thing that I have written" (*LJ*, IV, 174).

Shelley scholars, carried away with his treatment of the legend, usually maintain that it was Shelley who first suggested the subject to Byron when they talked together during their long stay on Lake Geneva, but as a matter of fact, the suggestion in all probability came the other way round. As Professor Chew has pointed out, the references to Prometheus in Byron's poetry and in his correspondence before the two poets met in 1816 are legion; the references to Prometheus in Shelley's poetry or letters are practically nonexistent.[18] When he did refer to him in the notes to the youthful *Queen Mab*, it was only as the villain who had by the gift of fire first enticed man away from his vegetarian diet (note to Act VIII).

Although Byron centered no major work on the rebellious Titan, it is easy to credit his statement that the drama had a profound effect on all of his poetry. It is to the figure of Prometheus, more than to the figure of the Gothic villain, that we owe the more mature conception of the Byronic Hero as he exists in the dramas. For Prometheus was an individualist, a skeptic, and a rebel, and all of these things Byron was too; and Prometheus was Greek – in a sense he epitomizes Greece and Greek culture, at least as Byron saw it – and Greece was always a symbol and an ideal in Byron's mind, from the days of his schoolboy studies at Harrow, and from his first pilgrimage to Greece in 1809, to his final return in his thirty-sixth year.

◆ PART THREE. BYRONIC HEROES

IX *CHILDE HAROLD*

EVEN the casual reader of Byron's *juvenilia* can see that the earliest Byronic Hero did not spring full-grown and unprepared for from the mind of the young poet on his Grand Tour. Something like the poetic character of Childe Harold had already appeared in the early *Hours of Idleness* – in the figure of the eighteen-year-old student who fondly recalls his past "childhood" at Harrow, for instance, and the tombstone on which he was wont to lie and meditate on autumn evenings ("On a Distant View of Harrow"). Or in the figure who opines in "Childish Recollections" that he is a "Hermit" straying alone in the midst of crowds. The Gloomy Egoist of the "Elegy on Newstead Abbey," the "last and youngest of a noble line," views with poetic melancholy the "mouldering turrets" and the "damp and mossy tombs," and finds that even the grass "exhales a murky dew" from the "humid pall of life-extinguished clay." Still, Byron's first volumes, being only the subsidized publications of another poetizing young nobleman, were not notably successful, and it is probably safe to say that by 1812 few remembered the derivative *Hours of Idleness* or their traditional poetic characters. If Byron was remembered at all, it was as the author of *English Bards and Scotch Reviewers*, the free-swinging Giffordesque satire prompted by the poor reviews of his first publications, and these heroic couplets gave little promise of *Childe Harold*.

Scott was therefore expressing the views of the general public when he said he was pleasantly surprised by *Childe Harold* I and II, since this was not the kind or the quality of poetry which he had come to expect of Byron. That the reading public was favorably impressed is of course amply evident in the fact that both poem and poet became legendary and lionized almost in a matter of days. Of course the character of the Childe is not the poem's only interest, or even perhaps its chief interest: *Childe Harold* is also a great poetic travelogue, a moving rhetorical account of scenes and events described with uncommon sensitivity and intensity. Even in our anti-Byronic twentieth century a Donne enthusiast like H. J. C. Grierson writes, "As a descriptive poem alone . . . *Childe Harold* is the greatest of its kind, the noblest panoramic poem in our literature." [1] Our concern here is with heroes, however, and not primarily with poetic description, and, as is commonly acknowledged, Childe Harold is the first important Byronic Hero, and the prototype of all the rest.

It has been almost as commonly supposed, however, from Byron's day to our own, that Childe Harold is in reality none other than Lord Byron himself, or at least his conception of himself, and this, of course, in spite of Byron's repeated protestations to the contrary, both in his letters and in a long passage in the Preface to Cantos I and II, in which he refers repeatedly to Harold as a "fictitious character" and a "child of the imagination." Critics and the public have goodnaturedly ignored his distinction, however, and have made the identification of poet and poetic character the subject of endless biographical and critical discussion. The fact is, of course, that Byron was himself in part responsible for this popular misconception of his poem.

In reality the first two cantos of the poem have no less than three different poetic characters, none of which is kept clearly distinct from the others. There is first of all the Childe himself, who is largely a traditional literary Romantic hero or an agglomeration of hero types. Second, there is in the first canto, at least, a minstrel-narrator whose archaic diction and occasional moralizing comment are in the tradition of Scott's romances or of Beattie's *Minstrel.* Finally, there is Byron's own persona, who breaks in with personal elegies, or with poetic diatribes against war and tyranny, and who is not really consistent in voice or character with the other two persons in the poem. Byron does not really clear up the confusion until the fourth canto, when he drops the first and the second poetic characters, and retains only the third.

Byron had both a precedent and an apology for this confusion of poetic characters or voices. Sir Walter Scott frequently confuses narrators in his romances. In *Marmion*, for instance, he sets up as the narrator of his story a moral harpist with the characteristic attitudes of a pious Catholic late-medieval minstrel, but frequently he drops this pose for that of a nineteenth-century Scots Romantic poet. The confusion is even more evident in Beattie's *The Minstrel*, one of Byron's acknowledged models for *Childe Harold*. The ballad-minstrel persona of the first book with a "Gothic Harp" and a medieval mind, who reports sympathetically the facts and myths of the Child of Nature's rearing, becomes in the second book a contemporary Scottish moral philosopher, at home in the Age of Reason. Byron obviously chose to follow the pattern of having a minstrel-narrator, for the sake of the objectivity and impersonality of third-person description of his pilgrim. When Dallas, who was following the poem through the press, asked Byron whom the "he" referred to in the closing elegy of the second canto, Byron replied, somewhat piqued, "The 'he' refers to 'Wanderer' and anything is better than the *I I I I* always *I*" (*Works*, II, 161, note).

The minstrel-narrator is plainly in evidence in the opening of the third-person description of the Childe in Canto I. His archaisms and shocked moral tone are clear in the second stanza:

> Whilome in Albion's isle there dwelt a youth,
> Who ne in Virtue's ways did take delight;
> But spent his days in riot most uncouth,
> And vexed with mirth the drowsy ear of Night.
> Ah me! in sooth he was a shameless wight,
> Sore given to revel and ungodly glee . . .[2]

But even in the first canto Byron is inconsistent. The sentiments of the stanzas on the Convention of Cintra, for instance, seem peculiarly unfit either for the Childe or for the aged Minstrel, so in the next stanza (27), the poet catches himself with a "So deemed the Childe," and apologizes by noting that although the Childe was not accustomed to such reasoning, "here a while he learned to moralize." (For the dissipated young cynic portrayed in the first few stanzas, this is a transformation indeed.) The Minstrel seems to breathe his last in the closing stanza of this canto, however, when he tells us that after this "one fytte of Harold's pilgrimage" we may find "some tidings" in a "future page, / If he that rhymeth now may scribble moe."

In the second canto, the Minstrel having disappeared, we are left for the most part with Byron's own persona. Even the literary Childe of the first canto – the young-old Wandering Jew or Hero of Sensibility with Gothic sins – seems largely to have been eclipsed. The canto opens with a long *vanitas vanitatis* passage including a malediction on Lord Elgin and all despoilers of Greek ruins, and then the poet continues: "But where is Harold? Shall I then forget / To urge the gloomy Wanderer o'er the wave? / Little recked he of all that Men regret . . ." (II, 16) – in the last line dissociating the literary Childe from the sentiments of the poet's persona in the prologue. Through most of the canto, then, the Childe is used only for occasional and casual asides (usually "So deemed the Childe"), or for easy transitions ("Then rode Childe Harold" into the next landscape).

The third and fourth cantos were of course written much later, in 1816–17, after Byron's four eventful years in England – the years of his greatest fame, and, after the scandalous separation, of his greatest ignominy. Byron must have grown as a man during those years, and certainly he grew considerably as a poet. Yet something of the same confusion of poetic characters persists in *Childe Harold*, at least through Canto III. The literary Childe appears again in this canto, but he, like his creator, has grown more mature. There was something adolescent about the hero of the first cantos, but the new figure is more like the traditional rebellious Romantic Hero. Like Byron, he has returned to society, but unable to resist Beauty and Fame, he has again been "burned," and has finally realized that he is "himself the most unfit / Of men to herd with Man," since "He would not yield dominion of his mind / To Spirits against whom his own rebelled, / Proud though in desolation . . ." (III, 12) – including for the first time, I believe, an echo of the Satan of *Paradise Lost*. The identification between the literary Childe and Byron's own persona is of course quite close in this canto, and in the Preface to Canto IV, Byron drops all pretense at keeping the two distinct:

With regard to the conduct of the last canto, there will be found less of the pilgrim than in any of the preceding, and that slightly, if at all, separated from the author speaking in his own person. The fact is, that I had become weary of drawing a line which every one seemed determined not to perceive: like the Chinese in Goldsmith's *Citizen of the World*, whom nobody would believe to be a Chinese, it was in vain that I asserted, and imagined that I had drawn, a distinction between the author and the pilgrim; and the very anxiety to preserve this difference, and disappointment at finding it unavailing, so far crushed my efforts in composition, that I determined to abandon it [i.e., the "difference," not the "composition"] altogether – and have done so. (*Works*, II, 323)

It is still important to note, however, that throughout the poem and even in Canto IV Byron and his persona are two different beings. The latter is of course a fabrication, an achievement of the poet's imagination, comparable, I believe, to Beattie's Edwin, and an even more "literary" personality than Wordsworth's "I" of the *Prelude* of 1850. The Byron of this period was no solitary, for instance, as Harold most certainly is; Byron was always the most social of poets, and even a casual reading of his letters proves that he realized the fact. Perhaps the distinction between the poetic and the real personalities is nowhere more evident than in the matter of a sense of humor or a capacity for irony. It is this capacity which Harold notably lacks, and it is this capacity which Byron himself, as seen in his letters and in his conversations, was never without. One need only note the manner in which he refers, in a letter to his friend Hodgson, to some of the most passionate concerns of the first cantos:

I have attacked De Pauw, Thornton, Lord Elgin, Spain, Portugal, the *Edinburgh Review*, travellers, Painters, Antiquarians, and others, so you see what a dish of Sour Crout Controversy I shall prepare for myself . . . *Vae Victis*! If I fall, I shall fall gloriously, fighting against a host. (*LJ*, II, 46–47)

This is not to say, of course, that these concerns were insincere, but the passage does demonstrate that Byron was even in 1812 capable of that mixture of irony, pathos, and bravado, largely missing in *Childe Harold*, but which was to make *Don Juan* his masterpiece.

These, then, are the three poetic characters in *Childe Harold*: The minstrel-narrator one need not be concerned with; he is a traditional poetical mouthpiece, and in any case he disappears after Canto I. The Childe himself is at first largely a traditional figure, a combination of sometimes incongruous traits from the heroes most popular in the Romantic age. He is kept distinct from Byron's own persona, however, only occasionally in the first two cantos; the distinction largely disappears in the third canto, and it is nonexistent in the fourth. Of course the earlier picture of the Childe colors all the rest of the poem, and the composite figure of the later cantos, while gaining in depth of distinctive personality as the first great Hero of Sensibility in English Romantic literature, retains many of the features he had acquired in his first traditional appearances in Cantos I and II.

Childe Harold of the first two cantos is indeed an imaginary literary figure, however many details of ancestry or biography he may have acquired from Byron's personal life, and in spite of the fact that he has also taken a Grand Tour. In personality he is a compound of many distinct and even disparate elements of the heroes discussed in the last chapters. In age and in some of his attitudes he is a Child of Nature; in his appearance and with his burnt-out passions and secret sins he bears a resemblance to the Gothic Villain, especially to the sentimentalized villain of Gothic drama; and in his meditations and in his personal reactions toward man and nature he resembles most closely those eighteenth-century types, the Gloomy Egoist and the Man of Feeling.

Insofar as he is a Child of Nature, Harold belongs of course to the romanticized late eighteenth-century type; he has not the aggressive ebullience of a Belcour or a Hermsprong, but rather the tender sensibilities of Fleetwood, or of Beattie's Edwin. (As we have seen, this hero was already on the wane at the turn of the century, and it could therefore be expected that this would be the least important aspect of Harold's personality.) First, his tender age is repeatedly emphasized. He is a youth "of Albion's isle," "scarce a third" of whose days have "passed by"; a "youth so raw," "One who, 'twas said, still sighed to all he saw" (I, 2, 4, 33). Like Beattie's Edwin, the Childe is also accomplished in rude minstrelsy, and in moments of solitude he turns to his lute to compose impromptu songs for the consolation of his drooping spirits: "He seized his harp, which he at times could string, / And strike, albeit with untaught melody, / When deemed he no strange ear was listening . . ." (I, 13).

Mostly, however, Harold is a Child of Nature in his attitude toward the natural world. Like Beattie's Edwin, or Fleetwood, or perhaps the poet *manqué* of *The Prelude*, he loves "To sit on rocks – to muse o'er flood and fell – / To slowly trace the forest's shady scene, / Where things that own not Man's dominion dwell . . ." (II, 25). In another passage Harold himself calls nature his mother, and himself her child:

> Dear Nature is the kindest mother still!
> Though always changing, in her aspect mild;
> From her bare bosom let me take my fill,
> Her never-weaned, though not her favoured child . . .
>
> (II, 37)

(Two manuscript variations help to explicate the last enigmatic adjective: "her weakly child," or "her rudest child.") Finally, we find that as with most of the Children of Nature, Harold, too, is fond of his "mother" in her more sublime and terrible aspects. Beattie's Edwin "was a strange and wayward youth, / Fond of each gentle and each dreadful scene. / In darkness and in storm he found delight . . ." [3] So also Childe Harold exclaims:

> Oh! she is fairest in her features wild,
> Where nothing polished dares pollute her path:
> To me by day or night she ever smiled,
> Though I have marked her when none other hath,
> And sought her more and more, and loved her best in wrath.
>
> (II, 37)

These features of the Child of Nature seem somewhat incongruous in combination with characteristics of the next of Harold's prototypes – the Gothic Villain. Harold, as were the Gothic Villains, is of "lineage long" which was "glorious in another day" (I, 3). This resemblance is perhaps adventitious, but the same cannot be said of the Childe's haughty pride and cold reserve, his burnt-out passions, his secret sins, and his flashes of half-hidden remorse.

It is interesting to note first of all that in a variant reading of one manuscript Harold is given two of the Gothic Villain's most typical characteristics, the first, pride, almost a hallmark. We are told that

> An evil smile just bordering on a sneer
> Curled on his lip . . .
> [He] deemed ne mortal wight his peer
> To gentle dames still less could he be dear . . .
> (*Works*, II, 21, note)

The finished picture is less blatantly Gothic, but his relationship to his villain cousin of the drama or novel is nevertheless still clear:

> Strange pangs would flash along Childe Harold's brow,
> As if the Memory of some deadly feud
> Or disappointed passion lurked below:
> But this none knew, nor haply cared to know;
> For his was not that open, artless soul
> That feels relief by bidding sorrow flow,
> Nor sought he friend to counsel or condole,
> Whate'er this grief mote be . . . (I, 8)

That Byron had ample literary precedent for giving Harold these past and secret sins and the attendant remorse has I think been proven in the preceding chapters. The glamour, the irresistible romance of a secret and sinful past was one of the prime attractions of the original Gothic Villain, and, as we have seen, the intensity of remorse, sentimentalized in the hero-villain of the Gothic drama, had carried over into the character of the Noble Outlaw, long before Byron began to write. It is especially interesting to note that Byron gave the Childe these secret sins in his first appearance in Canto I, presumably before Byron had any of the sins of the rumored incest or of his marriage on his conscience, and when, from the evidence of his letters and the testimony of his personal friends, he seems to have been "not sated . . . not cheerless . . . not unamiable," but "all a-quiver with youth and enthusiasm and the joy of great living."[4] This seems clear evidence for the conclusion that this aspect of the Byronic Hero, in its earliest manifestation, at least, was inspired by literature, not by life.

Of course Gothic Villains were passionate actors in sensationalistic drama, and Childe Harold is not; he is above all a "pilgrim," not in the sense of being a tourist, on the one hand, or as a real penitent, on the other, but as marked and cursed of sin, wandering over the face of Europe in an almost hopeless search for self-restoration, and fearing that this can never come about, even in death. In other words, Harold is Byron's first Cain or his Wandering Jew. Now this is not to say that the Cain or Ahasuerus stories gave much direct inspiration for *Childe Harold*; these stories were themselves creations of the Romantic Movement, and they illustrate typical themes – eternal remorse, wanderlust, ennui, and *Weltschmerz* – which *Childe Harold* also illustrates. In other words, these are classic themes of the Romantic literary tradition; they are by no means personal to Byron. And, as might be expected, Byron does not leave implicit this association of Harold with his fellow remorse-stricken wanderers. We are first told of the Childe that "life-abhorring Gloom / Wrote on his faded brow curst Cain's unresting doom" (I, 83), and later, the Childe himself names his malady:

> It is that settled, ceaseless gloom
> The fabled Hebrew Wanderer bore;
> That will not look beyond the tomb,
> But cannot hope for rest before.
>
> ("To Inez": I, following 84)

These are still not the most important of his prototypes, however: most of all in his meditations (and most of the poem is meditation), the Childe of the first two cantos is an eighteenth-century Gloomy Egoist, or a Man of Feeling.

One of the purposes which *Childe Harold* served was to furnish eager readers with an imaginary Grand Tour, and this at a time when Englishmen had been obliged for years to sit at home, through wars and rumors of wars on the Continent. Of course then, as now, the commonest tourist sites in Europe were ruins, tombs, and monuments of glories past. Childe Harold was therefore making a natural choice when he selected such sites as settings for his meditations, and they were given an especial poignancy for his readers by the fact that many of the conflicts commemorated were of recent wars, and wars in which Englishmen had taken a prominent part.

Yet the general elegiac tone of the first two cantos of the poem, and the recurring themes of *ubi sunt* and *sic transit*, are very much in the tradition of the Gloomy Egoists of the preceding century. There are many passages reminiscent of such poems as Hervey's *Meditations among the Tombs*, or passages one might imagine having come from a later and secularized Edward Young. Beckford's deserted mansion at Quinta da Monserrate provides a setting for one such meditation:

> Here giant weeds a passage scarce allow
> To Halls deserted, portals gaping wide:
> Fresh lessons to the thinking bosom, how
> Vain are the pleasaunces on earth supplied;
> Swept into wrecks anon by Time's ungentle tide! (I, 23)

There is a long meditation on a skull in the second canto which reminds one not only of a Hervey or Young, but perhaps also of Hamlet in the graveyard:

> Look on its broken arch, its ruined wall,
> Its chambers desolate, and portals foul:
> Yes, this was once Ambition's airy hall,
> The Dome of Thought, the Palace of the Soul:
> Behold through each lack-lustre, eyeless hole,
> The gay recess of Wisdom and of Wit . . . (II, 6)

The personal elegies which close each canto remind one particularly of Young's *Night Thoughts*. At the close of the first canto, in a long note, Byron himself reminds the reader of Young's lines: "Insatiate archer! could not one suffice? / Thy shaft flew thrice, and thrice my peace was slain . . ." [5] The second canto closes with an echo of the same passage: "All thou couldst have of mine, stern Death! thou hast; / The Parent, Friend, and now the more than Friend: / Ne'er yet for one thine arrows flew so fast" (II, 96). Harold's elegies hold out no Christian consolation of an immortality beyond the grave, however. The Pilgrim, in part a follower of Young or of Hervey, is a secularized Gloomy Egoist, closer to the classics (in theme, at least) than to his ecclesiastic forebears of the previous century. In the long *vanitas vanitatis* passage with which Canto II opens (reminiscent of Lucretius, perhaps, but also of the Preacher), Harold can only conclude that man is a "Poor child of Doubt and Death, whose hope is built on reeds." [6]

Finally, the Childe of the first two cantos, in many of his poses, is a Man of Feeling. He is suffering from unrequited love; in spite of his often-confessed preference for solitude and his dislike for mankind, he is a humanitarian – sternly against war and tyranny in all its forms; and in his meditations on the natural world he adopts many of the attitudes characteristic of Mackenzie's Harvey (*The Man of Feeling*) or of the sentimental heroes of Mrs. Radcliffe's Gothic novels.

His unfortunate love affair is merely hinted at, and never developed. We are told from the first that he "Had sighed to many though he loved but one, / And that loved one, alas! could ne'er be his" (I, 5). He is impervious now to Cupid's arrows, even while watching dark-eyed Spanish maids dancing in the moonlight: "For not yet had he drunk of Lethe's stream; / And lately had he learned with truth to deem / Love has no gift so grateful as his wings" (I, 82).

Harold's affinity with the Man of Feeling is shown more clearly in his prevailing human sympathy. He is solitary and antisocial, but as with the typical Man of Feeling, more because of his exquisite sensibilities than because of anything basically misanthropic in his nature. Like most Romantic poetic personalities, he has been "fated," set apart from other men, alienated from the social world of which he would otherwise gladly be a part:

> Still he beheld, nor mingled with the throng;
> But viewed them not with misanthropic hate:
> Fain would he now have joined the dance, the song;
> But who may smile that sinks beneath his fate? (I, 84)

Again, like most Men of Feeling, he cannot stand war or violence, and he sympathizes with the "rustic" who shrinks from viewing "his vineyard desolate, / Blasted below the dun hot breath of War" (I, 47). In his description of his first experiences with Spanish bull-fights, he concludes that the sport is barbaric, and his sympathies go out to the gored horse and the dying bull, reserving nothing but contumely for the "vulgar eyes" that watch (I, 72–80).

Finally, the Childe of the first two cantos belongs with the Man of Feeling in his attitude toward external nature. One can quite imagine Harold joining Mrs. Radcliffe's Emily St. Aubert in enraptured contemplation of the more rugged reaches of the Pyrenees or of the mountain fastnesses around Udolpho. As Professor Lovell has so thoroughly demonstrated, the early Childe, at least, belongs in that long and persistent tradition of landscape painters in English pre-Romantic literature.[7] The scenes are carefully sketched and balanced, with just the proper tinting, and just that note of the fearful-lovely sublime which so attracted painters and poets through the latter half of the eighteenth century. One of the more famous of the scenes serves to illustrate the point (note the "harmonizing" blue of the sky, and the definition of the sublime in the last line):

> Monastic Zitza! from thy shady brow,
> Thou small, but favoured spot of holy ground!
> Where'er we gaze – around – above – below,–
> What rainbow tints, what magic charms are found!
> Rock, river, forest, mountain, all abound,
> And bluest skies that harmonise the whole:
> Beneath, the distant Torrent's rushing sound
> Tells where the volumed Cataract doth roll
> Between those hanging rocks, that shock yet please the soul.
>
> (II, 48)

The traditional literary figure of Childe Harold in Cantos I and II is indeed, then, a potpourri or an agglomeration of the characteristics of the heroes discussed in the last two chapters: the Child of Nature; the Gothic Villain (unregenerate, as in the novel, or remorseful, as in the drama or in Scott's romances); the accursed Wanderer; the Gloomy Egoist, meditating on ruins, death, or the vanity of life; and the Man of Feeling, suffering from a lost love, or philanthropically concerned with the suffering caused by war or oppression.

That such a literary character could not but contain some incongruities is perhaps obvious enough, but I think it is highly probable that the very breadth of the selection of heroic characteristics accounts in large part for the poem's immediate and astounding acclaim. Here was a poetic character who combined in his person many or most of the characteristics the age found attractive: though suffering from "misfortuned" love and from the ennui of spent passions and remorse, at the same time he could appreciate the beauties of natural scenery and could moralize with the best of the meditative egoists on the passage of fame and glory and on the vanity of life. In a preceding chapter I noted that Scott's *Rokeby* was a very treasure trove of Romantic hero types, offering a virile Child of Nature, a youthful Man of Feeling (given to solitary walks and musical extemporizing), and no less than two Gothic Villain-Heroes. But here, in the person of Childe Harold, Byron has rolled all of these into one, and added to boot the characteristics of a meditative moralist. Such a hero could not fail to attract in the Romantic age. This, then, is the character of the Childe Harold of the first two cantos: he is striking, if largely traditional, and he was vastly popular, even if somewhat inconsistent.

The Childe of Cantos III and IV is in some ways a different person. Like the verse of the later poems, he is less rhetorical, and more poetic; less traditional, and far more personal. The important transformation, as has been commonly noticed, is that the Childe becomes assimilated to Byron's own persona, although some colors of the original portrait remain, not only in the mind of the reader, but in sporadic passages of the later poems. The scandalous "past" of the Childe has become actual, and the "exile" of the Harold of Canto III has become real, not merely a literary device. In other words, the new figure is not so far from the old but that many of his sentiments fit into the traditional pattern set in the first two cantos. There is, however, less of cynicism, and more of suffering; less of sin and guilt, and more of being sinned against. In a word, there is less of the

Gothic Villain and more of the first important English Hero of Sensibility.

But let me first admit that there are passages in the later cantos in which the suffering becomes too personal to remain literary, in which the emotion is too specific to be generalized and made objective. The most offensive of these is the famous "appeal to Nemesis":

> if calmly I have borne
> Good, and reserved my pride against the hate
> Which shall not whelm me, let me not have worn
> This iron in my soul in vain – shall *they* not mourn?
> . . . .
> Not in the air shall these my words disperse,
> Though I be ashes; a far hour shall wreak
> The deep prophetic fulness of this verse,
> And pile on human heads the mountain of my curse!
> . . . .
> That curse shall be Forgiveness . . .
> Have I not suffered things to be forgiven?
> (IV, 131–135)

Such a passage is not only too personal, but too petty and vindictive. One could perhaps maintain that this sentiment is in the "Christian" tradition, as does Professor G. Wilson Knight, who goes so far as to call these stanzas "Promethean," and points to them as the source of Shelley's innovation in the Prometheus legend – the Christian ideal of forgiveness which Prometheus exhibits toward Zeus.[8] In the Alexandrine above there is probably an echo of St. Paul: "If thine enemy hunger, feed him; if he thirst, give him to drink: for in so doing thou shalt heap coals of fire on his head" (Romans 12.19–20). But the sentiment remains inconsistent in *Childe Harold* – and, one might add, in the New Testament. It is far more characteristic of the Byronic Hero to say:

> Meantime I seek no sympathies, nor need –
> The thorns which I have reaped are of the tree
> I planted,– they have torn me,– and I bleed:
> I should have known what fruit would spring from such a seed.
> (IV, 10)

But enough has been written on the autobiographical in *Childe Harold* III and IV. Comparatively little in these cantos is so strictly personal as the passage just quoted, but that little has been much exaggerated by those critics and biographers who are legitimately more concerned with the poet's life than with his work. What I am more interested to point out here is that the Childe becomes in these cantos one of a long line of Heroes of Sensibility, a line which begins in the Romantic movement and continues through the remainder of the nineteenth century.

In an earlier chapter I defined the Hero of Sensibility as having emerged from a union of a secularized Gloomy Egoist with the ethically uncommitted Man of Feeling. His essential characteristics are that he is always passive, not acting but being acted upon (as was Harvey, the *Man of Feeling*); that he is given to prolonged, intense, and sometimes even morbid self-analysis, especially of his emotional states (as was Parson Yorick, or the later Werther); that since he is always egocentrically self-concerned, the whole world becomes colored with his own particular ennui and world-weariness (as is the case certainly with Edward Young's persona, and is pre-eminently the case with Werther); and finally, that most of these characteristics stem from his peculiar psychic malady of *Weltschmerz*: the tension in his personality that results from the conflict of two contradictory drives, one toward total commitment, toward loss of self in a vision of absolutes, the other toward a skeptical and even aggressive assertion of self in a world which remains external and even alien.

Perhaps Rousseau's St. Preux (or Rousseau himself) was the first of these Romantic Heroes of Sensibility. Certainly Werther belongs to this line of development; his anguished cry for self-commitment I have cited earlier as a prime expression of *Weltschmerz*. Faust himself, with his lonely and discouraged search for absolutes, and his subsequent resolve that "The highest, lowest forms my soul shall borrow, / Shall heap upon itself their bliss and sorrow / And thus, my own sole self to all their selves expand . . ." [9] belongs in part in the same tradition.

That the later Childe Harold has the first of these characteristics of the Hero of Sensibility needs really no proof, I suppose. He is certainly passive, intensely self-analytic, and given to projecting his peculiar ennui and suffering on the whole world of his vision. He is one of those "Wanderers o'er Eternity / Whose bark drives on and on, and anchored ne'er shall be" (III, 70); one of those, in their "aspirations to be great," whose "destinies o'erleap their mortal state," and "claim a kindred with the stars" (III, 78). But he is also the first great English victim of the Romantic malady of *Weltschmerz*.

It has long been recognized that in the third canto Childe Harold has Wordsworthian visions of an ordered and ensouled natural universe. E. H. Coleridge pointed this out in his edition of the poems, and every other Byron scholar or critic has noticed and commented upon it:[10]

> I live not in myself, but I become
> Portion of that around me; and to me
> High mountains are a feeling, but the hum
> Of human cities torture . . .
>
> the soul can flee
> And with the sky – the peak – the heaving plain
> Of Ocean, or the stars, mingle – and not in vain.
>
> . . . .
>
> Are not the mountains, waves, and skies, a part
> Of me and of my Soul, as I of them?
>
> . . . .
>
> Then stirs the feeling infinite, so felt
> In solitude, where we are *least* alone;
> A truth, which through our being then doth melt,
> And purifies from self . . . (III, 72, 75, 90)

This is the vision of the absolute "truth" to which the Hero of Sensibility longs to commit himself; it implies a loss of personal identity (it "purifies from self"), as does perhaps all religious or mystic commitment, and it was the "escape" of most of the Romantic generation, from Blake through Wordsworth and Shelley to Emerson or Whitman.

The Byronic Hero of Sensibility feels too positive a sense of identity to be able so to commit himself, however. In one sense, since this self-assertion frustrates any total commitment, it brings about what Professor Lovell calls the "failure of a quest," and it is the disappointment of this failure which Werther expresses when he says, "When we hurry toward it . . ., everything is as before, and we stand in our poverty, in our own narrowness, and our soul languishes for the refreshment which has eluded our grasp." [11] Childe Harold feels at times the same disappointment:

> Could he have kept his spirit to that flight
> He had been happy; but this clay will sink
> Its spark immortal, envying it the light
> To which it mounts, as if to break the link
> That keeps us from yon heaven which woos us to its brink.
>
> (III, 14)

Still, it is not all disappointment and frustration; it is also in a sense a return to life: ". . . for waking Reason deems / Such over-weening phantasies unsound, / And other voices speak, and other sights surround" (IV, 7). There is certainly a note of defiance in the tone of this affirmation of the reasoning self, and this, perhaps, is Byron's final answer to all forms of Romantic mysticism:

> Yet let us ponder boldly —'tis a base
> Abandonment of reason to resign
> Our right of thought — our last and only place
> Of refuge; this, at least, shall still be mine:
> Though from our birth the Faculty divine
> Is chained and tortured — cabined, cribbed, confined,
> And bred in darkness, lest the Truth should shine
> Too brightly on the unpreparéd mind,
> The beam pours in — for Time and Skill will couch the blind.
>
> (IV, 127)

The same tone of skeptical self-assertion and humanistic self-reliance forms the keynote of *Manfred* and *Cain*, and this, I believe, is Byron's last word, and the typical stance of the Byronic Hero. This is also, after all, the position of the narrator-persona of *Don Juan*, although in that case the vision of the cosmic tragedy of human self-assertion in an alien universe has been reinforced by the resurgence of Byron's capacity for "Romantic" irony. *Don Juan* illustrates that life must be conceived as tragedy (as Yeats says), and the human predicament may be an absurdity (as Sartre says), but the poem also asserts that life is infinitely varied, intensely exciting, and at times even invigoratingly comic.

This is to anticipate a resolution of the conflict, however, which the Hero of Sensibility in *Childe Harold* never achieves. The tension remains, and in the closing stanzas of Canto IV the mood again returns, and Harold longs once more for that obliviousness of self, that annihilation of the ego:

> I love not Man the less, but Nature more,
> From these our interviews, in which I steal
> From all I may be, or have been before,
> To mingle with the Universe . . . (IV, 178)

But in the splendid rhetoric of the address to the sea which follows—"Roll on, thou deep and dark blue Ocean—roll"—this first English Hero of Sensibility gives a vivid impression of a natural world impersonal and alien, totally indifferent to man and all his aspirations.

This agonized Hero of Sensibility was Byron's legacy to the literature of the age which succeeded him—not the healthy, ironic but life-affirming message of his great satire. Until almost the end of the century, both in England and on the Continent, Byron was remembered primarily as the author of *Childe Harold*, not of *Don Juan*. The agonized Hero of Sensibility appears again and again in the literature of the succeeding age: sometimes morbidly analytic of his own emotional and spiritual states, and in his *Weltschmerz* longing for some engagement to absolute truth which will rid him of his painful self-consciousness; longing to "mingle with the universe," but being continually frustrated in this desire by the reassertion of his skeptical, sometimes cynical, and sometimes remorseful ego. This hero and his central problem reappear in the poetry of De Musset, for instance, or in Pushkin's *Eugene Onegin*, and certainly this problem of commitment, this intense and longdrawn self-analysis, the agonized passiveness (some kind of "engagement" being necessary for action) reappear in England as the dominant traits of heroes in Arnold's *Empedocles*, in much of Tennyson's work (see *The Ancient Sage*, or passages of *In Memoriam*), especially clearly in Clough's *Dipsychus*, and even in Pater's *Marius*.

But I think it is not going too far to say that the climax of this hero's passion, and perhaps of his poetry, appears in Byron's *Childe Harold* III and IV.

X FOUR TURKISH TALES

C*HILDE HAROLD* I and II had appeared in March of 1812, and within months Byron was being toasted and feted in all London society. It is surprising that in the next two years of his life he found time to write at all: in addition to taking an active part in London social life, he delivered three speeches in the House of Lords, had two prolonged "affairs" (with Lady Oxford and with Lady Frances Webster), and began his unfortunate courtship of Annabella Milbanke.

But in the brief period of a little over a year – from June 5, 1813 to August 6, 1814 – he published the four first and most important of his verse romances, the "Turkish Tales": *The Giaour* (June 1813), *The Bride of Abydos* (December 1813), *The Corsair* (February 1814), and *Lara* (August 1814). Since the public had been prepared by *Childe Harold*, each romance was immediately and astonishingly successful. John Murray accepted *The Giaour gratis*, and on his own risk, Byron being skeptical as to the possibilities of its success, but by December it had gone through seven editions. *The Bride* sold six thousand copies in a month. *The Corsair*, the most successful of the three, sold ten thousand copies on the day of publication ("a thing perfectly unprecedented," as Murray remarked), and in just over a month it had gone through seven editions totaling twenty-five thousand copies. *Lara*, even after the first enthusiasm for these works had waned, sold six thousand copies in five days, and Byron finally released the copyright to Murray (the first for which he accepted money personally) for £700.[1] Moreover, the success of these romances was not only popular; it was critical in a degree as well. The poems were reviewed and praised by such eminent men of letters as George Ellis, the famous Jeffrey, and Byron's friends Rogers and Moore. Gifford, the satirist and poet Byron most respected, was especially pleased with *The Corsair*, and as late as 1830, Scott still paid tribute to the "depth of [Byron's] thought," and the "eager abundance in his diction" which eclipsed Scott's former undisputed rule of the domain of verse romance.[2]

Such facts testify to the popularity not only of Byron's poetry but of his hero, since all of these romances depend primarily on their protagonists, rather than on plot or verse, for their effect. Still, the romances need not concern us so much in the development of the Byronic Hero. In the first place, verse romances in general have since become a dead *genre*, having been entirely superseded by prose fiction; on the other hand, *Childe Harold*, some of the dramas, and *Don Juan* are still being read. It is a pity, in a way, that these romances have been so eclipsed, since some of them – Scott's and Byron's, for instance – are good spirited stories, if read quickly and for total effect rather than detail. Byron's, especially, are still stirring in description and in narrative. As T. S. Eliot says of him: "he has the cardinal virtue of never being dull"; and again: "As a taleteller . . . I can think of none other since Chaucer who has equal readability, with the exception of Coleridge . . . and Coleridge never attempted narratives of such length." [3] But dead these verse romances certainly are, except in the curricula of some of our more conservative secondary schools. Even in a study such as this, which is not primarily concerned with literary value, the romances are not of first importance since they do not show much advance in the development of the hero beyond *Childe Harold*. Byron's choice of characteristics for these heroes was more selective, however, and therefore they are more consistent; they do not need to serve in the multiple roles of the Childe, who had to be not only romantic "villain-hero," but sightseer and meditative moralist as well.

It was generally acknowledged at the time, even by partisans of the older poet (George Ellis, for instance), that in this form of verse

Byron eclipsed Sir Walter Scott. There were other poets writing verse romances – Southey, Moore, or Campbell, for example – but they did not come near these two giants either in popularity or in technique.

A number of reasons account for Byron's having won out, besides the adventitious factor of his notoriety in the role of Childe Harold. In the first place, Byron's verse has greater intensity and facility than Scott's. Byron is frequently awkward, but his verse or his story are always in motion; Scott notoriously pads his verse, and his divagations often do not heighten the suspense, as Byron's do almost invariably. Byron also drops the medievalism of Scott's romances, and introduces instead the exoticism of the contemporary Orient. He had been preceded in this by Southey in *Thalaba* (1801), but although Southey was a better scholar, he had not the benefit of Byron's first-hand experience in mid-Eastern travel, nor, one might add, Byron's flair for culling the most "romantic" or sensational details from such sources as Henley's notes to Beckford's *Vathek*.[4]

The main reason for Byron's victory over Scott, however, was in the greater focus, intensity, and subjectivity of his romances. This shows first in the plots of Byron's poems, which are invariably simple and uncomplicated, whereas the plots of *Marmion* and *Rokeby*, for instance, would do better for Waverley novels. It shows mostly in the two poets' respective heroes. Scott had gone a long way toward the development of the Gothic Villain turned sensitive Noble Outlaw, it is true, but he still retained a weak sentimental "hero" in almost all of his romances. In *Rokeby* he went so far as to spread his interest over the full range of heroes, from an unregenerate Gothic Villain (Oswald), through a Noble Outlaw (Bertram), to a weak Man of Feeling (Wilfred) and a Child of Nature (Redmond). Byron concentrates each of his romances on one dark hero, and the rest of the characters scarcely matter. Both Scott's and Byron's heroes are Noble Outlaws, but Byron's have much more in them of the Hero of Sensibility (possibly under the influence of the Gothic drama), and consequently their passions are far more subjective, and far more intense. This shows up most vividly in the passion of love. Scott confesses himself unable to draw a convincing lover: "But the Devil is, that your true lover, notwithstanding the high and aristocratic rank he inherits in romance and poetry, is in my opinion the dullest of human mortals, unless to his mistress – I know nothing I dread more in poetry than a love scene . . . "[5] Perhaps for this reason, he gives this passion to his sentimental heroes; Marmion alone of his Noble Outlaws is a lover, and he betrays his passion for the sake of a marriage for gain. Byron's heroes, on the other hand, are all lovers – for most of them it is the ruling passion in their lives – and they remain faithful, in true romantic fashion, until death.

The Byronic Heroes of these four romances, then, vary in character largely between two poles: that of the Gothic Villain and that of the Hero of Sensibility. They are all, however, Noble Outlaws, and are therefore active, not contemplative, as are Childe Harold, Manfred, and Cain. The Giaour, the least developed of the four, is largely a remorseful Gothic Villain. Selim, of the *Bride*, is almost pure Hero of Sensibility and Noble Outlaw: his soft, almost feminine character makes him the exception in the group. Conrad-Lara is definitely a Noble Outlaw in love, but the power of his remorseful defiance makes him stand closest, perhaps, to the type of Karl Moor.

The first thing to be noted about *The Giaour* is the fragmentary nature of its composition and publication, since this causes difficulties of interpretation. Byron's original intention was to tell a tale of "disjointed fragments" (as he writes in a preface), but he further confused it by adding passages both before and after publication. The final poem, in the seventh edition, is in twenty different fragments, with three different narrators (a Mohammedan fisherman, a pious Christian monk, and Byron's own persona), with many confusing flashbacks without transitions, and with a long monologue by the Giaour himself.

This is the story, insofar as one can make it out (and Byron obligingly added a one-sentence synopsis in the "Advertisement"): The Giaour, a Venetian "Christian" in a Moslem land, has somehow managed to win the affections of Leila, the wife of Hassan, a Turkish and feudal lord. One night while Hassan is celebrating a festival, Leila steps out for a trip to the local baths. Actually, in the likeness of a "Georgian page," she keeps a love tryst instead, and "wrongs" her husband with "the faithless Giaour" (456–458); the epithet refers of course to his lack of Mohammedan conviction. Hassan discovers the treachery, and, following "the Mussulman manner," has her sewn in a sack and thrown into the sea (presumably with the help of the fisherman-narrator). For this heartless deed the young Venetian vows revenge, and with his rebel band of Arnauts, he ambushes Hassan and his bodyguard and kills him, although in fair and single combat. His remorse for the death of Leila is not reduced by this revenge, however, so he retires to a Christian monastery. There, after depositing an indefinite sum of money, he is allowed a cell, and he finishes his life as a "penitent," although he persistently refuses the offices or comforts of the church. It is interesting to note that the lady disguised as a page appears in this tale for the first time, as she had appeared in Scott's *Marmion*, and as she was to appear again in *Lara*.[6] Then, too, the Giaour does qualify as a Noble Outlaw, since he apparently leads the Arnaut band, but admittedly not much is made of this.

The Giaour is primarily a sensitive Gothic Villain – in his appearance, in his air of the fallen angel, in his "remorse," and in his defiance. He has first of all the looks of a Gothic Villain, especially in those three tell-tale features, the brow, the eye, and the smile. His "fearful brow," "whose ghastly whiteness aids its gloom," is also "that sallow front / . . . scathed by fiery Passion's brunt" (194–231). His "bitter smile" is infrequent but unforgettable:

> Not oft to smile descendeth he,
> And when he doth 'tis sad to see
> That he but mocks at Misery.
> How that pale lip will curl and quiver!
> Then fix once more, as if for ever . . . (850–854)

But his most strikingly Gothic feature is his "evil eye," that traditional hallmark of such varied figures as Mrs. Radcliffe's Schedoni, Schiller's Armenian (*Der Geisterseher*), Beckford's Eblis (*Vathek*), Lewis's Wandering Jew (*The Monk*), and the Ancient Mariner (several scholars have attributed it to the fad of Mesmerism, but Byron had heard of "the evil eye" in the Middle East):

Oft will his glance the gazer rue,
For in it lurks that nameless spell,
Which speaks, itself unspeakable,
A spirit yet unquelled and high,
That claims and keeps ascendancy;
And like the bird whose pinions quake,
But cannot fly the gazing snake,
Will others quail beneath this look,
Nor 'scape the glance they scarce can brook.
(837–845)

The Giaour also has the air of the fallen angel, the gentle soul perverted, the mind born for nobler things. This characteristic had also become traditional, in Lewis's Ambrosio, in Schiller's Karl Moor, and in subsequent Noble Outlaw types—all stemming in this respect from the fallen angel of *Paradise Lost*:

A noble soul, and lineage high;
Alas! though both bestowed in vain . . .
It was no vulgar tenement
To which such lofty gifts were lent . . .
If ever evil angel bore
The form of mortal, such he wore:
By all my hope of sins forgiven,
Such looks are not of earth nor heaven!
(869–873, 912–915)

(Of course it should be remembered that these words come from a pious monk who is quite unsympathetic, and who does not believe the Giaour should be allowed in the monastery.)

Finally, the Giaour is like the sympathetic Gothic Villain in his mixed attitude of remorse and defiance. It is interesting to note that both Schedoni (of Mrs. Radcliffe's *Italian*) and the Giaour retire to monasteries, although in Schedoni's case the cassock was not a penitent's robe, but a disguise. Still, this description of the Giaour could have been applied with equal fitness to Schedoni: "Dark and unearthly is the scowl / That glares beneath his dusky cowl" (832–833). Julian, of Sotheby's *Julian and Agnes* (performed 1801), forms a closer parallel: he not only retired to a monastery, but like the Giaour refused the offices of the church, at least for a time.

But the Gothic Villain-Heroes of the drama all eventually made their peace with God and the church; it is a distinguishing feature of Scott's and of Byron's Noble Outlaws that they do not. These are among the last words of the Giaour to the father who hears his "confession" (presumably for the sake of the hero's monologue, since the Giaour remains unrepentant):

> Waste not thine orison, despair
> Is mightier than thy pious prayer:
> I would not, if I might, be blest;
> I want no Paradise, but rest. (1267–1270)

This is the same sure note of defiance that one hears from all the Byronic Heroes, from Childe Harold and the Giaour through Manfred and Cain. Their remorse is not for "sins" in the sense of transgressions of orthodox moral codes. The Giaour, for instance, does not repent of having slain Hassan, but he repents because Leila has been sacrificed for love: "I grieve, but not, my holy Guide! / For him who dies, but her who died" (1121–1122). For with Byronic Heroes "The mind is its own place"; each hero is, in a sense, *jenseits von Gut und Böse*; he creates his own human values, and the "sins" of which he repents are transgressions of his own peculiar moral codes. For the commandments of religion or for common social morality he has nothing but defiance and contempt.

Still, like all of these Romantic heroes, the Giaour too has something in him of the Hero of Sensibility. He once enjoyed nature, but after Leila's death, he confesses, "every hue that charmed before / The blackness of my bosom wore" (1198–1199). He has been taught by Leila the truth of romantic love:

> To die – and know no second love.
> This lesson yet hath man to learn,
> Taught by the thing he dares to spurn:
> The bird that sings within the brake,
> The swan that swims upon the lake,
> One mate, and one alone, will take. (1166–1171)

And finally, in an epitaph for Leila, he rises to the best lines in the poem:

She was a form of Life and Light,
That seen, became a part of sight;
And rose, where'er I turned my eye,
The Morning-star of Memory! (1127–1130)

Byron's next Turkish Tale, *The Bride of Abydos*, is a more finished and much less confusing work. One good reason for this is that Byron had finally solved the problem of the narrator-persona. He becomes his own narrator, and the lyrics are in their proper places, framing the two cantos of the poem, from the opening "Know ye the land where the cypress and myrtle" (inspired by Goethe's "Kennst du das Land") to the effective denouement of the white rose and the nightingale (Selim), whose song "Will shape and syllable its sound / Into Zuleika's name (II, 1193–1194).

The story needs no more than a short summary, since it has a simple plot, and since *The Bride* is probably the most widely read of Byron's romances. Selim and Zuleika have been brought up as the son and daughter of an old and very fierce "Giaffir," a rich Turkish landowner. In reality, however, Selim is not the Giaffir's son, but his nephew, and thereby hangs the tale. For, as we and Zuleika discover at last (Selim has been told the story, without his uncle's knowing it, by an ancient and loyal slave), the Giaffir has poisoned Selim's father (the Giaffir's brother) in order to gain his property, and has concealed the murder. Then the Giaffir decides upon a January-May marriage for his daughter; and Selim, who in rare absences from the palace has become a pirate chief, plans an abduction. He makes an appointment to meet Zuleika in a seaside garden for the escape, but in the long delay caused by his explanations and persuasions, they are discovered by the irate father and his slaves; Selim is killed and Zuleika dies of a broken heart.

There is, however, one problem in this poem which has often been made much of by both biographers and critics – the rejected theme of incest. Byron admits that in his first sketch of the poem he "had nearly made [Selim and Zuleika] too much akin to each other; and though the wild passions of the East, and some great examples in Alfieri [*Mirra*], Ford [*'Tis Pity*], and Schiller [*The Bride of Messina*] (to stop short of antiquity), might have pleaded in favour

. . ., yet the time and the north . . . induced me to alter their consanguinity and confine them to cousinship" (*LJ*, II, 309). The theme remains in the story only in that until his dramatic exposé on the seashore, Zuleika believes Selim to be her brother. The autobiographical aspect of the problem need not concern us, although one might add that in the Romantic age Byron's claim of precedent was not unjustified, and he might have added to his list Horace Walpole (*The Mysterious Mother*), and "Monk" Lewis, who had made far more sensationalistic use of the theme in his famous novel. Still, the incest is not entirely superfluous in the story, as so many critics have maintained. It was necessary for Selim and Zuleika to be supposed brother and sister in order for the Giaffir to allow them to consort in innocence together, since according to Moslem custom Zuleika could be allowed no intercourse with strangers, at least until her marriage. Above all, the theme adds one more element of mystery and suspense to the story.

The mystery of his birth, the shadow over his parentage, is one of the few characteristics which Selim shares with the Gothic Villain. He has also the "eye," from which "glances more than ire / Flash forth, then faintly disappear," but this feature, as we have seen, he shares with many characters less awesome than Schedoni. The story is also a drama of blood-vengeance for family honor, as is Walpole's *Otranto*, but then so is *Hamlet*, in a way, and the fratricide by poison resembles Shakespeare's plot more closely.

For Selim is notable among the Byronic Heroes of the romances in that he is almost pure Hero of Sensibility. He is first introduced as having just returned from a walk with Zuleika to the cypress groves, where they were beguiled with "Mejnoun's tale, or Sadi's song," and the fierce Giaffir reproves him as one who "Must pore where babbling waters flow, / And watch unfolding roses blow" (I, 72, 88–89). The taunt of the Giaffir—"let thy less than woman's hand / Assume the distaff—not the brand"—seems almost justified by a certain feminine softness in Selim's manner, as, for instance, when we see him gazing "through the lattice gate, / Pale, mute, and mournfully sedate" (I, 99–100, 255–256). Like Childe Harold, Selim also shows a touch of humanitarian sympathy when he condemns the Giaffir as a tyrant, and bids Zuleika "ask the squalid peasant how / His gains repay his broiling brow!" (II, 740–741) Most of all, as with all Byronic Heroes, he shows his sensibility in his love for Zuleika. He can be as passionate as the Giaour in his confession and persuasion in the sea-side cave, but he can also be as tenderly affectionate as the older brother who walked with Zuleika in cypress groves and listened to sad tales of love.

Byron's heroes all have this softness in them, this capacity for the tender feelings of a Hero of Sensibility, especially in their attitude toward women. Selim, however, in this respect especially, looks forward to Sardanapalus, who with all his effeminate love of luxury is still capable of rising to brave leadership in battle, and to Don Juan, who is truly such another combination of masculine courage and feminine tenderness, even passivity.[7]

In spite of the absence of the traits of the Gothic and in spite of the emphasis on sensibility, Selim still belongs in this group of Byronic Heroes, because he is the first of Byron's fully developed Noble Outlaws. He is related to Scott's border chiefs, although as a pirate translated to the shores of the Mediterranean. He has first of all ample reason for his outlawry, as have all Noble Outlaws: he has been robbed of his inheritance by the murderer of his father. In his personality he has also that sense of authority, immediate and unquestioned, which was the common heritage of every outlaw chief or robber baron since Götz von Berlichingen: "high command / Spake in his eye, and tone, and hand" (II, 629–630). Finally, Selim himself gives to Zuleika the first of Byron's apologies for piracy:

> " 'Tis true, they are a lawless brood,
> But rough in form, nor mild in mood;
> And every creed, and every race,
> With them hath found – may find a place:
> [With] open speech, and ready hand,
> Obedience to their Chief's command;
> A soul for every enterprise,
> That never sees with Terror's eyes;
> Friendship for each, and faith to all,
> And vengeance vowed for those who fall . . ."
>
> (II, 845–854)

Here, in ten short lines, is the Noble Outlaw's creed. There is something attractive about it, as Scott said of the times of his own border bandits, or of the robber barons of Germany: the open society, with close ties of personal loyalty, quick and sure justice, ample opportunity for the display of courage, and a leader "organically" related to his band. In one aspect, of course, this is mere adolescent play – Robin Hood, or cops and robbers, surviving today in Western movies or in neighborhood street gangs. This creed has also more serious implications, however. It is certainly related to that fascination with "organic societies" with born culture leaders which grew up in the Romantic period and lasted all through the nineteenth century. Carlyle's or Hegel's heroes, with their contempt for ballot boxes and due process, with their inborn surety of command and of obedience, are certainly related, however distantly, to Goethe's Götz or Scott's and Byron's Noble Outlaws. These poets and philosophers, alienated in a modern world, all felt a desire for the personal loyalties of an organic society with a *Führerprinzip*; most Romantics, like Scott or Byron, projected these dreams into the past or into the exotic distance: Hegel and Carlyle projected their dreams into the future.

In any case, Byron was obviously aware that in the Noble Outlaw theme he had a good thing, because his next two romances were both centered on an outlaw hero who is probably the most striking of all: Conrad-Lara. Byron obviously intended *Lara* to continue *The Corsair*; the "Advertisement" Byron prefixed to the later poem reads in part: "The reader . . . may probably regard [Lara] as a sequel to the Corsair; – the colouring is of a similar cast, and although the situations of the character are changed, the stories are in some measure connected." They are indeed connected: the corsair of the first romance, grief-stricken with the death of his beloved, returns in the second tale to his ancestral home.

The Corsair opens with a forty-line chorus, in which the pirates sing (in heroic couplets) the praises of life in an outlaw band. Then their leader appears: Conrad, whose "name on every shore / Is famed and feared" (I, 61–62). In a tower overlooking the bay he lives with Medora, the one love of his life.

We soon find that the neighboring Pacha of Coron has organized an expedition to destroy the pirate band, but Conrad decides to anticipate the battle by attacking Coron while the Pacha and his host of warriors are having a premature celebration. Conrad and his band raid the palace, the Pacha is put to flight, and the day is almost won, when on Conrad's ear ". . . the cry / Of women struck, and like a deadly knell / Knocked at that heart unmoved by Battle's yell" (II, 805–807). The palace has been fired, and the Pacha's maids and wives have been cut off. Conrad succeeds in saving the women, but the delay costs him the battle. The robbers are defeated, and their wounded leader is captured. He is languishing in prison, awaiting a particularly gruesome execution by impalement, when Gulnare, the Pacha's first wife, whom Conrad had personally carried from the flames, arrives secretly to offer her savior release. Conrad is not anxious to be saved, but he at last relents for Medora's sake. When Gulnare attempts to persuade her husband to have the Corsair ransomed, however, the Pacha accuses her of infidelity. Her passions are aroused, she murders her husband in his sleep, and flies to the pirate's den with Conrad. They return too late; Medora, in fear for Conrad's death or worse, has expired, and in his agony of grief, Conrad disappears from the island forever.

Conrad, who "left a Corsair's name to other times, / Linked with one virtue, and a thousand crimes" (III, 1864–1865), is perhaps the most striking of Byron's Noble Outlaws. Like Selim he is a pirate, but with the Gothic character of the Giaour, painted even more dark. He has the familiar features of the Gothic Villain, the brow, the lip, the eye:

> Sunburnt his cheek, his forehead high and pale
> The sable curls in wild profusion veil;
> And oft perforce his rising lip reveals
> The haughtier thought it curbs, but scarce conceals . . .
> There breathe but few whose aspect might defy
> The full encounter of his searching eye . . .
>
> (I, 203–206, 215–216)

He too has the secret past, the burnt-out passions of his kind, and is the first of Byron's heroes to be made a misanthrope: "Feared—

shunned – belied – ere Youth had lost her force, / He hated Man too much to feel remorse" (I, 261–262). But as he is made the darkest so far of these heroes, his "fallen-angel" characteristics are accentuated: "His soul was changed, before his deeds had driven / Him forth to war with Man and forfeit Heaven" (I, 251–252). Like his fellow heroes, Conrad retains even yet something of a softer, more tender aspect of character, reflected in his love for Medora: "Yes, it was love – unchangeable – unchanged, / Felt but for one from whom he never ranged" (I, 287–288). We have already seen the manner in which he lost a battle and almost his life for the sake of the women of his enemy's harem. Finally, when Gulnare, who has not his sense of honor, offers to kill the Pacha while he sleeps, Conrad will not concur, and when she does so, in spite of Conrad's helpless protestations (he is in chains), he shrinks in horror from the tell-tale spot of blood upon her brow.

Conrad is above all a Noble Outlaw, however, and his sense of undisputed command and the undying loyalty of his comrades is the theme of half the poem. It is interesting to note that when Byron was attacked for presenting an impossibly incongruous character in the person of his hero, he fortified himself, in notes to subsequent editions of the poem, with references to historical or contemporary rebels or outlaws. One of these notes is particularly interesting: First Byron refers to Blackbourne, Archbishop of York (1658–1743), who was rumored to have been a returned and reformed buccaneer (*Works*, III, 296); this may have furnished the idea for *Lara*. Then, in further defense of his characterization, he quotes at length (from a story in an American newspaper) the legend of Jean Lafitte, a contemporary French pirate off the coast of Louisiana. To illustrate the fierce pirate's magnanimity, the reporter recounts how Lafitte had once captured and then released unharmed a former friend who had headed an expedition bent on the pirate's destruction. The account is more than half fiction, probably the creation of the myth-making imagination of the anonymous reporter, but the interesting point is that twice during the course of his narrative the reporter refers to "La Fitte" as a "modern Charles de Moor" (evidently he had read Schiller's drama in English from a French translation). So we have that ubiquitous first Noble Outlaw returning through pseudohistory to literature. Byron could himself have cited Schiller or Scott in his defense, but, proud of his sense of fact, and oversensitive as he was to charges of plagiarism, he preferred always to cite precedent from history rather than from literature, however reputable the literature and however disreputable the history.

As I have noted, Byron's last Turkish Tale, *Lara*, was a continuation of *The Corsair*. Conrad-Lara has returned to his family estate after a long, mysterious absence, accompanied only by a young foreign page called Kaled (*alias* Gulnare, although the color of her hair has changed from raven to auburn). Lara lives a solitary life in his family castle, obviously much disturbed emotionally by something in his secret past, until one evening he is invited to a festival in Lord Otho's hall. While there, a recently returned knight, Sir Ezzelin, recognizes him (presumably as Conrad), and after a preliminary quarrel, challenges Lara to answer his charges on the following day, Otho standing surety for Ezzelin's appearance. On that very night, however, Sir Ezzelin disappears mysteriously on his way home, and suspicion fastens on Lara, who, as we find in the epilogue, was probably the mysterious stranger seen throwing a heavy bundle into the river in the dark hours of that early morning. Meanwhile, at the appointed time, Lara appears in Otho's hall. Some strong words pass between him and his host, and in the ensuing duel Lara wounds Otho (although only slightly and by intention only slightly), and thereby incurs Otho's mortal anger. Fearing that the game is up, Lara then recruits serfs and wanderers from all over the land, promises them their freedom, and starts a rebellion, himself their leader. His recruits get out of hand, however, and are eventually defeated, and Lara himself is killed in the last encounter. He dies in Kaled's arms, spurning the cross and absolution. Kaled, who in her grief has fainted, is then accidentally discovered to be no page but a woman. Our last picture is of her, half mad with grief, mourning on the spot of Lara's death.

There are, as I have noted in a previous chapter, two interesting precedents for Byron's story. Bertram and Mortham, in Scott's *Rokeby*, were also returned privateers who kept their past a secret, and it may well have been this poem rather than the Bishop Blackbourne legend which gave Byron the initial idea for *Lara*. Then, too, both Lara and Goethe's Götz von Berlichingen are destroyed because they have become leaders of a peasant rebellion. Their stories are different, to be sure: Götz reluctantly accepts the leadership in order to try to control their slaughter, and Lara on the other hand incites the uprising with malice aforethought. But once begun, Lara also tries unsuccessfully to control the rebellion: "In vain he doth whate'er a chief may do, / To check the headlong fury of that crew . . . / The hand that kindles cannot quench the flame" (II, 935–938). Byron had probably read Scott's translation of the drama, since he read Scott's works with avid interest.

Not much is added to the character of Conrad to create the character of Lara. The latter is darker, more Gothic (perhaps in keeping with the setting in his and Otho's feudal halls), and altogether less sympathetic than Conrad – more on the order of a Marmion.

One passage of characterization, however, added after the completion of the original manuscript, deserves some particular analysis, since both critics and biographers have made so much of it. On the basis of this passage Du Bos builds his argument that the Byronic Hero (and therefore Byron) is a "fatal man," and a host of other critics, including such important figures as Mario Praz and T. S. Eliot, have followed Du Bos's lead:[8]

> There was in him a vital scorn of all [events]:
> As if the worst had fallen which could befall,
> He stood a stranger in this breathing world,
> An erring Spirit from another hurled;
> A thing of dark imaginings, that shaped
> By choice the perils he by chance escaped;
> But 'scaped in vain, for in their memory yet
> His mind would half exult and half regret:
> With more capacity for love than Earth
> Bestows on most of mortal mould and birth . . .
> But haughty still, and loth himself to blame,
> He called on Nature's self to share the shame,
> And charged all faults upon the fleshly form
> She gave to clog the soul, and feast the worm;

Till he at last confounded good and ill,
And half mistook for fate the acts of will.

(I, 313–322, 331–336)

The first two lines of the passage give the by now highly traditional pose of the grief-stricken and yet defiant villain turned hero, and one must remember that Conrad-Lara had just lost Medora. The next two lines make Lara a fallen angel, with this time a more particular reference than is usual to the Satan of *Paradise Lost* (an "erring Spirit from another hurled"). The lines beginning "A thing of dark imaginings" express first that particular bravado in the face of danger which has characterized the Noble Outlaws, but give evidence also of an acute bit of psychologizing on Byron's part: this is, after all, a description of something like the Freudian "death wish," and that a good hundred years before it received its definitive formulation. Formulated or not, however, we have seen that it affected in differing degrees most of the Romantic Heroes, from the Noble Outlaw Karl Moor through Faust and Cain-Ahasuerus to Prometheus. The next two lines, describing Lara's "capacity for love," carry out the theme of sensibility which we have followed through the entire range of these heroes. It is the last lines, then, with their reference to fate, which have become so crucial.

What Byron personally believed or did not believe, in regard to fatalism or any other tenet of faith, cannot be an issue here. A good many competent studies have been written on Byron's personal beliefs, and one of the few points on which they agree is that in his casual pronouncements and in his letters Byron was notoriously inconsistent.[9] The attitudes of the Byronic Hero are at issue here, however, and the fact is that whatever else he may have been, the Byronic Hero (*pace* Du Bos) was certainly not characteristically a fatalist. He may be "unfortunate"; he may seem in the context of the poem to be "fate-ridden," but that is another matter indeed. Oedipus is undoubtedly the most "fate-ridden" figure in literature, but he is not a fatalist. Had he been a fatalist, there would have been no drama.

E. H. Coleridge mentions three passages in *Childe Harold* which might be construed as expressions of a belief in fatalism (*Works*, II,

74, note). The first of these names the Childe as "Pleasure's palled Victim! life-abhorring Gloom / Wrote on his faded brow curst Cain's unresting doom" (I, st. 83). "Doom," here, of course implies "judgment," not "fate": because of his past sins the Childe has been condemned to wander, as was Cain, his first predecessor in crime. The second reference, oddly enough, is also a traditional reference to Cain, to Ahasuerus, or to the Flying Dutchman: "But there are wanderers o'er Eternity / Whose bark drives on and on, and anchored ne'er shall be" (II, st. 70). The third reference is admittedly less equivocal – to "melancholy bosoms" who "Deem themselves predestined to a doom / Which is not of the pangs that pass away" (IV, st. 24). The general passage is a meditation on Petrarch, but Byron's syntax does not make clear who these "melancholics" are: they may or may not include Childe Harold. On the other hand, it is Harold in his own person who says: "The thorns which I have reaped are of the tree / I planted . . ." (IV, st. 10).

The only "fatalistic" passage in *The Giaour* is one in which the hero wonders that a childhood friend's prediction that the dark hero would come to no good has been so fearfully fulfilled (1228f). Selim, in *The Bride*, makes one reference to the "fate" which forced him to love Zuleika (a myth of "romantic" love as old as Plato's *Symposium*), and another to the "fatal Nature" which makes man war against his fellow man (II, 898, 911). The latter may suggest a rather Hobbesian conception of the state of nature, perhaps, but is certainly no confession of fatalism.

Conrad, instead of excusing himself by appeals to fate, recognizes such appeals as weakness. He soliloquizes: "Is this my skill? my craft? to set at last / Hope, Power and Life upon a single cast? / Oh, Fate! – accuse thy folly – not thy fate" (I, 337–339). Lara is the only possible exception to this generalization, and it has already been demonstrated that of all the Byronic Heroes he is closest to the Gothic Villain, and the least sympathetic.

Byron realized that to have a hero appeal to fate as an excuse, or to attribute his "sins" (or his virtues, for that matter) to a power beyond his conscious control, would be to diminish seriously the stature of the protagonist as a man, and while this will do for unregenerate and unsympathetic Gothic Villains such as Schedoni or Ambrosio, it will not do for a hero. Byronic Heroes, from Childe Harold to Cain, all have too sure a sense of their independent egos and of their defiant wills to abdicate their moral responsibility in such a manner. They seem if anything at times almost proud of their sins, if for no other reason than that they are their very own.

Finally, it may be objected that Byron himself absolves his heroes from blame in such "fallen angel" passages as that earlier cited from *The Corsair*, and when he writes that Conrad's "heart was formed for softness – warped to wrong, / Betrayed too early, and beguiled too long" (III, 1830–1831). But in the first place, it should be noted that it is never the Byronic Hero who excuses himself in this manner; it is always the narrator-persona describing the hero. More important: this is not fatalism, but simple scientific determinism – the presupposition that for every event in the psychic as well as the physical world there must be a predetermining cause. Just as the psychologist as scientist (whatever libertarian notions he may hold as a man) must presuppose determinism, so must the literary artist.[10] We as readers require that characters be psychologically consistent, that we be able to "understand" them. We expect both the scientist and the poet to give us reasons, and if they do not, we accuse them of slipshod thinking. In existentialist terms, literature as well as psychology are in the realm of "essence," not the realm of "existence," and ordinary laws of cause and effect must apply in poems as well as in case histories.

The characteristic Byronic Hero, then, is not a fatalist. He accepts the burden of his conscience willingly, even defiantly; with the possible exception of Lara, he does not attempt to evade his moral responsibility. He has borrowed characteristics from the Gothic Villain, in his looks, his mysterious past, and his secret sins; and he has retained characteristics from the Man of Feeling in his tender sensibilities and in his undying fidelity to the woman he loves – but he is more than these: he is also a Romantic rebel. The sins for which he accepts responsibility are not those of his misdeeds which society considers most reprehensible. The Giaour is remorseful not because he has killed Hassan, but because Leila has been drowned, indirectly in consequence of their forbidden love. Conrad is grief-stricken not because he leads an outlaw life, but because Medora dies. In other words, not only are his sins his own, but his moral values are also his own; he chooses his values in open defiance of the codes of society.

Still, the hero of these Turkish Tales, since he is primarily a Noble Outlaw, is a creature of action, of impulse, even of instinct. He is a striking figure, certainly, and, in a dashing way, an attractive figure. He illustrates also an advance on Childe Harold (of Cantos I and II, at least), in that he is more thoroughly conceived and therefore has a more consistent character. To achieve his next advance in characterization, however, Byron turned to the realm of the lyrical drama (or, as he called it, the "metaphysical" drama), but he also returned to a hero more like Childe Harold in that he was not so much active as contemplative. Manfred, Lucifer, and Cain followed, and stand together as Byron's three greatest achievements among his more "philosophical" heroes.

XI TWO METAPHYSICAL DRAMAS

IN THE years just preceding his exile in 1816, Byron had served on the committee which selected plays for Drury Lane, and during the course of this service, he read literally hundreds of long since forgotten works, including, of course, a good many Gothic melodramas. (Among the plays with which he was personally concerned in preparing for the stage was Coleridge's *Remorse*.) It is certainly more than probable that this experience was on his mind when he made his first effort in the drama in the summer and fall of 1816, while living in Switzerland. He did not intend *Manfred* for the stage, of course (he always referred to it by its title as a "dramatic poem"), but it nevertheless shows the deep influence of the Gothic extravaganzas still holding the stage when he left England.

Manfred even now is discussed far more often for its autobiographical elements than for its historical significance or its literary merit, and especially for the possible personal reference of the hero's secret sin – presumably including incest – and his agony of remorse on that account. Now insofar as this is a question of biography it lies outside the scope of this study, but of course there is the internal literary question as to whether or not Manfred himself committed incest, and that is another matter. We can first review the facts as the drama presents them: Manfred does have a secret sin, and it involves Lady Astarte, who is of his "own blood," and who loved him "as we should not love" (II, i, 24–27). Moreover, her blood "was shed;" she was "destroyed," although not by Manfred's "hand," but by his "heart, which broke her heart; / It gazed on mine, and withered" (II, ii, 117–120). This is almost all the reader knows, except that whatever the fatal event was, it happened about twilight one evening when Count Manfred was alone with Astarte in his tower. It seems fairly certain that at the time of the drama Astarte is dead, although she is "without a tomb." How she died and under what circumstances remain a mystery (II, iv, 82). All that one can legitimately conjecture is that some incestuous act seems to have occurred. Astarte's death could not have come about through public disclosure and punishment, however, considering the secrecy surrounding the event; it may have been the untoward result of Manfred's Faustian experimentation with the demonic powers that rule the world.

The point is that it is impossible to reconstruct Manfred's crime and secret sin, and, as Bertrand Evans has proved, this is precisely in the tradition of the English Gothic drama.[1] The villain-hero must suffer remorse, but the reasons for his remorse remain vague and are often not divulged until the last act (if at all), in order to heighten the suspense, to deepen the mystery, and to retain as much sympathy as possible for the hero. The theme of incest was also traditional enough in Gothic novels and drama, and in Romantic literature in general. Byron had been preceded by the use of this theme in the very first of English Gothic dramas, Walpole's *The Mysterious Mother*, and also in the prose narrative, *René*, of his French contemporary, Chateaubriand.[2]

This brings up the question of the sources of Manfred, on which point there has been abundance of investigation, especially by German scholars of the last century. Professor Chew summarizes the list of important influences: Goethe's *Faust*, Chateaubriand's *René*, the *Prometheus* of Aeschylus, and the Satan of *Paradise Lost*. To these have been added *Werther*, Coleridge's *Remorse* and Maturin's *Bertram* (for minor details), Lewis's *Monk* (especially for Byron's rejected third act), Beckford's *Vathek* (for Arimanes and his throne), Shelley's *Alastor* (for something of the theme of investigation of death), and *Queen Mab*. Since these investigations Professor

Evans has added another likely source in Sotheby's *Julian and Agnes* (published in 1814 as *The Confession*).[3] I am not particularly concerned here with *Quellenstudien*, but it can be noted that most of these works have come up for discussion in the preceding chapters on the heroic tradition in Romantic literature. And this alone tells something about *Manfred*.

As Professor Chew wrote of the play: "More than any other English poem *Manfred* is typical of the Romantic Period; it is an expression of the mood of Romanticism, an epitome of the time." [4] This is a very positive assertion, but within the scope of this study, at least, it is no more than true. Manfred stands as the culmination of a long tradition of heroes. He is representative of almost every one of the hero-types of the Romantic movement, and he is the one hero in English literature of whom this can truthfully be said. Finally, this drama represents one of the few instances in English in which this tradition can be said to have produced an important literary work.

One concession must in all justice be made: the very fact that the hero is so representative makes the drama suffer, primarily from a confusion of theme. The Faustian idea that "Sorrow is Knowledge," that "The tree of Knowledge is not that of Life" (a variation of the *Weltschmerz* theme) is certainly important in the drama, and it is far more than merely Gothic: it comes near to the heart of Romanticism. The incest-remorse theme, however, is inherited from the Gothic tradition, and does not rise much above it. Moreover, it is only rather tangentially related to the more "philosophical" *Weltschmerz* theme. It is tempting to accept Professor Chew's contention that "The crime element is a concession to the literary fashion . . . the philosophical conception would have been the same had Manfred been portrayed as free from any stain of sin." Professor Chew maintains that Astarte is a kind of objective correlative for the play's theme: "Manfred's quest after knowledge thus ends in failure, and this failure is, as it were, embodied in the character of Astarte." [5] Tempting as this view may be, it goes too far; *Manfred* is still in the Gothic tradition, however much it may at times rise above it.

Still, Manfred is more than merely a remorseful Gothic Villain.

He is the Byronic Hero in the process of maturing, of taking on a philosophical and psychological depth which he certainly did not have in *Childe Harold* I or II or in the romances. This is shown in the accession of the Faust theme of knowledge and sorrow, in the hero's Titanism, and his defiant questioning not only of political or moral authority (as in the romances), but of ultimate philosophical and religious authority as well, and finally it is shown in the Satan-Prometheus themes of the "mind as its own place"– free to create its own scheme of order and value. Even if these various themes seem at times inconsistent with the traditional Gothic setting and tone, one feels that they are almost successfully fused in the glorious rhetoric of the soliloquies, and in the high poetry of the choruses and lyrics.

In appearance, in his lonely solitude, and in his aristocratic air of authority Manfred is like the traditional Byronic Hero of the romances. The chamois hunter recognizes that Manfred's "garb and gait bespeak thee of high lineage" (II, i, 7), and later, the Abbot concurs. Manfred could have been a leader, but his pride forbade it: "I could not tame my nature down; for he / Must serve who fain would sway; and soothe, and sue" (III, i, 116–117). He too has the characteristics of the fallen angel, for, as the Abbot says: "This should have been a noble creature . . . / A goodly frame of glorious elements, / Had they been wisely mingled . . ." (III, i, 160–164). Above all, of course, he is like the Gothic Villain of the drama in his secret sin and his remorse, the crushing agony of which drives him all through the play, and which makes him his "own soul's sepulchre." But notice that even his sins are of his own "judging," so to speak: he is not remorseful for his sinful seeking after forbidden knowledge or for his pride, but only because his passion has caused the death of the one thing in life which he loved.

This brings us to the other side of Manfred's personality. Like Childe Harold or any of the heroes of the romances, he, too, has a soul of sensibility beneath his Gothic exterior. He was even a Child of Nature in his youth:

> My joy was in the wilderness,– to breathe
> The difficult air of the iced mountain's top . . .

to plunge
Into the torrent, and to roll along
On the swift whirl of the new-breaking wave . . .
(II, ii, 62–69)

His lonely solitude was not the result of pride alone. The Hero of Sensibility is always isolated from birth because of his very sensitivity; he has a superfluity of soul and of imagination, and he has a private vision:

My Spirit walked not with the souls of men . . .
The aim of their existence was not mine;
My joys – my griefs – my passions – and my powers,
Made me a stranger . . . (II, ii, 51–56)

Of course the greatest of these feelings was his love; he had learned from Astarte the lesson which Selim learned from Zuleika, or the Giaour from Leila: "To die – and know no second love."

These are the traditional characteristics which Manfred shares with the Byronic Heroes of the first half of *Childe Harold* and of the romances. He is already a striking figure, to be sure, but some of the Gothic dramas had achieved almost as much, if with less of poetry. Manfred is destined to rise higher, however, and with his progress through the drama he takes on the characteristics of those greatest of Romantic hero-types: Ahasuerus, Faust, and Satan-Prometheus.

I have already noted that even in the early *Childe Harold* Byron had made use of Cain-Ahasuerus, even if only in casual allusion, and that in the progress of that poem he developed some of the themes associated with that most forlorn of Romantic heroes. In *Manfred*, however, the Wandering Jew motif is not merely incidental: it becomes of major importance. Manfred makes many references to the "power upon me which withholds, / And makes it my fatality to live" (I, ii, 23–24) to his "fierce thirst of death . . . still unslaked," to the barrenness of his "days and nights imperishable, / Endless, and all alike, as sands on the shore, / Innumerable atoms" (II, i, 48, 53–54). There is one longer and more vehement passage, addressed to the Witch of the Alps, which is remarkably reminiscent of the Eternal Wanderer:

I have gnashed
My teeth in darkness till returning morn,
Then cursed myself till sunset; — I have prayed
For madness as a blessing — 'tis denied me.
I have affronted Death — but in the war
Of elements the waters shrunk from me,
And fatal things passed harmless; the cold hand
Of an all-pitiless Demon held me back,
Back by a single hair, which would not break.
In Fantasy, Imagination, all
The affluence of my soul . . . I plunged deep,
But, like an ebbing wave, it dashed me back
Into the gulf of my unfathomed thought . . .
I dwell in my despair —
And live — and live forever. (II, ii, 131–149)

Shelley, we remember, had used Ahasuerus in *Queen Mab*, but he had changed the Jew's remorse to defiance, and had made him something of an argumentative atheist. In Schubart's original poem (much of which Shelley translates in a note) we find a Jew much closer to Byron's conception. There is first of all the agonized remorse, fully as intense as that of the hero-villain of Gothic drama. The "Ungeheuer Einerlei" of Schubart's Jew corresponds to the barren sameness of Manfred's days and nights, "endless and all alike." Manfred, too, has made Schubartian trials of death — by water, fire, and the sword — and as the Jew is always rescued by an avenging angel, so Manfred is rescued by an "all-pitiless Demon" (and Ahasuerus tries to leap into Aetna, as Manfred tries to leap from the Jungfrau). Finally, both figures have been cursed with an eternal life of wandering, a "fatality to live," and "live forever."

The passage is most interesting, however, in exhibiting that death wish so characteristic of the remorseful Jew, and in exhibiting it in a manner to show its intimate connection with the longing for self-oblivion characteristic of that pervasive Romantic mood of *Weltschmerz*. This dominant attitude forms the point of contact between Cain-Ahasuerus, Faust, and the Hero of Sensibility. Manfred here longs for self-oblivion — in madness, in death, and in "Imagination" — but each time he is defeated, and he returns to self and the "fatality to live."

The parallels between the character of Manfred and the character of Faust are even closer, however, and more essential to the "philosophical" theme of the play.

The facts of Byron's relationship with Goethe and his writings are familiar enough. Byron had heard parts of *Faust* translated to him by the inveterate Germanophile, "Monk" Lewis, during the summer of 1816, at the Villa Diodati, when Byron was beginning *Manfred*. Byron at first denied any significant influence of *Faust* on *Manfred*, but one must remember that at the time he had been charged with outright plagiarism – and certainly that charge is untrue. Later, after Goethe had himself written of the influence and complimented Byron on his use of *Faust*, Byron was not displeased to acknowledge his debt.[6]

Faust, like Manfred, was also a solitary from birth, and largely for the same reasons – because of his great powers of imagination and sensibility. Moreover he had become a Titan in literature even before Goethe turned to him, and he had become that because of his superior sensibility, because he was an aristocrat of suffering. He could have said with Manfred: "I can bear . . . / In life what others could not brook to dream, / But perish in their slumber" (II, i, 76–79).

There is a more distinctive parallel in the way in which the two heroes have so far spent their lives. Faust opens his drama with a lament for the uselessness of his long life of study – of philosophy, law, medicine, and theology. Manfred also admits that "Philosophy and science, and the springs / Of Wonder, and the wisdom of the World, / I have essayed . . . / But they avail not" (I, i, 13–17). That this unbridled search for knowledge is "sinful" both Faust and Manfred implicitly acknowledge, but that is not why they have left off. They have forsaken the search because they have both come to the same sad conclusion, that science is "But an exchange of ignorance for that / Which is another kind of ignorance" (II, iv, 61–63). They are both too skeptical and too proud and self-assertive to submit to those truths others have found absolute. In other words, in the search for truth they are victims of that same *Weltschmerz* which becomes the plague of the Hero of Sensibility. They long for some sort of truth to which they can commit themselves, for in that commitment only can they find "Oblivion – self-oblivion! / Can not ye wring from out the hidden realms / Ye offer so profusely – what I ask?" (I, i, 145–147). Finally, in the frustration of their search and in the desperation of their longing, they turn from their books to direct communion with demons and spirits. Faust calls up the Earth-Spirit, and then meets Mephistopheles himself. Manfred calls up natural spirits and destinies, and finally meets their chief, Arimanes.

But here, of course, the themes diverge. Faust, in desperation, to be sure, but nevertheless willingly, makes a pact with the Prince of Darkness; this Manfred disdains to do. This difference caused Georg Brandes to say that *Manfred* exhibits a higher conception of man than does *Faust*.[7] For Manfred is too proud to submit to anyone; although twice tempted to do so, both by the Spirits and by the Witch of the Alps, he refuses disdainfully. In this respect he bears a resemblance to the last two of the Romantic heroes: Satan and Prometheus.

It was in regard to *Manfred* that Byron wrote: "The *Prometheus*, if not exactly in my plan, has always been so much in my head, that I can easily conceive its influence over all or any thing that I have written" (*LJ*, IV, 174). And in the summer of 1816, when he began *Manfred*, he wrote his famous lyric apostrophe to Prometheus. Whether Shelley inspired Byron with an interest in the Titan or whether Byron inspired Shelley (the latter I think the more likely) is not very material. Prometheus was the very type of the Romantic rebel: as we have seen, he had an independent revival in the "Great Man" movement in German literature, and his parallel development in so many Romantic minds is owing undoubtedly to the spirit of the times. That Satan was also on Byron's mind needs no further proof than the echoes of *Paradise Lost* which can be found in several of the crucial passages in *Manfred*. For both Shelley and Byron, Satan and Prometheus had come to stand for the ultimate in titanic rebellion: a rebellion which asserted the independence of the individual and the primacy of his values not only in the face of society, but even in the face of "God."

Since Prometheus and Satan are by nature rebels, their characters are defined in part by that against which they both rebel. I have noticed in a previous chapter that the universe of the original Aeschylean drama was split in a curious way into three levels: the Promethean level, on which humanist values prevail; the "order" of Zeus, which is capricious, repressive, and antihuman; and the order of Fate, a mysterious power, only vaguely defined but obviously above both Prometheus and Zeus. In Goethe's fragment Prometheus remained largely as he was, a titanic sufferer and defender of man, but Zeus became for Goethe the personal God of orthodox religion. The higher order to which Prometheus appeals is not defined. In Shelley's drama the two lower orders remain the same, but the "Fate" of Aeschylus or of Goethe becomes "Demogorgon," who, according to one interpretation, at least, is nothing more or less than a personification of the natural and scientific laws of the universe. Perhaps it is only reasonable that this development should take place: in an age of human self-sufficiency and extreme individualism such as the Romantic age, it could be expected that Prometheus (and Satan, for that matter) would come to stand for man's assertion of humanistic values in a natural or "naturalistic" universe.

The "levels of order" in the universe of Manfred are much the same as they had been in Goethe's drama, and as they were to become in Shelley's. Manfred, as the titanic sufferer, stands for the individual man (although it must be freely admitted that since he is in the Gothic tradition, he is no philanthropist). Arimanes and his host of demons who rule the material world by means of their spiritual essences take great delight in persecuting mankind with shipwrecks, wars, and the Congress of Vienna – and in persecuting Manfred in particular, whom they curse to "immortal" torments. But just as Prometheus refers to an overruling Fate or to Demogorgon, so Manfred refers to a higher order which he variously calls the "Powers deeper still beyond," the "over-ruling Infinite," "the Maker," or "the Unknown." These levels of order in *Manfred* are usually interpreted as implying at least a degree of Manichaeism or of Zoroastrianism (as in Lucifer's speeches in *Cain*), but I think one need look no further than the legend of Prometheus. There is no identification of this "over-ruling Infinite" with the Christian God, the God of the Abbot whom Manfred scorns. These powers are as distant and impersonal, in terms of the play, as is Demogorgon in Shelley's drama, or the Fate of Aeschylus's *Prometheus Bound.*

In the final act, however, Manfred goes one step further than the Prometheus of Shelley or Goethe in solitary rebellion. Byron's Manfred is in this respect in the same position as Byron's Prometheus; in his torment he leads a "sad *unallied* existence." The Prometheus of Aeschylus had Fate and time on his side, and Shelley's Prometheus knew that the ultimate victory, through Demogorgon, would be his. But Byron's Manfred and his Prometheus stand utterly alone. If they are to conquer, it is only in the independence of their own minds, even in death: "Triumphant where it dares defy, / And making Death a Victory," or, as Manfred says to the Abbot: "Old Man! 'tis not so difficult to die!"[8]

There is one other of Manfred's defiant speeches which deserves some analysis, I believe, since it shows the ultimate development of the idea that "the mind is its own place"– that speech of Satan which became of peculiar and quite un-Miltonic significance for some Romantics. Manfred addresses the Spirits who at the close of the drama have come to bear him away, as Faust had been borne away:

> Thou hast no power upon me, *that* I feel;
> Thou never shalt possess me, *that* I know:
> What I have done is done; I bear within
> A torture which could nothing gain from thine:
> The Mind which is immortal makes itself
> Requital for its good or evil thoughts, –
> *Is its own origin of ill and end –*
> *And its own place and time*: its innate sense,
> When stripped of this mortality, derives
> No colour from the fleeting things without,
> But is absorbed in sufferance or in joy,
> *Born from the knowledge of its own desert.**
>
> (III, iv, 125–136)

In the first place, these lines bear a striking resemblance to the close of Byron's address to Prometheus, who leads

* Italics mine, except in first two lines.

a sad unallied existence:
To which his Spirit may oppose
Itself — an equal to all woes —
And a firm will, and a deep sense,
Which even in torture can descry
Its own concentered recompense. . . . (52–56)

The "mind is its own place"— in an alien universe it creates its own values ("Is its own origin of ill and end"), and finds its satisfaction or its infinite remorse in fulfilling or in failing its own free commitments.

Perhaps one should hesitate to call this attitude existentialist: the term has been already too much used and abused and has gathered so many extraneous connotations. Yet what Byron describes here through Manfred or Prometheus comes very close to the core of the existentialist dilemma: man alone in an alien and godless universe, with nothing much of his own except the "dreadful freedom" to create his own system of value, and, in a sense, to create his very self. It is this aspect of the Byronic Hero which so appealed to Nietzsche that he made Byron's dramas the subject of one of his earliest and most ambitious juvenile essays, and, in one of his last works, rated *Manfred* above *Faust*.[9]

Of course I do not mean to say that Byron reasoned his way to such conclusions: Byron's reasoning was often sporadic and inconsistent. But Byron came at the crest of a great heroic tradition in literature, and from its very beginnings, in the *Sturm und Drang* of German literature and in the Gothic drama and the literature of sensibility in England (not to speak of *Paradise Lost* and its reinterpretations), this was a tradition of extreme subjectivity, of extreme individualism, and often of total rebellion. In such a context and with such a background Byron could very well speak better than he knew.

The fact remains, however, that in spite of its blazing rhetoric and flaming lyrics, *Manfred* is not entirely successful as a "metaphysical" drama (to use Byron's term). It may well be, as Professor Chew writes, that "the philosophic conception would have been the same had Manfred been . . . free from any stain of sin."[10] He is not free of sin, however, since he is not only a Faust-Prometheus, but also a Gothic Villain turned hero, and the latter figure is from a different and somewhat inconsistent level of literature. In Byron's next effort in a "metaphysical way," his drama *Cain*, he was more consistent and therefore more successful intellectually, although except in isolated passages I do not believe he reaches the same level of poetry.

As Byron's statement in *Cain* is more clear, so are his sources fewer. That he had once in his nonage read Gessner's *Der Tod Abels*, and that he had read *Paradise Lost* many times, he acknowledges in his preface. Faust, with his thirst for knowledge, has also entered into Byron's conception of his hero. Beyond these three undisputed sources, the only ones which have been discovered are the apocryphal book of Enoch, which probably gave Byron some hints (beyond *Paradise Lost*) for the flight through space, and Pierre Bayle's *Dictionary*, from which Byron has evidently gleaned some of his skeptical arguments.

There were a few of Byron's contemporaries who assessed *Cain* as drama, and three of them – Scott, Shelley, and Goethe – accorded it very high praise indeed. Scott wrote that Byron had "matched Milton on his own ground"; Shelley wrote that "*Cain* is apocalyptic; it is a revelation never before communicated to man"; and Goethe concluded, "Its beauty is such as we shall not see a second time in this world" (see *Works*, V, 204).

These estimates were not at all typical, however; for the most part *Cain* was received as another and worse effusion of the Chief of the "Satanic School" of poetry: it was viewed as a theologically subversive tract, and not much more.[11] This interpretation has dogged the drama through the last century and into our own. The furor raised at the time of its appearance occasioned not only irate reviews by such eminent clerics as Bishop Heber, but also pamphlets and entire books of refutation by other outraged orthodox theologians and scholars. Even later in the century, with such anticlerics as Georg Brandes and Nietzsche, *Cain* was still discussed more as an antitheological tract than as a drama. Brandes's eccentric evaluation of Byron is based largely on his viewing the poet not only as the apostle of liberty, but as the most popular freethinker of the century – and in both of these respects Brandes was of course Byron's most zealous disciple.

With the turn of the century, if not before, theological interest in the questions Byron had raised began to wane, and so did interest in *Cain*. Stopford Brooke, that pious and broadminded clergyman-critic who sounds like a voice from another age, has been the last but one to give the play serious theological consideration, and he did so only to save Byron for a somewhat sentimentalized Christianity.[12] Byron, Brooke maintains, was torn by his hatred for Calvinism to "do battle" with his own religious beliefs; but Brooke comes to the somewhat remarkable conclusion that in the long run Byron served the interests of "true" Christianity, since he brought into the open such vicious untruths as the doctrines of predestination and of original sin. Finally, Professor Fairchild, in his monumental work on religious opinion in English poetry, is less kind to Byron, to say the least, but he also views *Cain* as a theological essay.[13] If Professor Fairchild has little to say for the "Romantic religion" of poets like Wordsworth and Coleridge, however, he has even less to say for Byron. He finds that Byron's arguments in *Cain* are puerile, vain, and blatantly egoistic. But Brooke and Fairchild are exceptions among twentieth-century critics of the play: most critics take the view that *Cain* is indeed a tract, but that since the issues are dead, so is the play. This point could perhaps be argued. Our age has seen the revival of the doctrine of original sin in the dramas of T. S. Eliot, and, on the other side of the issue, Archibald MacLeish's recent modernization of the book of Job, in which the devil is as much of a hero as he is in Byron's biblical drama.

My point is not to discuss *Cain* as theology, primarily, but as a drama – although as a heroic drama of metaphysical rebellion. The parallel here with *Paradise Lost* seems to me particularly apt. As a theological dissertation Milton's poem is also "dead" to the modern reader (though it still was not a century ago); we no longer read it for its theme – the justification of "God's ways to man." Still, *Paradise Lost* remains a great poem, for it is also an intensely moving personal tragedy, or perhaps a domestic tragedy, as E. M. W. Tillyard suggests.[14] The same can be said, I believe, of Byron's *Cain.* Moreover, although I would not want to compare the two poems as poetry, I think one could argue that for most modern readers, Byron's drama is more consistent and even more appealing, intellectually, than is Milton's epic. Not being bound by the religious orthodoxy of Milton's theme, Byron does not feel constrained to introduce God and his difficult argumentation. Lucifer's views stand unchallenged by anything except Cain's quite human questioning, and the thorny problems of theodicy and of original sin remain in the play as mysteries.

The two heroes of *Cain*, Lucifer and the first murderer, show the Byronic Hero in the last stage of his development. They are true Romantic rebels, and free as they are from the taint of Gothic melodrama, they show this heroic tradition for what it was: a metaphysical rebellion in the cause of Romantic self-assertion.

In a previous chapter I reviewed briefly the rise of the Satan of *Paradise Lost* in the estimation of critics and poets of the century and a half following its publication. Satan was always sublime, but this aspect of his person was increasingly emphasized by critical apologists. Toward the close of the eighteenth century he was also being sentimentalized, in a sense humanized (Milton's imitator, Klopstock, led one of his demons to repentance and to the gates of heaven). With the advent of Romanticism, as *hubris* became a virtue rather than a cardinal sin, Satan came to symbolize romantic rebellion for such poets as Blake, Shelley, and Byron. This was, after all, only a revival of a heresy which had a long if *sub rosa* tradition in Western culture: even in the medieval mind Satan had some Promethean attributes. In such German literature as was not touched by Milton's influence, however, Satan had remained more orthodox. Mephistopheles of Goethe's *Faust* is a sophisticate, to be sure, but he is not a Titan: he is purely negative and destructive, a naysayer to everything life holds.

The Lucifer of Byron's *Cain* is far closer in this respect to Milton's devil than to Goethe's. He is first of all defiant, one of those "with courage never to submit or yield":

> I have a Victor – true; but no superior . . .
> I battle it against him, as I battled
> In highest Heaven – through all Eternity,
> And the unfathomable gulfs of Hades,
> And the interminable realms of space,
> And the infinity of endless ages,
> All, all, will I dispute! (II, ii, 429–435)

He is also, like Milton's demon, a fallen angel who has not yet left all his brightness off. When Cain sees him for the first time and is as yet unaware of his identity, Lucifer seems "A shape like to the angels / Yet of a sterner and a sadder aspect / Of spiritual essence . . ." (I, i, 80–83). In rather better poetry, the simple Adah, Cain's wife, compares Lucifer with the "other angels": "as the silent sunny noon, / All light, they look upon us; but thou seem'st / Like an ethereal night . . ." (I, i, 509–511).

But Lucifer's most important relationship with Milton's Satan is in his development of the doctrine also echoed by Manfred, that "the mind is its own place." This characteristic Lucifer shares with Byron's Prometheus: "Nothing can / Quench the mind, if the mind will be itself / And centre of surrounding things – 'tis made / To sway" (I, i, 213–216). The theme is repeated once more in Lucifer's parting advice to Cain:

> *One good* gift has the fatal apple given, –
> Your *reason*: let it not be overswayed
> By tyrannous threats to force you into faith
> 'Gainst all external sense and inward feeling:
> Think and endure, – and form an inner world
> In your own bosom – where the outward fails;
> So shall you nearer be the spiritual
> Nature, and war triumphant with your own.
> (II, ii, 459–466)

This is the same skeptical and rebellious doctrine developed by Childe Harold in the later cantos, and which Manfred expresses just before his death. (Oddly enough, this passage seems also to echo Michael's parting advice to Adam to find a "Paradise within thee, happier far." But surely this is Milton the humanist speaking, not Milton the theologian.)

In one important respect Lucifer is much unlike Prometheus, however, and this I believe forms the crux of the drama. Lucifer stands for defiance, for reason, and the thirst for knowledge, but he cannot love, and this gives the play its dramatic conflict. This is the only point in their long arguments on which Cain gets the best of his princely antagonist. Lucifer tries several evasive subterfuges, but Cain continually recurs to the questions: "Dost thou love nothing?" When Lucifer tries to turn the issue on Cain with his "I pity thee who lovest what must perish," Cain replies, "And I thee who lov'st nothing" (II, ii, 337–338). In other words, Lucifer is in most respects a typical Byronic Hero, in his courage and in his skeptical self-assertion, but he lacks that softness, that sensibility, which the true Byronic Hero is never without. In this respect the tragedy of *Cain* shows a definite advance on the theme of *Manfred*. Though not granted the poetry of *Manfred*, or at least not so much of it, in conception *Cain* rises above the Gothic into the realm of tragedy.

For like Manfred, Cain is a Faust, titanic in his self-assertion, in his thirst for knowledge, in his *Sehnsucht nach Unendliche*, but he is also a Hero of Sensibility, capable of strong and impassioned love, and he has none of Manfred's Gothic misanthropy. The conflict between these two forces in his personality, which Lucifer exploits, gives the drama its tragic conflict and eventual resolution.

Cain is depicted from the first as capable of moods of tenderness, in spite of his soul's sickness. He shows his soul of sensibility best in a speech like the following, an expression of his love for all he sees, but above all for his gentle wife,

> My sister Adah. – All the stars of heaven,
> The deep blue noon of night, lit by an orb
> Which looks a spirit, or a spirit's world –
> The hues of twilight – the Sun's gorgeous coming –
> His setting indescribable . . .
> The forest shade, the green bough, the bird's voice . . .
> All these are nothing, to my eyes and heart,
> Like Adah's face: I turn from earth and heaven
> To gaze on it. (II, ii, 259–269)

Cain's sensibility is only one aspect of his personality, however:

the other is his passionate longing for knowledge, for truth. The issue is clear-cut from the beginning: Cain has reasoned with his parents that "it *was* the Tree of Knowledge; / It *was* the Tree of life: knowledge is good, / And Life is good; and how can both be evil?" (I, i, 35–38). Eve answers: "Content thee with what *is*. Had we been so, / Thou hadst been contented." But Cain is too much of a Romantic to be satisfied that "Whatever is, is right," and when Lucifer appears and tells him "If thou dost long for knowledge, I can satiate / That thirst," Cain too readily succumbs (I, i, 558–559). Lucifer stands for reason and knowledge, but knowledge uninformed with love: he tells Cain that he must "Choose betwixt Love and Knowledge – since there is / No other choice," and Cain, even if only temporarily, chooses knowledge (I, i, 429–430). He refuses to "bow down" to Lucifer, but as the latter justly observes, this isn't really necessary.

From there on, Cain's destruction is assured. With Lucifer as guide, he takes his trip through ethereal space, and sees things "Beyond all power of my born faculties, / Although inferior still to my desires / And my conceptions" (II, i, 80–83). He marvels at the stars till he becomes "Intoxicated with eternity," and he cries to the "gods": "Let me die, as atoms die / . . . or know ye in your might and knowledge" (II, i, 113–115). But all he sees serves only to make him even more dissatisfied with what he is: "I am sick of all / That dust has shown me – let me dwell in shadows" (II, ii, 108–109). And when Lucifer reproaches him: "Didst thou not require / Knowledge? And have I not, in what I showed, / Taught thee to know thyself?" Cain can only answer: "Alas! I seem / Nothing" (II, ii, 418–421).

In this mood of sorrow and misery at his human plight (and not his alone, but the plight of all who will come after him, to whom he will give life), at the absurdity in man's finite nature filled with infinite longings, Cain murders his brother Abel.[15] This is, of course, the drama's catastrophe, but it was inherent in Cain's first climactic choice of knowledge over love.

Immediately repentant, Cain bends over his dead brother's body: "Oh! for a word more of that gentle voice, / That I may bear to hear my own again!" And he refers to his preceding thoughts, to the anger of frustration which had driven him to murder: "I am awake at last – a dreary dream / Had maddened me . . ." (III, i, 356–379).

It is important to note, however, that, like Manfred, Cain remains defiant to the end toward both Lucifer and God.[16] I do not mean merely in his asking the Angel if he is his brother's keeper; that speech is indeed a blot on the drama, as Professor Chew suggests, and certainly inconsistent with Cain's new-found realization of the primacy of love.[17] Byron was driven to include this speech only because of his unwise resolve to retain as many as possible of the literal words of Genesis. But toward the close of the act Cain concludes: "That which I am, I am; I did not seek / For life, nor did I make myself . . ." (III, i, 509–510). This is certainly the same note of defiance one might hear from Manfred or Lucifer, but what follows shows that Cain has progressed beyond their negative defiance: he begs to be able to give his life to return that of his brother, and on this note of remorse for his failing in the positive human value of love the play closes. Like Adam and Eve, Cain and Adah leave (with their child) for a life of penance: "Eastward from Eden we will take our way: / 'Tis the most desolate, and suits my steps" (III, i, 552–553). For all the unevenness of its poetry, and for all that it is marred by too much philosophical rhetoric, the drama becomes at the end a moving personal tragedy.

The moral universe of the drama can be compared with that of *Manfred* and that of *Prometheus*, the better to define these last two of Byron's Titanic heroes. Here the only rule to follow is that the order of the dramatic universe must be the vision presented by the drama's most sympathetic characters.

The first fact one must consider is that God nowhere appears in the tragedy, and there is no one who puts up any convincing arguments for his side of the case. Abel is made too simple-minded to argue, and the position of Adam and Eve can be summed up in Eve's admonition to Cain: "Content thee with what *is*." Moreover, neither of the first parents is made sympathetic. Adam's first reaction upon learning of Abel's death is to blame Eve, as the ultimate source of this new evil (this Byron probably learned from *Paradise Lost*: Adam's first reaction there also is to turn the blame on his wife). Eve's reaction is to deliver a curse on the head of her eldest son which vies in intensity and vehemence with those vivid curses from the lips of the old Queen Margaret in *Richard III*.

The view of the world presented by Lucifer is a mixture of Manichaeism in metaphysics and of proud stoicism in ethics. This Manichaean skepticism is probably derived, as Byron's critics immediately pointed out, from Pierre Bayle's *Dictionary*, but it is not, after all, an intellectually disreputable position, as Bayle himself acutely demonstrated. Moreover, Lucifer's views are nowhere controverted in the drama by anyone of equal authority. In his stoicism he is not far from Milton's Satan, except, of course, in that his stoicism is not reinterpreted for the reader in deprecatory remarks from the narrator, as is Satan's stoicism in *Paradise Lost*.

But Cain is himself the drama's one sympathetic character, since he and not Lucifer has the capacity to love. He is not wholly taken in by Lucifer's arguments as to the ultimate nature of the universe, but on the other hand he is not convinced by his parents. His final position is best summed up in his own words: "That which I am, I am; I did not seek / For life, nor did I make myself . . ." In other words, his view is not very different from that of Manfred: he can see the "absurdity" of his situation in a world he did not make. But he can also see more than Manfred—in the value of his love for Adah, for his son, and for all of his posterity.

It seems to me that one has every right to take this as the final position of the Byronic Hero, and to take Lucifer and Cain as representing the final stage in that hero's development. There is still something in him of the Satanic, certainly, but very little of the Gothic Villain. In his skepticism and in his defiant self-assertion he is certainly antireligious, but then the whole of the heroic tradition of which he was the ultimate English expression was a rebellion against orthodoxy of all kinds, including religious orthodoxy. And the final message of this Byronic Hero is after all an approach to the message of *Faust II*, if expressed in less than *Faust's* poetry. On this point, however, it is only fair to remember that had Goethe, too, died at the age of thirty-seven, the poetry for which he would be remembered would not differ markedly in philosophy or outlook from that left by Byron in *Cain*, and Goethe would have to his credit no *Don Juan*.

Although the public had received Byron's *Childe Harold* and his romances with open hearts and had not even balked at *Manfred* (although there was some questioning of the metaphysical implications of the final scene), they could not accept *Cain*. Lucifer and Cain do no more than carry out the development of the Byronic Hero to its logical conclusions, dropping the Gothic trappings, but the full implications of this titanic rebellion were too much for Byron's public. Comparing himself with that greatest of the age's historical heroes, Napoleon, Byron later wrote in *Don Juan*:

> But Juan was my Moscow, and Faliero
> My Leipsic, and my Mont Saint Jean seems Cain;
> *La Belle Alliance* of dunces down at zero,
> Now that the Lion's fallen, may rise again . . .
>
> (XI, st. 56)

And so, indeed, they did.

XII THE BYRONIC HERO AND HEROIC TRADITION

IN THIS study of the types and prototypes of the Byronic Hero one major point, at least, has become clear: there was in the Romantic Movement a distinctive heroic tradition – an aspect of Romanticism which perhaps deserves more scholarly attention than it has so far received. The tradition began in Germany in the *Sturm und Drang*, and culminated in Goethe's *Faust*, Romanticism's greatest achievement. It is probably true to say that the "hero aspect" of Romanticism was always more important in Germany than in England; but English Romanticism too has its representatives in this tradition – indeed, England has a prior claim at least to the Gothic Villain-Hero and to Satan. Our one major English representative, however, is Byron; if Faust must stand in this respect for German Romanticism, the Byronic Hero must stand for England. This gives the Byronic Hero a special significance for the student of English letters: he is our natural contact with this last great heroic tradition in our literature.

To recognize the existence of the family of Romantic heroes, however, is to see first that it is distinctive in the broader tradition of the literary hero, and second that whatever it may have been, it is now no longer alive either in our literature or in our general culture. These heroes claim at least a historical significance, however, and perhaps also a contemporary significance, and for this reason it is worthwhile, even at the risk of oversimplification, to outline in this concluding chapter their place in heroic tradition, to summarize the major reasons for their demise, and, finally, to consider what possible relevance a study of these Romantic heroes can have for an understanding of our own age and literature. These topics could all serve as subjects of separate studies, but a summary treatment of them here should help place the Byronic Hero and the whole family of Romantic heroes in perspective.

The norm for any discussion of heroic tradition is usually the description of the hero in the *Poetics*. Aristotle is of course concerned mainly with plot, not with character, but he does mention incidentally a few of the hero's major characteristics. First of all the hero must be "bigger than life"; he must be above the common level, with greater powers, greater dignity, and a greater soul. He must have the qualities of an ordinary mortal so that we can see ourselves in him, but he is an idealization, a man whose capacities have been multiplied and enlarged so as to make him a giant among men. Furthermore, in spite of his tragic flaw, he must be "better," more "virtuous," than the average man. With the introduction of virtue one is likely to run into difficulty: if a hero must be virtuous in the usual modern sense of the term, most Romantic heroes (and most Shakespearean heroes, for that matter) would not qualify. Surely the point to remember, however, is that when Aristotle spoke of virtue he did not, of course, use the term with anything like the Christian meaning. One gets a better understanding of heroic virtue from the famous description of the "magnanimous" man in the *Ethics*, for here Aristotle notes that magnanimity (often translated "pride") is the "crown of all virtues." The magnanimous man is "not given to admiration, for nothing to him is great"; he seeks honors only from equals; he is generous only from a sense of strength, not from a sense of duty; and above all, he knows his own worth, and he is sure of himself because he does. The hero's basic virtue, in other words, is close to what Nietzsche in the *Genealogy of Morals* calls "self-respect," and it is very distant indeed from any ideal of Christian meekness, or even of ordinary modesty.[1] This portrait may not seem at first so appealing to a modern mind, but in general it is a faithful likeness of the heroes of Western culture, both in literature and in history. One need only think of Shakespeare's Hal or Henry V, or of Coriolanus, or in history, of men from Caesar to Charlemagne to Napoleon who have become legendary heroes in our culture.

If we now return with this formula to the heroes discussed in the previous chapters, we see first of all that the eighteenth-century types will not qualify at all: none of them is sufficiently "heroic." The Child of Nature, the Gloomy Egoist, and the Man of Feeling can be called heroes only for the sake of convenience (protagonist is an awkward word), and at the cost of some confusion of terms. The Hero of Sensibility does become a hero – almost in *Werther*, and certainly in Byron's works – but his is a borrowed glory, borrowed from the tradition of which he is a part. He had not been a hero in Sterne's and Mackenzie's novels, and when he survives into the Victorian age – in the poetry of Arnold or Clough or Tennyson – he survives only as a solitary and sensitive sufferer: with the loss of his titanic passions, his pride, and his certainty of self-identity, he loses also his status as hero.

This Aristotelian formula does indeed apply to the Romantic heroes, however, from the Gothic Villain-turned-Hero of the drama, through the Noble Outlaw (from Götz and Karl Moor to Marmion and the Corsair), and through the various Faust-figures, to Satan and Prometheus. Each of these heroes is "bigger than life"– by virtue of his intellectual powers, his personal dignity, and his capacity for feeling – and all of them are certainly activated by a very self-conscious pride, even in their suffering.

Some of these figures, such as Prometheus, were always heroes, and Romanticism did no more than revive them for literature. Others, however, were raised to heroic stature in the Romantic age, and some of them from very humble origins. The Noble Outlaw, for instance, had been a figure only in ballads and subliterary romances before Götz and Karl Moor. Faust rose from the level of buffoonery to which he had fallen in English farce, or from his puppet-stage appearances on the Continent, to become the most popular literary hero in eighteenth-century Germany. Ahasuerus, who was at worst a decrepit shoemaker and at best an encyclopedic traveling lecturer, becomes a Titan in the poetry of Schubart, of Shelley, and of others beyond. And Cain, from the villain-buffoon of the medieval Mystery, is first sentimentalized in Germany, and then Prometheanized in Byron's tragedy.

If the Romantic heroes have the necessary features to entitle them to a place in the broader heroic tradition in literature, they have also characteristics which make them distinctive in that tradition. Of these I believe two are most important – their sensibility and their Satanism.

All of these heroes have souls of sensibility: Götz and Karl Moor no less than Byron's Manfred or Cain. They appreciate natural beauty (unless, like some of the Gothic Villains, they are too preoccupied with their sin and remorse); often they long for some kind of absorption in the universe around them (as do Werther, Childe Harold, and Cain); and above all they have almost infinite capacities for feeling: especially, of course, for the tenderness and the passion of love. This aspect of the Romantic Hero is not difficult to account for: the individualistic temper and extreme subjectivity of the movement as a whole has often been noticed. Then, too, one must remember that the Romantic Hero appeared in the ebb of that vast wave of sentiment which inundated northern Europe in the last half of the eighteenth century: there is a direct connection between Sir Charles Grandison, Yorick, and Werther, even if only the last qualifies as a true hero. There were limits, however, to these sensibilities; for the most part they were intensely personal – even egocentric – and the typical Romantic Hero is not, as a Marxist would say, "socially concerned." Prometheus is the one major exception, and even he figures in Goethe's and Herder's fragments or in Byron's poetry primarily as a metaphysical rebel, not as a savior of man.

The other dominant characteristic of the Romantic Hero is his Satanism, a trait that seems at first more difficult to account for. It is unquestionably there, and it is not the impress of the author's personality, either: authors of such diverse temperaments as Schiller, Scott, Shelley, and Byron portrayed Satanic heroes.

One cause of this Satanism must be accounted adventitious: the influence of *Paradise Lost*. The putative villain of Milton's poem was heroic in almost everyone's eyes, and it would be difficult to overemphasize the influence of this epic, not only in England – on Blake, Byron, and Shelley – but also on the Continent. Schiller alludes to the poem as having furnished a model for Karl Moor; Klopstock imitated it in *Der Messias*; and in *The Laocöon* Lessing refers to it as the greatest of modern epics.

A more important cause for this heroic Satanism, however, lies in the eighteenth-century pietistic movement, which was perhaps even more influential in Germany than in England. It has long been recognized that sentimentalism is related to pietism: both foster a deep inner concern with one's emotional states, an exacerbating, sometimes even morbid, self-analysis. But Satanism is also directly related to pietism, although as a form of rebellion. This is especially evident in Blake's reaction against the repressive effects of religious dogma (especially sexual repression, but also social), and against the ever present danger of hypocrisy in pietism, but I think it is also evident in Byron's *Don Juan*, or in Shelley's youthful and militant atheism. And fifty years later it is still evident in Nietzsche's reaction against the Lutheran pietism of his own early environment.

Finally, I think there is a deeper reason in a fact I have often referred to in the previous chapters; the Romantic movement was a rebellion in the name of individualism, and there has perhaps always been an alliance between aggressive humanism, self-reliance, and Satanism, on the one hand, and God-reliance, total commitment to Absolutes, and consequent self-immolation on the other. Milton's Satan and Marlowe's Faustus share a common sin, the sin of *hubris*, but one must also admit that it is this very human pride or self-reliance which gives them the nobility of tragic heroes.

Whatever their peculiarities, and whatever the origins of these peculiarities, these Romantic heroes represent an important tradition in our literature. Almost every great Romantic in Germany became in some way implicated: Goethe and Schiller both inaugurated their popular literary careers with Noble Outlaws; the Faust story was written and rewritten by German poets from the neoclassical Lessing to the pessimistic Lenau; and the fragmentary German dramas, epics, or novels which featured Prometheus, Ahasuerus, or Cain are almost innumerable. In England we have a reinterpreted *Paradise Lost*, a number of Gothic novels and dramas (few of which reached into the realm of literature), the heroic romances of the younger Scott, some of the poetry of Shelley, and the works of Byron. In all of these works the Byronic Hero is the one protagonist who in stature and in temperament best represents the tradition in England.

There are probably a number of reasons, accidental or otherwise, why Byron became the English Romantic hero-poet, but there are two which I think are most significant. First, Byron was a cosmopolitan aristocrat, not only by birth, but by temperament; and second, he was probably more open to heterogeneous influences, both intellectual and emotional, than was any other of the major English Romantic poets.

There is certainly an unpleasant tone of aristocratic condescension in Byron's frequent references to Wordsworth, Southey, and Coleridge as the "Lakists," or in his references to their "underlings" of the "Cockney School," including Keats (although neither epithet was of Byron's coinage), but there is also a more honorable reason for his attitude. For Byron was in and of the "great world" in a way that the other English Romantics were not. Sometimes they seem almost provincial beside him, however much they may surpass him as poets. Scott meant praise as well as irony when he wrote that Byron "manages his pen with the careless and negligent ease of a man of quality," [2] and W. H. Auden refers humorously to the same characteristic in one of his *Letters from Iceland*:

> You lived and moved among the best society
> And so could introduce your hero to it
> Without the slightest tremor of anxiety;
> Because he was your hero and you knew it,
> He'd know instinctively what's done, and do it.[3]

This may at first seem trivial, but no matter how much he may be in a tradition, a poet still writes of what he feels and experiences most personally, and it was Byron, not Wordsworth or Coleridge, who enjoyed the worldly, literate, and intelligent conversations at

Holland House, who chatted with Sheridan or Colman in the Green Room at Drury Lane, and who later in Switzerland spent many pleasant hours with that fascinating old queen of Romanticism, Madame de Staël. Byron was in touch with the "great world" and with his times in a way that no other English Romantic could be, whatever his reading or his intelligence.

The other of Byron's personal characteristics which helps account for his being our English hero-poet, is his open-mindedness, what one critic, taking a cue from *Don Juan*, has called his "mobility." [4] Shelley was more widely read than Byron, and Coleridge more deeply, but none of the other Romantics exhibits the breadth of Byron's interests: he was very much impressed – too much, perhaps – with Gothic novels and drama; in spite of his basic skepticism he was capable of entertaining in *Childe Harold* III a Wordsworthian concept of Nature; isolated classics of his schoolboy reading (Aeschylus's *Prometheus*, for instance) made such deep impressions on his mind that they colored all of his own works, or survived in memory (Gessner's *Abel*) to bear fruit many years later; and Byron was almost alone among the English Romantics to be influenced by *Faust*, and to appreciate Goethe's greatness. Of course Byron's intellectual mobility was his weakness as well as his strength. The confusion of theme in *Manfred* and the confusion of character in *Childe Harold* bear witness to this. Such eclecticism is more appropriate in *Don Juan*; when an earlier poem gives a unified impression, it is because of the vivid characterization of a Byronic Hero, not because of any fusion of the poem's intellectual content. Whatever the reasons of temperament or of genius, Byron was able to fashion a hero from the heterogeneous elements of this tradition who was not only to bear his name, but who was to leave so striking an impression on the minds of future readers as to almost efface the memory of such English predecessors as Mrs. Radcliffe, Scott (in his romances), or the Gothic dramatists.

To recognize this distinctively Romantic heroic tradition, with its German and its English representatives, is also to recognize that this last great age of heroes has passed. The causes for the demise of the hero are too broad and too complex to be more than listed here, and some of them have been studied quite exhaustively by contemporary scholars and critics.[5] In order even to outline this decline, however, I think it is useful to make a distinction between a literary heroic tradition and a philosophical, or a political-prophetic tradition. Perhaps the distinction is ultimately artificial, since both developments are intimately associated, but it is still useful. Byron, for instance, belongs in the literary tradition, and only by implication in the political-prophetic, insofar as he or his legend became involved in rebellions for liberation. Carlyle, on the other hand, belongs certainly in the political-prophetic tradition, but his Abbot Samson and even his Frederick and Cromwell are to an extent creations of a literary imagination.

The literary tradition died in England almost with Byron, although a few notable exceptions represent its attempted continuation. Benjamin Disraeli's *Vivian Grey* (1826) displays some heroic characteristics, for instance, and Disraeli included Byron himself in *Venetia* (1837). Rochester, in *Jane Eyre*, is certainly a descendant of the Gothic Villain-Hero, and Emily Brontë's Heathcliff is not only Byronic, but a great literary achievement. Generally speaking, however, the Romantic heroes did not survive in important works of Victorian literature. There are no Fausts at all; there is only one undisputed Wandering Jew, the emaciated protagonist of George Croly's *Salathiel* (1829); and the only notable Titan is in Robert Bridges' *Prometheus, the Firegiver* (1884).

The literary tradition had a more vigorous life on the Continent, especially in Germany. The first enthusiasm of the *Sturm und Drang* was short-lived, it is true, but Prometheuses, Fausts, and traditional Don Juans (not like Byron's) continued to be written through most of the nineteenth century. The influence not only of Byron's works, but also of his legend, out of all proportion to his reputation in England, reinforced this tradition. His name became a household word, and "Childe Harolds" and "Manfreds" were written in almost every European literature. Moreover, heroic poems written in English in this tradition are now dead works, but often on the Continent they have become classics of their various national literatures. Nikolaus Lenau's *Faust* (1836), or his fragmentary *Don Juan* (1851), both written more under the influence of Byron than of Goethe, are among the greatest treatments of these two legends. In far-off Russia, writing within a few years of Byron's death, Pushkin became an avowed disciple of Byron, and Russia's first national poet. His *Boris Godunov* (1829) is certainly a remorseful Gothic Villain-Hero, and *Eugene Onegin* (1837) is a direct descendant of Childe Harold or Manfred.

Eventually, however, this literary heroic tradition died both in England and on the Continent. The factors responsible are various, but two of the most important can paradoxically be ascribed in part to Romanticism itself.

The antiheroic factor most frequently mentioned is realism in art and "scientism" in our culture generally. In common with all forms of ideals, heroism and hero-worship require a certain mystique in order to thrive, and this the objectivity of realism or of science does not allow. The hero can survive in a "naturalized" universe – one regularized by science and left free both of wonder and of moral order – indeed, some of the Romantic heroes did. If the hero can find no moral order in the universe of *things* (and I think it can be argued that even Shakespeare doubted one could find such an order – in *Lear*, for instance), he can still find a moral order in himself, as man. But the hero cannot survive the kind of analysis (in later realism, or in scientific naturalism) which strips him of his idealized attributes and reduces him to nothing more than a half-conscious product of his environment.

The other most commonly mentioned antiheroic factor in modern culture was also inherent in Romanticism: the rise of bourgeois democracy and of the cult of the common man. One can see this inconsistency in Emerson, who in his historical essays preached a doctrine of hero-worship not very different from that of Carlyle, and who on the other hand, in *The American Scholar*, urged poets to "embrace the common . . . [to] sit at the feet of the familiar, the low," to sing of "the meal in the firkin, the milk in the pan."

Carlyle is the one important English prophet of heroism. Indeed, as Byron represents the creator of heroes in nineteenth-century England, so Carlyle represents the worshiper of heroes. His lecture series *On Heroes, Hero-Worship, and the Heroic in History* was immensely popular, his essays such as *Past and Present* were widely read and widely influential, and much of his history, especially his monumental *Frederick the Great*, is hero-worship objectified. (It is perhaps symbolic of the bitter end of the tradition in English literature that toward the close of his life Carlyle tried to make a hero of the notorious Governor Eyre.)

Prophets of heroism like Carlyle flourished on the Continent, too, philosophers and poets of what Eric Bentley has called "heroic vitalism"—especially Wagner, Nietzsche, and Stefan George—and on these prophet-poets the influence of Byron's literary heroes was particularly important, as it was not in England. Bertrand Russell, in his *History of Western Philosophy*, devotes an entire chapter to the Byronic Hero, giving Byron the credit for establishing on the Continent a type of "aristocratic rebel"—a rebel not concerned with social revolution or remedial legislation, but with some "intangible and metaphysical good." This rebellion "takes the form of titanic cosmic self-assertion, or . . . of Satanism. Both are to be found in Byron." Moreover, this "aristocratic philosophy of rebellion . . . has inspired a long series of revolutionary movements, from the Carbonari after the fall of Napoleon to Hitler's *coup* in 1933."[6] All of this would have to be qualified, of course. Byron did not originate even the literary type; it began in the German *Sturm und Drang*. Schiller's *Die Räuber*, for instance, was popular on the German stage all through the nineteenth century, and Karl Moor is certainly both "Titanic" and "Satanic." But Russell's main point, I suppose, still stands. The type did take Byron's name, and Byron did inspire patriots in Italy from Mazzini to D'Annunzio, although not (and the point is worth noting) Mussolini.

The highly controversial question of the relationship of this tradition to Fascism, particularly in Germany, is a problem which deserves and has received some very careful study, and by scholars more conscientious than Bertrand Russell.[7] All I can do here is attempt very briefly to point out some of the complexities of the issue which might indicate that most generalizations on the subject are facile, and some are absurd.

It became very fashionable during the second World War (when Russell's *History* was written) to draw a line of influence which included the following names: Fichte and Hegel, Byron and Carlyle, Wagner and Nietzsche, Stefan George and Oswald Spengler, sometimes D. H. Lawrence, and – Hitler. (Which of these men were emphasized and which omitted depended largely upon the individual scholar's peculiar bias.) It cannot be denied that these men, as writers and as thinkers, all belong to what can loosely be called the political-philosophical heroic tradition, but here are a few of the complexities: Carlyle, however unjustly, told his reader to close his Byron and open his Goethe. Goethe, by the way, not Napoleon, was most consistently Nietzsche's candidate for the type of the *Uebermensch.* As Carlyle was influenced by Fichte and Hegel, so he influenced Emerson (see the latter's *Representative Men*, or his essay "On Heroes") – and Emerson has always been considered a great apostle of democratic individualism. Nietzsche, too, was fond of Emerson, as well as Byron, and read both with interest.[8] Nietzsche himself became the "official philosopher" of Nazi Germany posthumously, and largely through careful editing and reinterpretation, inspired at first by his proto-Nazi sister.[9] In actuality, he consistently expressed contempt both for German nationalism and for anti-Semitism (the basis of his break with Wagner). Finally, it is certainly obvious that the Byronic Hero (and the same is probably true of Nietzsche's *Uebermensch*) is far too individualistic ever to be involved seriously with nationalism, and he is also too passionately concerned with individual freedom. The Byronic Hero might consent (as Byron did) to lead a small band of *Carbonari* or of Greek patriots (although Manfred and Faliero disdain even that), but I cannot conceive either Byron or his hero remaining in England to stage a *putsch* from a local pub.

There are very few generalizations that one can safely and honestly make on the subject. In the first place, two political and philosophical doctrines are at work here, not one: the doctrine of the organic state, which certainly owes its origin to Fichte and Hegel (or before them to Herder); and that of hero-worship, which tends to be individualistic and "metaphysically rebellious," and which probably owes its origin to the *Sturm und Drang* and to such Romantics as Byron. The doctrines become closely associated in the ideal of the "culture leader," as in the works of Carlyle, but they are by no means inseparable, and several of the important figures who wrote of heroes (Byron conspicuous among them) have little or nothing to do with nationalism in any form. Byronic Heroes were individualists, not collectivists. A second important generalization is that a great many of these writers, especially Byron, Carlyle, Emerson, and Nietzsche, were "sensationalists": that is, they expressed their opinions in a manner definitely calculated to shock the unwary reader; and the opinions of a sensationalist, from the very fact that they are always extreme, can of course be perverted to uses completely aside from the author's original intention. Often this can be done, as with Nietzsche or Emerson, merely by taking the statements out of context, and taking them literally (for example: "Consistency is the hobgoblin of little minds"; the context – Emerson's objective idealism).

But the political-prophetic tradition which supposedly culminated in Fascism is only tangentially related to the literary tradition of heroes – and in any case, both traditions are dead. In the political sphere the antiheroic philosophies of Marxism and Benthamite democracy have triumphed. The latter perpetuates the cult of the common man at the expense of the hero, and the former the cult of the proletariat. In the sphere of literature, this century has seen the ultimate triumph of what has been called the principle of the antiheroic.

In our own age any study of the Byronic Hero and of the Romantic heroic tradition in general has, I believe, three major values – one literary, one historical, and a third more broadly philosophical.

Anyone must admit that this Romantic tradition produced much rant, rhetoric, and fustian. A great deal of it (even in Byron) seems to us almost unreadable. No one, for instance, would seriously suggest that one revive for general reading (aside from scholarly purposes, that is) the vast majority of the Gothic dramas written with such expenditure of energy all through the Romantic period (including Byron's *Werner*). Even the metrical romances – aside from a few of Scott's and Byron's – are, and probably should remain, unread. But on the other hand some of this literature can still be read for enjoyment, and in that class I would include some of Byron's romances (*The Corsair*, for instance), many of his dramas (especially *Manfred*, *Sardanapalus*, and *Cain*), and much of *Childe Harold*. One cannot expect the polished craft of Keats or of some of Coleridge, the lyric grace of Shelley, or the mystic profundity of Wordsworth; but once one has become accustomed to the rhetoric, there is in these works a fire and an enthusiasm – much the same as what Arnold called "sincerity"– which makes one forgive Byron's occasional awkwardness.

The historical value of such a study lies in a better understanding of Romanticism – specifically English Romanticism. Germany is in no danger of overlooking the *Sturm und Drang* rebellion of the age: *Die Räuber* and *Götz* are still being produced on the stage, and *Faust* (there is much *Sturm* in part one) has become the great classic of German literature. By an odd accident of fortune, however, the English Romantic movement is now represented largely by poets such as Wordsworth, Coleridge, and Keats, who were not the popular poets of the day (as were Schiller and Goethe in Germany), and who do not by any means represent the whole of Romanticism: Byron and Scott come far closer, but unfortunately they were not such great poets.

Finally, I believe it is important to understand the whole of Romanticism also for what I would call, broadly speaking, philosophical reasons: an understanding of this tradition and of the Byronic Hero in particular can help us see more clearly what Albert Camus has recently called the "philosophy of rebellion." [10] For the Byronic Hero may be only rather tenuously related to the tradition of the heroic which culminated in Wagner or possibly in Fascism, but he is most intimately related to that other tradition, also originating in Romanticism (or in the French Revolution, as Camus says) – the tradition of "metaphysical" or "total" rebellion. It is total rebellion because it is a rebellion not only on a political level, but also on the philosophical and religious level – and sometimes, in nihilistic extremes, against life itself.

This tradition of total rebellion has remained up until our own time largely literary, artistic, and even esoteric, on occasion breaking out more broadly in Russian nihilism, in forms of surrealism, or in pre-war Parisian existentialism. In our own age, however, it has become far more widespread. Secular existentialism, with Sartre and Heidegger as leaders, is perhaps the dominant philosophy in Paris, and most certainly dominant in Germany. Although in America the tradition has not made much of an impression in academic philosophical circles, it has had a great vogue since the war in American letters, both in and out of the academy.

Understanding this philosophy of rebellion has therefore become a prime concern for all of us, whether or not we feel ourselves personally implicated, and if we are to understand it fully, we must be able to trace its history and its sources. It is not hard to see, I think, that the Romantic heroic tradition, with its subjective sensibility and especially with its rebellious Satanism, gave the first articulate or literary signs of this modern rebellion. Manfred, with all his prototypes and his successors, has indeed cast a long shadow – not only over Europe, but over America.

Our problem is not only to understand this rebellion, however, but somehow to overcome it. As Camus says, and as many of his critics agree (even if they do not agree with his conclusions), some means must be found to reaffirm the validity of basic human values in the chaotic or absurd universe in which this rebellion has left us. Camus maintains that the means for this reaffirmation of values can be found in the very definition (but his critics say it is a stipulative definition) of the concept of revolt. Rebellion must recognize "limits" if it is to be "genuine," and those limits must lie in a respect for others as independent and individual existences.

What we are left with at the end of *Manfred* may be (as I believe it is) a close approximation of the modern existentialist predicament, and if so, it lies at the nihilistic extreme of that position. For Manfred's only final consolations are that "the mind is its own place," and that even death can be an act of defiance. *Cain*, however, goes beyond *Manfred* in this respect. Here, if I interpret the drama correctly, Byron exploits the old Romantic theme of the inevitably tragic search for absolute knowledge versus the satisfaction of a limited and human love. And certainly *Cain* ends with a reaffirmation of this most basic of human values, in the quiet close in which the hero leaves—"Eastward from Eden"—with his beloved Adah and their only son. We are left with human love as the one sure value in a world of irrational conflict. Then, too, Cain's sincere remorse (for the drama is a tragedy), not for his pride, but for his rebellious murder, is certainly a sign that he has learned to see what Camus calls "the proper limits of rebellion." But whatever one says of *Cain*, there can be no doubt of the interpretation of *Don Juan*.

I did not include Byron's Juan in the range of Romantic Heroes because he would have appeared oddly out of place in the company of the Corsair, of Manfred, or of Cain—the traditional Don Juan would not, but Byron's would. The narrator-persona of *Don Juan*, however, does retain many of the characteristics of the usual Byronic Hero—he is still skeptical and still defiant—but as the poem develops he takes on characteristics quite different from those of Childe Harold or Manfred, and the final impression the poem leaves (especially in the last cantos) is of a Byronic Hero become strangely tolerant, for all his satiric wit, of a rebel who has found his "limits," as Camus calls them. He is against war, against every form of tyranny, and he has a deadly hatred for all cant and hypocrisy. One thing alone he advocates without equivocation: a respect for the rights of indvidual men.

In other words, I believe *Don Juan* is finally an optimistic poem, but the optimism is not of the facile sort based on a willful blindness to the evil in man and to the "irrational" elements in the universe—an optimism all too common in the works of other Romantics. The narrator of *Don Juan* has experienced the universe depicted in *Manfred* or *Cain*, but he has come through. Not by reason or philosophy, admittedly—he is never strong on that—but by a broad sense of humanity and a skeptical common sense. Perhaps if we are to survive the philosophy of rebellion, these are the virtues we will need.

NOTES, BIBLIOGRAPHICAL APPENDIX, AND INDEX

NOTES

I have used the standard edition of *The Works of Lord Byron*, ed. E. H. Coleridge (London: John Murray, 1898–1904), in 13 vols.: *Poetry*, ed. E. H. Coleridge, vols. I–VII; *Letters and Journals*, ed. Rowland E. Prothero (Lord Ernle), vols. I–VI. These are abbreviated in the text to read: *Works*, I–VII, for the poetry; and *LJ*, I–VI, for the letters. In regard to individual poems or dramas, however, I have made reference in parentheses only to act, stanza, or line. In references to *Childe Harold* (especially in Chapter IX), I have used Roman numerals for the canto, but instead of the lower case Roman numerals common in editions of Byron I have used Arabic numerals for stanza numbers, for obvious typographical reasons.

All translations in the text, unless otherwise acknowledged, are my own.

INTRODUCTION

[1] In *Forschungen zur neueren Literaturgeschichte*, VI (München, 1898).

[2] *The Haunted Castle* (London: George Routledge, 1927).

[3] In *University of California Studies in English*, XVIII (Berkeley and Los Angeles: University of California Press, 1947).

[4] I have used the second edition, trans. Angus Davidson, reprinted as a Meridian Book (New York, 1956).

[5] Praz, pp. 26–27 (italics mine).

[6] Praz, p. 66.

[7] Praz, pp. 76, 80.

[8] Albert C. Baugh, *et al.*, *A Literary History of England* (New York: Appleton-Century-Crofts, 1948), p. 1124.

[9] *The Byronic Teuton* (London: Methuen, 1940), pp. 8–9.

[10] Hentschel, pp. 9–10.

[11] *A Survey of English Literature, 1780–1830* (New York: Macmillan, 1905), II, 149.

[12] In *From Anne to Victoria*, ed. Bonamy Dobrée (New York: Scribner, 1937), pp. 604f. Reprinted in Eliot's *On Poetry and Poets* (New York, 1957). For Quennell, see *Byron: The Years of Fame* (London: Collins, 1941).

[13] From a conversation quoted in Ernest J. Lovell, Jr., *His Very Self and Voice* (New York: Macmillan, 1954), p. 434.

CHAPTER I. OUR LAST GREAT AGE OF HEROES

[1] In *Works*, ed. Lady Trevelyan (Philadelphia: The University Press, n.d.), II, 180–186.

[2] Cited in Samuel C. Chew, *Byron in England: His Fame and Afterfame* (New York: Scribner, 1924), Chap. xii.

[3] See Arthur O. Lovejoy, *The Great Chain of Being* (Cambridge: Harvard University Press, 1936), Chap. vi.

CHAPTER II. THE CHILD OF NATURE

[1] *Nature's Simple Plan* (Princeton: Princeton University Press, 1922), p. 88.

[2] Ernest Bernbaum, *The Drama of Sensibility* (Cambridge: Harvard University Press, 1925), p. 237.

[3] The play is reprinted in *British Dramatists from Dryden to Sheridan*, ed. G. H. Nettleton and A. E. Case (Cambridge: Harvard University Press, 1939), pp. 719–757. The quotations in my text are from I, ii, 11–14; I, v, 72–74; III, vii, 142–146; IV, iii, 22–25; V, viii, 128–130.

[4] Reprinted most recently in an edition with an introduction by Vaughan Wilkins (London: Turnstile Press, 1951).

[5] Hoxie N. Fairchild, *The Noble Savage* (New York: Columbia University Press, 1928), p. 299.

CHAPTER III. THE HERO OF SENSIBILITY

[1] For a selective list of bibliographical references to these theorists, see the paragraph devoted to the Man of Feeling in the Bibliographical Appendix.

[2] James R. Foster, in his *History of the Pre-Romantic Novel in England* (New York: The Modern Language Association, 1949), is the first to do full justice to Prevost. An earlier scholar, Benjamin N. Woodbridge, in "Romantic Tendencies in the Novels of the Abbé Prevost," *PMLA* XXVI (1911), called attention to a possible line of influence of Prevost, through *René*, on the Byronic Hero.

[3] *A Sentimental Journey*, Everyman ed. (London: J. M. Dent, 1927), p. 121. Note the interesting parallel between this sentiment and Byron's "the great object of life is sensation – to feel that we exist, even though in pain" (*LJ*, III, 400): the difference between the eighteenth-century Man of Feeling and the Romantic Hero of Sensibility – but a difference more of degree than of kind.

[4] *The Man of Feeling*, ed. Hamish Miles (London: The Scholartis Press, 1928), pp. 121, 45–46.

[5] See *The Confessions*, trans. J. M. Cohen (London: Penguin Books, 1953), pp. 400–401, 408.

[6] James H. Warner, "The Basis of J. J. Rousseau's Contemporaneous Reputation in England," *Modern Language Notes*, LV (1940), 272.

[7] Part III, Book IX, *Dichtung und Wahrheit*; in *Sämtliche Werke*, Jubiläumsausgabe (Stuttgart: J. B. Cotta'sche, 1902–12), XXIV, 163–164.

[8] *Kampagne in Frankreich*, in *Werke*, XXVIII, 164–165.

[9] Stuart Pratt Atkins, *The Testament of Werther in Poetry and Drama* (Cambridge: Harvard University Press, 1949), p. 17.

[10] *Die Leiden des jungen Werthers*, ed. Max Herrman, in *Werke*, XVI, 7.

[11] *Werther*, pp. 4, 10.

[12] *Werther*, p. 30.

[13] *Werther*, p. 73.

[14] *Loc. cit.*, note 7 above.

[15] There is no modern edition of the poem, so I have used *The Poetical Works*, Aldine ed. (London: Bell and Daldy, n.d.).

CHAPTER IV. THE GOTHIC VILLAIN

[1] Ann Radcliffe, *The Italian* (London, 1811), I, 15, 246.

[2] See Eino Railo, *The Haunted Castle* (London: George Routledge, 1927), Chap. iv, and James V. Foster, *History of the Pre-Romantic Novel in England* (New York: Modern Language Association, 1949), *passim*.

[3] Among lesser-known Gothic Villains, Harriet Lee's Kruitzner, from "The German's Tale," a novelette in vol. II of *Canterbury Tales* (London: Colburn and Bentley, 1832), has the best claim to have influenced Byron's heroes. Byron borrowed this story, sometimes almost *verbatim*, for his *Werner*, and admits that it had a great influence on his works. Kruitzner has most of the characteristics of a Byronic Hero, including the sense of guilt, although his sin – a self-centered love of luxurious living – is not Byronic. His son Conrad turns out to have been the true unregenerate Gothic Villain.

[4] Radcliffe (note 1 above), pp. 69–70.

[5] M. G. Lewis, *The Monk*, ed. E. A. Baker (London: George Routledge, 1922), p. 9.

[6] Radcliffe, pp. 69–70; *Lara*, I, st. 5. Italics are Praz's in both cases: *The Romantic Agony* (New York: Meridian Books, 1956), p. 85, note 30.

[7] *Gothic Drama from Walpole to Shelley*, University of California Publications in English, XVIII (1947). Evans gives his own reasons for this development of the villain of the drama: see pp. 86–89 for a summary.

[8] *Plays on the Passions*, in *Works*, 2nd ed. (London: Longman, Brown, Green, and Longmans, 1853), Act III, Sc. ii (p. 88).

[9] Evans, p. 137.

[10] Evans, p. 178.

CHAPTER V. THE NOBLE OUTLAW

[1] In this section and what follows I make no consistent attempt to distinguish between the period of *Sturm und Drang* and Romanticism proper in Germany. In a study centered on English Romanticism the distinction seems superfluous, not only because there was no *Sturm und Drang* in England (the Age of Sentiment is quite another matter), but also because the German writing of this period had its influence in England not in the 70's or 80's, but during the Romantic Movement proper.

[2] Preface to *Goetz von Berlichingen*, in *The Poetical Works of Sir Walter Scott* (Edinburgh, 1834), XII, 447. I have used this translation of *Götz*, although it is not very accurate, since this was the version which influenced the English Romantics, particularly Byron, who could read no German. For a similar statement about the chivalric and bandit life of the Scotch Border country, see the preface to *The Lay of the Last Minstrel*.

[3] Schiller's prose drama seems to me as melodramatic and as histrionic as anything Byron wrote, but it is being successfully produced in Germany today.

[4] I, ii; in Schiller's *Sämtliche Werke* (München und Leipzig: Georg Müller, 1910), vol. I.

[5] *Ibid.*, in the textual variant cited on p. 498.

[6] On his first reading of the play he wrote to Southey: "Why have we ever called Milton sublime? that Count de Moor horrible wielder of heart-withering virtues? Satan is scarcely qualified to attend his execution as gallows captain," in *Collected Letters*, ed. E. L. Griggs (Oxford, 1956), I, 122. See Frederic Ewen, *The Prestige of Schiller in England, 1788–1859* (New York: Columbia University Press, 1932); but in overrating the influence of this drama on Wordsworth's *Borderers* Ewen seems to be following Margaret W. Cooke, "Schiller's 'Robbers' in England," *Modern Language Review*, XI (1916), 156–175.

[7] In *Poetical Works*, ed. Thomas Hutchinson, Oxford Standard Authors (1910), Act I, 60–65; 1115–1120.

[8] See E. de Sélincourt, "The Hitherto Unpublished Preface to Wordsworth's 'Borderers'," *Nineteenth Century and After*, C (1926), 723–741.

[9] I, xxi. I have used the *Poetical Works*, Cambridge ed. (Boston: Houghton Mifflin, 1939). References to canto and stanza are hereafter included in the text.

CHAPTER VI. FAUST

[1] William Rose, *From Goethe to Byron: The Development of Weltschmerz in German Literature* (London: George Routledge, 1924), pp. 5–11.

[2] *Faust I*, 1765–1774. I have used the translation of Bayard Taylor (1870); World Classics ed. (Oxford: Oxford University Press, 1932), pp. 54–55.

[3] It is worth noting that Mario Praz, in *The Romantic Agony*, sees this and similar passages as evidence of a pervasive Romantic agolagnia. This seems to me an unnecessary stretching of terms: Byron surely means that he is most fully self-aware when he is undergoing profound feeling, not that he takes a perverse pleasure in pain. Note the parallel with Parson Yorick's "*Patior, ergo sum.*"

CHAPTER VII. CAIN AND AHASUERUS

[1] In this connection it is appropriate to note that in some late Jewish legends it was the fallen angels who instructed man in most of the arts and sciences, including agriculture and the working of metals, and astronomy as well as astrology. See Moncure Daniel Conway, *Demonology and Devil-Lore*, 3rd ed. (New York: Henry Holt, 1889), II, 279, or Louis Ginzberg, *The Legends of the Jews* (Philadelphia, 1909–1913), I, 125.

[2] There were other even more minor treatments of Cain in eighteenth-century Germany, the most important being "Maler" Müller's "Adams erstes Erwachen und erste seelige Nächte" (1778) and "Der erschlagene Abel" (1775). See the Bibliographical Appendix for references.

[3] Bertha Reed's *The Influence of Solomon Gessner Upon English Literature* (Philadelphia: Americana Germanica Press, 1905) is in many respects an absurd example of *Quellenstudien* (among other verbal and thematic parallels, Miss Reed writes, in regard to Byron's *Cain*, "It is important to note that Cain and Abel marry their sisters, as in the *Death of Abel*," p. 102). But in all justice it must be admitted that whatever parallels there are, Miss Reed has found, and she has also compiled an impressive collection of passages from periodicals to trace Gessner's English reputation. John Livingston Lowes, in *The Road to Xanadu* (Boston: Houghton Mifflin, 1927), has detailed Gessner's influence

on Coleridge, and Lowes has of course a balanced estimate of the poem's worth.

[4] Quoted in Reed, p. 5.

[5] Coleridge, *Poetical Works*, ed. E. H. Coleridge (Oxford: Clarendon Press, 1912), II, 285–292.

[6] See J. Minor, *Goethes Fragmente vom ewigen Juden und wiederkehrenden Heiland* (Stuttgart und Berlin: J. B. Cotta'sche, 1904), p. 51. This includes a thorough study of Goethe's plans for the projected epic.

[7] I am indebted for the information in this paragraph to Lowes (note 3 above), Chap. xiv.

[8] I have used the *Works*, ed. Thomas Hutchinson, Oxford Standard Authors (1905). References hereafter are in the text.

[9] C. F. D. Schubart's *Sämtliche Gedichte* (Stuttgart, 1839), IV, 68.

[10] "Von den Hinterweltlern," *Also Sprach Zarathustra.*

CHAPTER VIII. SATAN AND PROMETHEUS

[1] This applies, of course, only to the period of this study. Satan was already a Titan in Grotius's *Adamus Exul* (1601), and in Vondel's *Lucifer* (1654), either or both of which may have influenced Milton, and also in Marino's *Strage degli Innocenti* (see Mario Praz, *The Romantic Agony*, Chap. ii, "The Metamorphosis of Satan").

[2] There is a recent and well-reasoned attempt to rehabilitate Satan in William Empson's "The Satan of Milton," *Hudson Review*, XIII (1960), pp. 33–59; see also his *Milton's God* (London: Chatto and Windus, 1961), especially Chap. ii.

[3] See Maximilian Rudwin, *The Devil in Legend and Literature* (Chicago: Open Court, 1931), pp. 241f.

[4] Dryden, *Essays*, ed. W. P. Ker (Oxford: Oxford University Press, 1900), II, 165; Addison, in "Defects in Milton," No. 297 of the *Spectator.*

[5] I am indebted for the references in this paragraph to Arthur Barker, "'. . . And on His Crest Sat Horror,' Eighteenth-Century Interpretations of Milton's Sublimity and of His Satan," *University of Toronto Quarterly*, XI (1942), 421–436.

[6] *Shelley's Prose*, ed. David Lee Clark (Albuquerque: University of New Mexico Press, 1954), pp. 327, 290.

[7] Printed in Clark, pp. 264–275.

[8] See Gilbert Murray, *Aeschylus* (Oxford: Clarendon Press, 1940), pp. 101f., and, for a view largely consonant, E. A. Havelock, *The Crucifixion of Intellectual Man* (Boston: Beacon Press, 1951). This transformation of Zeus's character is considered not at all "likely," however, by H. J. Rose, *A Commentary on the Surviving Plays of Aeschylus* (Amsterdam: Noord-Hollandsche Uitgevers Maat-schappij, 1957), I, 11.

[9] See Tertullian, for instance (*Adv. Marc.* I, i): "Verus Prometheus, deus omnipotens, blasphemiis lancinatus . . .," cited by R. J. Zwi Werblowsky, *Lucifer and Prometheus* (London: Routledge and Kegan Paul, 1952).

[10] The influence of Shaftesbury and the Prometheus legend on the poetry and esthetics of the *Sturm und Drang* is covered thoroughly in Oskar Walzel, *Das Prometheussymbol von Shaftesbury zu Goethe*, 2te Auflage, in *Wortkunst*, Heft VII (München, 1932).

[11] *Characteristics*, ed. J. M. Robertson (London: G. Richards, 1900), I, 135–136.

[12] So Karl Heinemann, *Die tragischen Gestalten der Griechen in der Weltliteratur*, in *Erbe der Alten*, Heft III (Leipzig, 1920), Band I, 21.

[13] There are of course other German treatments of the legend, including Herder's *Der entfesselte Prometheus* (1802), which although of not much literary value, is interesting in that his Prometheus, who learns forgiveness through suffering, anticipates the transformed and "Christian" hero of Shelley's drama.

[14] *Prometheus Unbound*, in *Poetical Works*, ed. Thomas Hutchinson, Oxford Standard Authors (1905), p. 201, hereafter referred to in the text.

[15] See Carl Grabo, *Prometheus Unbound: An Interpretation* (Chapel Hill: University of North Carolina Press, 1935).

[16] Act I, 77–89, in Goethe's *Sämtliche Werke*, Jubiläumsausgabe (Stuttgart und Berlin: J. B. Cotta'sche, 1902–1912), XV, 14.

[17] Georg Brandes, *Main Currents of Nineteenth Century Literature* (New York: Macmillan, 1903), IV, 300f. In *Ecce Homo* (Sect. 4 of "Warum ich so klug bin") in *Gesammelte Werke*, Musarion-Ausgabe (München, 1928), XXI, 200, Nietzsche writes: "Ich habe kein Wort, bloss einem Blick für Die, welche in Gegenwart des Manfred das Wort Faust auszusprechen wagen. Die Deutschen sind *unfähig* jedes Begriff von Grösse . . ."

[18] In *Modern Language Notes*, XXXIII (1918), 306–309, Samuel Chew lists references to Prometheus in Byron, including many not included in the indices of Coleridge's edition of the *Works*.

CHAPTER IX. CHILDE HAROLD

[1] "Lord Byron: Arnold and Swinburne," The Warton Lecture on English Poetry, printed in *Proceedings of the British Academy, 1919–1920* (London, 1920), p. 444.

[2] Canto I, stanza 2. References hereafter will be in the text. For obvious typographical reasons, I am using Arabic numerals for stanza numbers.

[3] *The Minstrel*, in *The Poetical Works of James Beattie*, Aldine ed. (London, n.d.), p. 46.

[4] E. H. Coleridge, in his introduction to *Childe Harold* (in *Works*, II, xiv).

[5] "Night One," in *Poetical Works* (London, 1854), p. 5.

[6] II, 3. The two stanzas following 3, beginning "Yet if, as holiest men have deemed, there be / A land of souls beyond that sable shore . . .," were written at the request of R. C. Dallas (Byron's "editor" of Cantos I and II) to replace a rabidly anticlerical and antireligious stanza in the original manuscript. They are superior as poetry, but not consistent with the frankly skeptical tone of the rest of the canto.

[7] Ernest J. Lovell, *Byron: The Record of a Quest* (Austin: University of Texas Press, 1949), especially Chap. IV, "Byron and the Picturesque Tradition."

[8] In *Byron: The Christian Virtues* (New York: Oxford University Press, 1953), pp. 249f. It is worth noting in this connection, since Knight points to this passage as having influenced Shelley, that both Shelley and Hobhouse were strongly against Byron's printing of this "appeal to Nemesis": see *LJ*, IV, 259 and note, and *Lord Byron's Correspondence*, ed. John Murray (London: John Murray, 1922), II, 69, note. Needless to say, Professor Knight does not note the possible echo of St. Paul's epistle in this passage.

[9] *Faust I*, 1771–1773; translation of Bayard Taylor (1870), as in *Faust*, World Classics ed. (Oxford: Oxford University Press, 1932), p. 55.

[10] Manfred Eimer, in his *Byron und der Kosmos*, in *Anglistische Forschungen*, XXXIV (Heidelberg, 1912), built an entire *Weltanschauung* for Byron largely on the basis of these passages. The most thorough study of the whole matter is in Professor Lovell's study (note 7 above).

[11] *Die Leiden des jungen Werthers*, ed. Max Herrman, in Goethe's *Werke*, Jubiläumsausgabe (Stuttgart: 1902–12), XVI, 30 (see the chapter above on the Hero of Sensibility). In reference to Lovell, it is only fair to say that although he considers this a "failure of a quest" on Byron's part, he also makes it an important basis for Byron's "modernity": see the last chapter of his study (note 7 above): "The Contemporaneousness of Byron." For a similar attitude, see P. E. More, "The Wholesome Revival of Byron," *Atlantic Monthly*, LXXXII (1898), 801–809, and the essays by Willis W. Pratt ("Byron and Some Current Patterns of Thought") and Leslie Marchand ("Byron and the Modern Spirit") in *The Major English Romantic Poets*, ed. Clarence Thorpe, *et al.* (Carbondale: Southern Illinois University Press, 1957), pp. 149–168.

CHAPTER X. FOUR TURKISH TALES

[1] For these publication figures, see Coleridge's Introduction to *The Corsair* (*Works*, III, 217), and Leslie Marchand's *Byron* (New York: Alfred Knopf, 1957) I, 433, 467.

[2] See his 1830 Introduction to *Rokeby*, in *Poetical Works*, Cambridge ed. (Boston, 1900), p. 230.

[3] "Byron," in *From Anne to Victoria*, ed. Bonamy Dobrée (New York: Scribner, 1937), pp. 610–611, 605–606.

[4] For other literary sources of the Turkish background in these poems, see Harold S. L. Wiener, "Byron and the East: Literary Sources of the 'Turkish Tales,'" in *Nineteenth-Century Studies*, ed. Herbert Davis *et al.* (Ithaca: Cornell University Press, 1940).

[5] *Letters*, ed. H. J. C. Grierson (London: Constable and Co., 1932–37), III, 185–186.

[6] Of course Lady Caroline Lamb had used the disguise of a page to gain access to Byron's rooms, but then perhaps she had also read *Marmion* – or, for that matter, *Cymbeline* or *Twelfth Night*.

[7] G. Wilson Knight, in "The Two Eternities: Essay on Byron," in *The Burning Oracle* (London, New York: Oxford University Press, 1939), develops this theme of a masculine-feminine hero, especially in *Sardanapalus*.

[8] Charles du Bos, *Byron and the Need of Fatality*, trans. Ethel C. Mayne (London: Putnam, 1932); Mario Praz, *The Romantic Agony*, 2nd ed., trans. Angus Davidson (New York: Meridian Books, 1956); T. S. Eliot, see note 3 above.

[9] The two most recent studies of Byron's "philosophical" attitudes are: E. W. Marjarum, *Byron as Skeptic and Believer*, in *Princeton Studies in English*, No. 16 (1938), and Ernest J. Lovell, *Byron* (Austin: University of Texas Press, 1949). Marjarum concludes: "He was inconsistent to the last" (p. 83).

[10] I am not saying that a "libertarian" position (the belief that there is some freedom of will which is not accounted for in a deterministic scheme of things) is intellectually inconsistent. I mean only that the concept of free will which can be *illustrated* or *described* in literature is that of free will as self-determination, and not as causeless (or existential) choice.

CHAPTER XI. TWO METAPHYSICAL DRAMAS

[1] See his "Manfred's Remorse and Dramatic Tradition," *PMLA*, LXII (1947), 752–773.

[2] For a note on the influence of *René* on the Byronic Hero, see the Bibliographical Appendix below.

[3] Samuel C. Chew, *The Dramas of Lord Byron*, in *Hesperia*, 3te Heft (Göttingen and Baltimore, 1915), and Evans, note 1 above. See also William J. Calvert, *Byron: Romantic Paradox* (Chapel Hill: University of North Carolina Press, 1935), and Maurice J. Quinlan, "Byron's *Manfred* and Zoroastrianism," *Journal of English and Germanic Philology*, LVII (1958), 726–738.

[4] Chew, p. 74.

[5] Chew, pp. 78, 80.

[6] The most recent account of the relationship is in E. M. Butler's *Byron and Goethe* (London: Bowes and Bowes, 1956). Chew (note 3 above) includes in an appendix the parallels between *Faust* and *Manfred*.

[7] *Main Currents in Nineteenth Century Literature* (New York: Macmillan, 1905), III, 308.

[8] "Prometheus," lines 58–59; *Manfred*, III, iv, 151. Byron was enraged when Murray left this line out of the first edition: "You have destroyed the whole effect and moral of the poem . . ." (*LJ*, IV, 157).

[9] See "Ueber die dramatischen Dichtungen Byrons," in *Werke*, Musarion Ausgabe (München: Musarion Verlag, 1922), I; and *Ecce Homo*, in *Werke* (1928), XXI, 200.

[10] Chew, note 3 above, p. 78.

[11] See Samuel C. Chew, *Byron in England* (New York: Scribner, 1924), for an amusing account of the drama's reception by the general public.

[12] "Byron's Cain," in *Naturalism in English Poetry* (New York: E. P. Dutton, 1900), pp. 259–289.

[13] Hoxie N. Fairchild, *Religious Trends in English Poetry* (New York: Columbia University Press, 1949), III, 428–432. Professor Fairchild's attitude toward Byron and toward the entire Romantic heroic tradition is illustrated in a comment he makes on Ethel Mayne's biography of Byron. She had concluded that the famous epigram from *Faust I*, "Es irrt der Mensch / So lang er strebt," summed up the best in Byron's personality (*Byron*, II, 315). This, Professor Fairchild observes, is "Faustian rant" (p. 451).

[14] See his discussion of the "domesticating crisis" in *Paradise Lost*, in *The English Epic and Its Background* (New York, 1954).

[15] In a letter to Moore, Byron writes that "the Demon is to *depress* [Cain] . . . in his own estimation . . ., by showing him infinite things and his own abasement, till he falls into the frame of mind that leads to the catastrophe . . . from rage and fury against the inadequacy of his state to his conceptions . . ." (*LJ*, V, 470).

[16] In this view I am in agreement with C. N. Stavrou, "Milton, Byron, and the Devil," *University of Kansas City Review*, XXI (1955), 153–159.

[17] Chew, *Dramas*, p. 130. But note that the complaint speech, "The punishment is more than I can bear," etc., is given to Cain's wife, contrary to the biblical narrative.

CHAPTER XII. THE BYRONIC HERO AND HEROIC TRADITION

[1] *Ethica Nicomachea*, trans. W. D. Ross, in *Works* (Oxford: Clarendon Press, 1925), IX, 1123b–1125a. The resemblance between the Nietzschean *Ue-*

bermensch and the "magnanimous man" has been noted: see Walter Kaufmann, *Nietzsche* (New York: Meridian Books, 1956), pp. 327–329, or his *From Shakespeare to Existentialism* (Boston: Beacon Press, 1959).

[2] In a review of *Childe Harold*, in the *Quarterly Review*, XXI (October 1816).

[3] (New York: Random House; London: Faber and Faber, 1937), p. 52.

[4] Ernest J. Lovell, *Byron* (Austin: University of Texas Press, 1949), p. 25. The reference to *Don Juan* is to Canto XVI, st. 97.

[5] See, for instance, Eric Bentley, *A Century of Hero-Worship*, 2nd ed. (Boston: Beacon Press, 1957), or Mario Praz, *The Hero in Eclipse in Victorian Fiction*, trans. Angus Davidson (Oxford: Oxford University Press, 1956).

[6] (New York: Simon and Schuster, 1946), p. 747. This chapter is largely a reprint of his "Byron and the Modern World," *Journal of the History of Ideas*, I (1940), 24–36, although the latter is longer and does Byron better justice. There is nothing really new in either essay, and Lord Russell repeats many inaccurate clichés about Byron, including an assertion that Byron was always a devoted admirer of Napoleon until his abdication (p. 750), when of course Byron's admiration for Napoleon was always critical and qualified.

[7] See H. J. C. Grierson, *Carlyle and Hitler* (Cambridge, England, 1933), and Peter Viereck, *Metapolitics: From the Romantics to Hitler* (New York, 1941) for the Romanticism-to-Fascism argument. But see Bentley (note 5 above) and especially Ernst Cassirer, *The Myth of the State* (New Haven, 1946), for more carefully reasoned (and postwar) arguments of the whole problem.

[8] Kaufmann (note 1 above), p. 391, note. He cites Andler, *Nietzsche, Sa vie et sa pensée*, vol. I, in which Emerson is named one of Nietzsche's "précurseurs."

[9] See Kaufmann (note 1 above), pp. 15–29.

[10] *The Rebel*, trans. Anthony Bower (New York: Vintage Books, 1956). Camus does not have much to say specifically on the Byronic Hero, but see pp. 49f.

BIBLIOGRAPHICAL APPENDIX ON HERO TYPES

IN ILLUSTRATING the brief sketches above of Romantic and pre-Romantic hero types, I chose what seemed to me the clearest examples in each case, and the poems, plays, or novels in which they appear have been acknowledged in the text and notes; but to have made the same acknowledgment of the secondary bibliographical and critical sources would have been to overload the introductory paragraphs of each chapter with not very helpful footnotes. I hope this short appendix will serve instead, first, to acknowledge my indebtedness, and at the same time to provide a brief and basic annotated bibliography of studies of hero types. This list is by no means exhaustive, of course, but these are the works I have found most helpful, and the major studies in each field are included. The only bibliography in English which covers most of these subjects is Werner P. Friederich and Fernand Baldensperger's *Bibliography of Comparative Literature* (University of North Carolina Press, 1950), and the subsequent and current supplements in *The Yearbook of Comparative and General Literature*.

THE CHILD OF NATURE

The distinction I have made between the Child of Nature and the older Noble Savage is, I believe, an innovation, and most studies are simply of the Noble Savage or of primitivism generally. The standard work on primitivism in English Literature is still Hoxie N. Fairchild's *The Noble Savage* (Columbia University Press, 1928). See also Chauncey Brewster Tinker, *Nature's Simple Plan* (Princeton University Press, 1922) – a scholarly but entertaining monograph. Primitivism was well established in England before Rousseau, but he did of course give it added impetus, although probably because he was misunderstood. See A. O. Lovejoy, "The Supposed Primitivism of Rousseau's 'Discourse on Inequality,'" *Modern Philology*, XXI (1923), 165–186, and James H. Warner, "The Basis of J. J. Rousseau's Contemporaneous Reputation in England," *Modern Language Notes*, LV (1940), 270–280.

THE MAN OF FEELING

There is of course a vast bibliography of studies on English Sentimentalism. Two early but very important studies are by Ernest Bernbaum, *The Drama of*

Sensibility (Boston and London: Ginn and Co., 1915), and Paul Van Tieghem, "La sensibilité et la passion dans le roman européen an 18e siècle," *Rev. de littérature comparée*, VI (1926), 424–435. The best case for Shaftesbury as the apostle of sentiment is made by C. A. Moore in "Shaftesbury and the Ethical Poets in England, 1700–1760," *PMLA*, XXI (1916), 264–325, but R. S. Crane pushed the origins back to the Cambridge Platonists and late seventeenth-century Latitudinarians in "Suggestions toward a Genealogy of the 'Man of Feeling,'" *English Literary History*, I (1934), 204–230. The most comprehensive critical and bibliographical treatment of the sentimental novel, giving full credit also to the French, especially Prevost, is James R. Foster's *History of the Pre-Romantic Novel in England* (New York: The Modern Language Association, 1949). For a short and well-balanced study, if also early, see Edith Birkhead, "Sentiment and Sensibility in the Eighteenth-Century Novel," *Essays and Studies by Members of the English Association*, XI (Oxford, 1925), 97–116. For the English and European influence of *Werther* in particular, see Stuart Pratt Atkins, *The Testament of Werther in Poetry and Drama* (Harvard University Press, 1949), a model among such "influence" studies.

THE GLOOMY EGOIST

The name of this hero derives of course from the study by Eleanor M. Sickels, *The Gloomy Egoist* (Columbia University Press, 1932), which covers "post-Elegy" melancholy from Gray to Keats. Miss Sickels' work was designed to complement Amy Louise Reed's *The Background of Gray's Elegy* (Columbia University Press, 1924), which traces the melancholy meditator back to *Hamlet* and Burton. See also J. W. Draper, *The Funeral Elegy and the Rise of English Romanticism* (New York University Press, 1929); R. D. Havens, *The Influence of Milton on English Poetry* (Harvard University Press, 1922); and the second volume of Paul Van Tieghem's *Le Préromantisme* (Paris: F. Rieder, 1924–30).

THE GOTHIC VILLAIN

The area of the Gothic novel is undoubtedly the most well-plowed field in English literary history, in proportion to its worth. The studies which I have found most useful are Eino Railo's *The Haunted Castle* (London: George Routledge, 1927), and Edith Birkhead's *The Tale of Terror* (London: Constable, 1921). Montague Summers' *The Gothic Quest* (London: The Fortune Press, 1938), overwhelms one with its enthusiasm, and exhausts one with its inclusiveness. Almost the only, and certainly the definitive study of the Gothic drama is Bertrand Evans' *Gothic Drama from Walpole to Shelley*, in *University of California Publications in English*, XVIII (Berkeley and Los Angeles, 1947).

THE NOBLE OUTLAW

Most of the studies of the Gothic Villain also cover the Noble Outlaw (see especially Railo above), but see Agnes Murphy, *Banditry and Chivalry in German Fiction, 1790–1830* (University of Chicago Press, 1935), and also the introduction to L. A. Willoughby's edition of *Die Räuber* (Oxford University Press, 1922). For this influence on English literature, see F. W. Stokoe, *German Influence in the English Romantic Period* (Cambridge University Press, 1926).

FAUST

There are two collections of German treatments of the Faust story, with short introductions to each selection: K. G. Wendriner, *Die Faustdichtung vor, neben und nach Goethe*, 4 vols. (Berlin: Morawe und Scheffelt, 1913), and H. W. Geissler, *Gestaltungen des Faust*, 3 vols. (München: Parcus, 1927). There is a recent brief critical and bibliographical study in German by Karl Theens, *Doktor Johann Faustus* (Meisenheim an Glan: Anton Hain, 1948); and in French, Charles Dédéyan's thorough three-volume study, *Le Thème du Faust dans la littérature Européenne* (Paris: Lettres Modernes, 1954–59), traces not only the actual appearances of the legendary doctor, but also the general theme of a heroic thirst for sensation, knowledge, and power, through the literature of Germany, England (short chapters on Beckford, M. G. Lewis, Byron, and Shelley), and France. The entire history of Faust, however, from its origins in pre-Christian kingship rites to Thomas Mann, has been discussed in English with clarity and style by E. M. Butler, in three volumes (Cambridge University Press): *The Myth of the Magus* (1948); *Ritual Magic* (1949); and *The Fortunes of Faust* (1952). The last volume traces the literary Faust from the Faust book of 1587 to the present.

CAIN

The best interpretative study to date of Cain in literature is Auguste Brieger's *Kain und Abel in der deutschen Dichtung*, in *Stoff-und Motivgeschichte der deutschen Literatur*, No. 14 (Berlin und Leipzig, 1934), which covers the development of the story from the Christian fathers through German literature of the *Sturm und Drang*, with a brief summary chapter on the nineteenth century. Jacob Rothschild's *Kain und Abel in der deutschen Literatur* (Würzburg, 1933), is useful for its bibliography, from the Middle Ages to this century. There is no study of Cain in English literature, but see Bertha Reed, *The Influence of Salomon Gessner upon English Literature* (Philadelphia: Americana Germanica Press, 1905), and John Livingston Lowes, *The Road to Xanadu* (Boston: Houghton Mifflin, 1927).

AHASUERUS

Oddly enough, there is at this date no definitive study of the Wandering Jew in legend and literature, but this lacuna in scholarship will be filled in two or three years by Professor George K. Anderson of Brown University, who is working on a comprehensive critical and bibliographical study of the entire history of the legend. For the time being, however, his series of articles remains the most useful treatment of Ahasuerus in English: "The Wandering Jew Returns to England," *Journal of English and Germanic Philology*, XLV (1946), 237–250, gives a brief account of the legend in England up to 1640, including a transcription of the *Kurze Beschreibung*; "Popular Survivals of the Wandering Jew in England," *JEGP*, XLVI (1947), 367–382, covers folk themes and subliterature through the nineteenth century; and "The Neo-Classical Chronicle of the Wandering Jew," *PMLA*, LXIII (1948), 199–211, discusses the anonymous *Mémoires de juif errant* (1777) and two German eighteenth-century treatments of the story. Albert Soergel, in *Ahasver-Dichtungen seit Goethe*, in *Probefahrten* VI (Leipzig, 1905), gives a good critical discussion mostly of German Wandering Jews, and includes an extensive bibliography. Jos. J.

Gielen, in *De wandelende Jood in Volkskunde en Letterkunde* (Amsterdam: De Spieghel; Mechelen: Het Kompas, 1931), includes an impressive bibliography, but otherwise the critical discussion is beyond the linguistic sphere of most of us. A good brief treatment is that in Werner Zirus, *Ahasverus, Der Ewige Jude*, in *Stoff- und Motivgeschichte der deutschen Literatur*, No. 6 (Berlin und Leipzig, 1930), pp. 1–77. See also Lowe's *Road to Xanadu*, Chapter xvi, and Railo's *The Haunted Castle*.

SATAN

The most prolific authority on Satan (with emphasis on French literature) is Maximilian Rudwin. His *The Devil in Legend and Literature* (Chicago: Open Court, 1931), is the most comprehensive of his studies on the subject, and has references to the others. Any work on *Paradise Lost*, of course, discusses the origins of Milton's Satan, but the most interesting of these, I believe, is R. J. Zwi Werblowsky's *Lucifer and Prometheus* (London: Routledge and Kegan Paul, 1952). Werblowsky is professedly a Jungian, but he does not insist on Jungian terminology, and his discussion remains valid whether or not one accepts Jungian theory. See also "The Metamorphosis of Satan," Chapter iv of Mario Praz's *The Romantic Agony*, 2nd ed., trans. Angus Davidson (New York: Meridian Books, 1956). For the development of Satan in eighteenth-century England, see Arthur Barker, "'. . . And on His Crest Sat Horror,' Eighteenth-Century Interpretations of Milton's Sublimity and of His Satan," *University of Toronto Quarterly*, XI (1942), 421–436, and R. D. Havens, *The Influence of Milton in English Poetry*.

PROMETHEUS

There is also no definitive published study on the Prometheus legend in Western literature. Such general "classical-influence" guides as Douglas Bush's *Mythology and the Romantic Tradition in English Poetry* (Harvard University Press, 1937) are of course too broad to be of much help on one particular myth. John Bailey's discussion of Aeschylus, Goethe, and Shelley in "Prometheus in Poetry," reprinted in *The Continuity of Letters* (Oxford University Press, 1923), is more appreciative than critical. Albert Guérard, in "Prometheus and the Aeolian Lyre," *Yale Review*, XXXIII (1944), 483–497, presents briefly an interesting theory explaining the importance of the legend for the Romantics, and Oskar Walzel, in *Das Prometheussymbol von Shaftesbury zu Goethe*, 2te Auflage, in *Wortkunst*, VII (München, 1932), gives a thorough and scholarly account of the influence of the legend on poetic theory in the *Sturm und Drang*. Olga Raggio, in "The Myth of Prometheus; Its Survival and Metamorphoses up to the Eighteenth Century," *Journal of the Warburg and Courtauld Institute*, XXI (1958), 44–62, is of course concerned largely with iconography in works of art, but she does throw new light on the development of the legend in literature, at least through the Renaissance. There is a good brief treatment of the legend in Karl Heinemann's *Die tragischen Gestalten der Griechen in der Weltliteratur*, Band I, in *Das Erbe der Alten*, Heft III (Leipzig, 1920). There is an unpublished dissertation on the legend in English and French literature (with the addition of a "Promethean" theory of world history) by Lewis Awad: see *Dissertation Abstracts*, XIV (1954), 117–118 (Princeton). See also the brief essay on the provenance of the legend in Lawrence Zillman's variorum edition of Shelley's *Prometheus Unbound* (University of Washington Press, 1959).

BYRONIC HEROES

Besides the studies reviewed in the Introduction, and those cited in subsequent chapters on individual Byronic Heroes, a few more general studies should be added: the introduction and early chapters of Edmond Estève's *Byron et Romantisme Français* (Paris: Hachette, 1907), and Carl Lefevre's "Lord Byron's Fiery Convert of Revenge," *Studies in Philology*, XLIV (1952), 468–487 – both of these studies are largely analytic, not genetic. Ernest J. Lovell, in *Byron: The Record of a Quest* (University of Texas Press, 1949), sees in the Byronic Hero the "Zeluco theme"– the remorseful or antisocial hero's rejection of, and rejection by, Nature – exemplified in John Moore's novel *Zeluco* (1789), but also in much Romantic literature including Byron's works. The entire Don Juan legend, including Byron's adaptation of it, is covered critically and bibliographically in Leo Weinstein's *The Metamorphoses of Don Juan* (Stanford University Press, 1959). The two most recent studies of Byron's poetry – Paul West, *Byron and the Spoiler's Art* (London: Chatto and Windus, 1960), and Andrew Rutherford, *Byron* (Edinburgh: Oliver and Boyd, 1961) – are not concerned with the Byronic Hero's origins, but they do trace his development in Byron's works. Mr. West's analysis is imaginative, if somewhat subjective; Mr. Rutherford is more scholarly, if with a moral (and Leavisian) bias.

BYRON AND CHATEAUBRIAND

The possible influence of Chateaubriand's works, especially of *René*, on the Byronic Hero, has often been debated, since *René* has many Byronic characteristics, and since the story was first published in *Le Génie du Christianisme* in 1802, ten years before *Childe Harold* I and II. Chateaubriand himself had no doubts on the subject: he generously credited himself with the creation of the Byronic Hero, and reproved Byron for never having acknowledged the debt (see especially *Essai sur la littérature angloise*, in *Ouvres*, ed. Saint-Beuve (Paris: Garnier, 1860), XI, 781–782). English scholars in general have minimized the possible debt; French scholars have emphasized it, one scholar going so far as to say that Byron's private life – including the sin of incest – was in imitation of *René* (see L. Reynaud, in *Le Romantisme*, Paris, 1926). These, I believe, are reasonable conclusions: (1) Presumably Byron did read *René*, but probably not until he had become a celebrity and had met Madame de Staël, in 1812, and by that time the first Byronic Hero was already established; (2) The agonized remorse for secret sins and the likely incest theme make it possible that *René* did influence *Manfred*, although, as we have seen, both of these themes were already flourishing in England even before *René* was published in France; (3) René is a Hero of Sensibility, and obviously bears a resemblance to Werther, but René is no Titan – as a matter of fact, he is generally meek, repentant, and submissive, especially toward his elders and toward the church, as is no Byronic Hero. There is no mention of Chateaubriand or of *René* in Byron's letters or journals. There are two references in his poetry: in *The Bride of Abydos* (II, xx, note), in which Byron makes reference to an anecdote in Chateaubriand's travel writings, and in *The Age of Bronze* (714 and note), in which Byron makes sarcastic reference to Chateaubriand's politicking at the Congress of Verona. On the whole question, see Mario Praz, *The Romantic Agony*, pp. 67–69 and notes, and see Rolf Kaiser, "René und Harold," *Archiv für das Studium der Neueren Sprachen*, CLXX (1936), 185–196. Kaiser lists "thematic" parallels between *René* and *Childe Harold* I and II. *René* and *Atala* have appeared in the M.L.A. Translation Series, trans. Irving Putter (University of California Press, 1952).

INDEX

Works other than Byron's are listed under authors. Important heroes are cross referenced, with names that are also titles cross referenced as titles.